Oakeshott on Rome and America

British Idealist Studies Series
1: Oakeshott

Series Editor
Noël O'Sullivan, University of Hull

imprint-academic.com/idealists

OAKESHOTT ON ROME AND AMERICA

Gene Callahan

imprint-academic.com

Published in the UK by Imprint Academic
PO Box 200, Exeter EX5 5YX, UK

Published in the USA by Imprint Academic
Philosophy Documentation Center
PO Box 7147, Charlottesville, VA 22906-7147, USA

ISBN 9781845403133 (hardback)
ISBN 9781845406677 (paperback)

A CIP catalogue record for this book is available from the
British Library and US Library of Congress

imprint-academic.com/idealists

Contents

Acknowledgements

The author would like to thank David Boucher, Bruce Haddock, James Connelly, Peredur Roberts, Colin Tyler, Katherine Raymond, Noel O'Sullivan, Linda Feldman, Rosalind Davies, Jake Kawatski, Julian Velard, the members of the NYU Colloquium on Market Institutions and Economic Processes, Chris Rolliston, Dan Klein, Jeffrey Rogers Hummel, and George Selgin for generously offering their helpful comments on earlier drafts of this manuscript. This work is largely based on my doctoral thesis written at Cardiff University and completed in 2010, also titled *Oakeshott on Rome and America*.

In all instances, if emphasis is used in a quotation, it is in the original, unless specifically stated as otherwise.

Introduction

> When Montesquieu and the framers of the American Constitution articulated the conception of a limited constitution that had grown up in England, they set a pattern which liberal constitutionalism has followed ever since. Their chief aim was to provide institutional safeguards of individual freedom; and the device in which they placed their faith was the separation of powers. In the form in which we know this division of power between the legislator, the judiciary, and the administration, it has not achieved what it was meant to achieve. Governments everywhere have obtained by constitutional means powers which those men had meant to deny them. (Hayek, 1973: 1)

On July 19, 2005, a Sunni Muslim who was working on drafting Iraq's new constitution was gunned down outside a restaurant in Baghdad, along with two companions. This was apparently the fulfillment of the threat by Sunni militants to kill any Sunni Muslim cooperating with the Shi'ite majority in creating the document. The same day, 13 people died in an attack on a bus taking workers to a U.S. base. This followed a weekend in which 'scores of people lost their lives' in 'a series of bombings' (BBC News, July 19, 2005), including 98 in a truck bombing at a Shi'ite mosque.

For the year 2005 well over 30,000 insurgent attacks were recorded, killing many thousands of Iraqis and hundreds of American and British soldiers. The new constitution was ratified on October 15, 2005, but the violence continued to escalate, with the murder rate in Baghdad, by early 2006, estimated to have tripled over two years (Finer, 2006). At the end of that year, 14 months after the Iraqi Constitution was ratified, the Pentagon reported attacks on American forces were at an all-time high (Suarez, 2006). Even four years after the constitution was adopted, its existence seemed to make little difference; as Steven Lee Meyers reported in *The New York Times*:

> Instead, Iraqis treat their Constitution—like the benchmarks—the way they treat what few traffic lights operate here.
>
> 'So what?' a Kurdish lawmaker, Mahmoud Othman, said when asked about the risk of holding the election later than the Constitution demands. 'Nothing in Iraq is very legitimate.' (Meyers, 2009)

In the midst of such carnage, which some termed 'civil war', and the obviously deep divisions in Iraqi society at its root, what led the Anglo-American occupying force to place such faith in the efficacy of a written constitution as a palliative for these troubles? The answer, I suggest, lies in the continuing popularity of 'rationalism in politics', a phrase taken from the most widely known work of the British philosopher and political theorist Michael Oakeshott: his 1947 essay 'Rationalism in Politics'.[1] So, let us begin by examining what Oakeshott meant by the phrase.

What is rationalism in politics?

In his works on rationalism, Oakeshott criticizes the belief that the optimal, indeed, the only intellectually defensible method for choosing public policies and settling on general principles of governance is first to set aside all of the prejudicial influence of existing practices, wiping clean the mind to create a *tabula rasa* in which pure, abstract reasoning can generate universally valid political truths, and then to mold actual political practice to fit those ideals. As the 'politics of perfection', rationalism considers any concession made to existing institutions or practices that results in deviation from the ideals to be, for the rationalist, a betrayal of reason arising from an atavistic and deplorable attachment to one's prejudices. Oakeshott contends that this conception of what constitutes 'rational', and thereby commendable, conduct has dominated modern European thought, and in particular European political theory and practice, since the time of the Enlightenment.

However, Oakeshott argues that, far from being the best way to direct political activity, the rationalist program does not offer even a possible way to proceed. He sees it as springing from a fundamental misconception of the relationship between explicitly formulated rules and techniques and the concrete activity to which they apply. Such technical guidelines, he holds, are never generative of a form of practice, but instead only arise through practitioners coming to reflect upon an activity in which they are already engaged. Formal techniques and rules, although often of great utility, are never more than a highly abstract sketch of the rich vision that the skilled practitioner has of his field of expertise.

Although the rationalist must always fall short of living up to his own standard, Oakeshott contends that his attempts to realize his

---

[1] In fact, Oakeshott characterized 'nation building' long before George W. Bush ever engaged in it as a species of rationalism in which 'arrangements of a society are made to appear, not as manners of behaviour, but as pieces of machinery to be transported around the world indiscriminately' (1991 [1962]: 63).

ideals can still cause great mischief. A society under the spell of the rationalist charm will, in seeking to cope with novel difficulties, tend to neglect the resources with which its own political tradition might address these situations in stride, and instead will wind up staggering erratically forward, drawn this way, then that, by the promises to fix all its troubles that are offered by a succession of rationally devised schemes.

The alternative to rationalist politics presented by Oakeshott could be called 'practical politics'. This should not be understood as signifying an unwavering adherence to the current arrangements simply because of their existence, or the impossibility that reflection on present practices could point to ways of improving them. Rather, it suggests that the most promising path for genuine political reform lies in pursuing the 'intimations' of improvement already contained in what now exists. In describing Aristotle's — and, I believe, his own — conception of the proper role of the practically oriented political thinker, Oakeshott notes that Aristotle likened his task to that of a physician treating an ill patient. The physician's job is to return the person to the healthy condition that it lies in his nature to enjoy, not to transform him into some other sort of being altogether.

Comparing the theory with some evidence

However inherently plausible or intuitively appealing Oakeshott's thesis may be, I can see no reason not to expose it to further scrutiny by examining its applicability to actual political episodes. This work aims to investigate the history of two different republics, the Roman and the American, in regard to how closely these concrete polities conform to Oakeshott's contrasting ideal types of the practical and the rationalist styles of approaching politics, and what evidence they provide supporting or undermining his thesis.

I suggest that this choice of 'test cases' promises to be particularly illuminating for two reasons: First, Oakeshott himself considered the Roman republic a notable exhibition of the practical style of politics, while offering the American founding as a prime example of the rationalist approach. Second, although the American founders drew great inspiration from their Roman predecessors, their fixation on the downfall of the Roman republic led them to abjure reliance on tradition, which had been the Romans' foremost guide to proper political action, in favor of placing their confidence in a document deliberately constructed upon abstract principles held to be universally true and applicable in all circumstances, hoping, thereby, to create a more perfect republic, clad in armor shielding it from the forces that had finally ended the Roman experiment with self-governance.

A consideration worth stressing as we launch our inquiry is that no concrete polity should be expected to provide an unalloyed sample of these pure concepts. Oakeshott himself stressed that the constructs he utilized 'as extremes … are ideal' (1996: 21). In order to remedy our natural susceptibility to the intellectual infirmity of cherry-picking just those events that support our abstract framework while passing over any inconvenient counterexamples, we periodically will call into question our hypothesis that our ideal types do more to advance than to hinder our understanding of the Roman and the American republics, by giving due consideration to how the actual histories of those two polities diverge from the theoretical constructs with which we have paired them.

An outline of this work

The remainder of this work will proceed as follows:

Chapter 1 will explore Oakeshott's concept of rationalism, and specifically rationalism in politics, in more depth.

In Chapter 2, we will trace how we can see the idea of rationalism forming a continuous thread from his earliest book to his latest writings, and show how the idea of the rationalist conceit, while always present in his work, was developed and refined as Oakeshott's thought matured.

In Chapter 3, we will survey a number of criticisms of Oakeshott's thesis on rationalism, with special emphasis as to how those various critiques present us with questions upon which our later historical analysis may shed some light.

Chapter 4 was motivated by two different, but interrelated, issues. The first of these being that when I presented earlier versions of various parts of the present work at conferences, a number of commentators questioned whether Oakeshott's ideas on rationalism are of contemporary relevance. These commentators' scepticism about this matter generally was phrased along the following line: 'True', they would say,

> this whole rationalism business was a major problem at the time Oakeshott was writing his chief essays on the topic, in the 1940s and 1950s, in the era of Hitler, Stalin, and Mao. But surely today, the whole notion of designing a society from the top down has been discredited to the extent that this is no longer really a live issue, is it?

So, one impetus behind the inclusion of this chapter is to show that, while rationalism in politics has been taught some modesty by the events of the last few decades, it is far from moribund. The second motive is that it became apparent to the author, while dealing with the historical material offered by the Roman and the American republics, that a crucial differentia between their approaches to politics, and one of which the American founders were keenly aware, has to do with how efficacious it is to plan out the basic form of a polity in advance — in other words, is there some distinct advantage a polity can gain by declaring the principles upon which it is to operate in written form, and, further, elevating that written statement of those principles to some plane seen as resting above the tumult of day-to-day politics? Because the American founders saw doing so as a prophylactic against the fate that befell the Roman republic, and because their view is still prevalent in both contemporary political theory and practice (as evidenced by the case of Iraq with which we opened this work), this chapter is somewhat of a linchpin tying together the previous, more theoretical chapters with the subsequent, more empirical ones.

Chapter 5 will be chiefly concerned with how justified Oakeshott was in his forwarding of the Roman republic as an exemplar of the pragmatic style of politics that he opposed to rationalism. It is a fairly short chapter, chiefly because the consensus of historians of the period so overwhelmingly supports Oakeshott's view. It would be quite possible to continue piling up witness after witness making Oakeshott's case, but this seems unnecessary.

Chapter 6 will take up the more controversial topic of the cause of the Roman republic's demise and whether additional injections of rationalist design might, as the American founders suspected they had, buttressed the republic against the historical forces that were acting towards its dissolution. Here it is important to assert my limited aims in examining this material, since several commentators on presentations of this chapter wondered just how it was that the author, who is not a specialist in this period, could be so immodest as to put forward his own explanation of the republic's downfall? My response is to assert that my work here has no pretension of historical originality; the only claim to originality present, the warrant of which I leave it to my critics to judge, lies in employing the findings of the historians deemed most authoritative on this era as evidence weighing for or against Oakeshott's thesis on rationalism, as well as for or against the American founders' notion that the fate of the Roman republic could have been forestalled by rational design.

Chapter 7 will examine to what extent Oakeshott was on target in seeing the American founding as a salient instance of political rationalism. It is, like Chapter 5, fairly brief, and for much the same reason: I find the testimony of the expert historians of this period fairly clear cut, and, while it would be easy to amass much more evidence supporting my conclusion here, space limitations lead me to believe that any additional words I am granted are better spent elsewhere.

Chapter 8 will explore some post-founding American history in light of Oakeshott's contention that the rationalist can never really proceed as he purports to do. This chapter presents evidence suggesting that the 'failure to follow the letter of the Constitution' is not, as some contemporary, 'strict constructionists' contend, a peculiarly modern phenomenon, beginning (depending on which strict constructionist one is attending to) with Lincoln and the American Civil War, with Roosevelt and the New Deal, with the Cold War, or with George W. Bush and the 'War on terror'. Instead, it is something that began almost as soon as the U.S. Constitution was adopted, and is not (primarily) a symptom of bad faith but, rather, an inevitable consequence of the fact that no such rationalist design can ever dictate subsequent practice in the way that it is meant to do.

Finally, we conclude by summarizing the results of our investigations. All along, our aim has been only to offer evidence that Oakeshott's thesis has applicability, and to suggest avenues for further research. While such a goal is far more modest than attempting to set forth a conclusive theory of politics, or attempting to 'prove' that Oakeshott was correct, I hope that it may be worthy in its own right, as well as, perhaps, being more in keeping with Oakeshott's own program of research than would be either of the above-mentioned alternatives. Furthermore, many recent republican theorists, such as Viroli (1999) and Pettit (1997), have advocated rational design as a way of ensuring the preservation of republican institutions. The results of our efforts tend to indicate that their project is ill-conceived.

The manner of enquiry

At this point, it is necessary to pause and explain the sort of enquiry we are conducting. In seeking empirical evidence that supports or weighs in against Oakeshott's thesis on the mistaken theory of conduct behind the rationalist understanding of politics, and the deleterious effects of any attempt to put that theory into practice, we necessarily will abstract from concrete, historical happenings certain salient aspects of those events that are relevant to our task, while leaving out a multitude of other, perhaps quite historically important, features characterizing those goings-on. In other words, we will be evaluating episodes from history with regard to what they have to say about the applicability of and illumination offered by the ideal types Oakeshott employed in constructing his theory, rather than purporting to offer comprehensive historical explanations for those episodes, let alone explanations of that kind that claim to be advances upon conclusions already forwarded by historians.

I suggest that Oakeshott, in his portrayal of rationalistic politics and its counterpart, is employing what Max Weber would refer to as *ideal types*. Per Weber, they ought to have two sorts of adequacy: explanatory adequacy (or, as Weber put it, adequacy on the level of meaning (Schutz, 1967 [1932]: 225) and causal adequacy. Explanatory adequacy means that we can comprehend why, if an actor or an action closely conforms to the ideal type in question, the phenomenon we actually observe is a result of the elements of that type. Causal adequacy means that we can find cases in the real world that proceed roughly as our ideal type says they should; in other words, our type is not only plausible, but it also helps describe various actual social goings-on. Demonstrating causal adequacy might involve the use of historical narrative or statistical studies. In the last four chapters of the present work, we will employ historical narrative to show the causal adequacy of Oakeshott's ideal types, while Chapter 3 will defend the explanatory adequacy of his types against various critics.

This approach is worth noting for several reasons. First of all, whatever originality this thesis can boast of consists not in any claim to historical discoveries but, rather, in its consideration of the relevance of the historical conclusions of others as they apply to the particular theoretical issues raised by Oakeshott and his critics concerning rationalism in politics. As such, while we will cite primary sources insofar as they bear on our topic, we will largely rely on the work of modern historians, specializing in the periods in question, to provide us with our evidence. Surely political theorists are entitled to employ those findings as 'given data', much as chemists cannot help but rely on the state-of-the-art theory available in molecular physics as a basis for their own work.

The second noteworthy aspect of our rummaging through history in search of episodes that more or less exemplify the specific ideal types having a hold on our attention is that Oakeshott himself, in his work on the philosophy of history, devoted some attention to this method of historical enquiry, and, while not dismissing it as without merit, regarded it as a means of comprehending past events that intrinsically fell short of acknowledging their historical character. The essential character of 'an historical past', as he understood it, was that it 'may be regarded as a passage of historical change' (1999: 121). However, in any attempt to understand past events by viewing them as instances of ideal types, which are posited as capturing some essential, more general pattern those events have in common with other historical goings-on, the primacy of change in a fully historical explanation necessarily will be suppressed. The construction and employment of such an abstract type inherently focuses the attention of the theorist wielding it upon an unchanging constellation of properties perceived to be present in each exemplar of the type, consequentially marginalizing the significance of the unique and contingent events that led up to any specific historical happening and the particularities by which each instance of the type differs from the idealization:

> [The ideal-type historian] purports to be anatomizing a bygone present situational identity in terms of its constituent occurrences. No doubt he recognizes himself to be concerned with a passage of time which contains genuine change; but his enquiry, centred upon the articulation of a situational identity, cannot properly accommodate this recognition … an engagement to anatomize an historical situation, in specifying its duration, recognizes it as an emergence and admits its evanescence; but the enquiry is not concerned to abate the mystery of its appearance upon the scene, to investigate the mediation of its appearance or to trace the vicissitudes of its evanescence. It is concerned only with correctly inferring an intelligible structure composed of notionally contemporaneous mutually related constituent occurrences. (1999: 65–66)

Oakeshott concluded that

> … although [history understood by means of ideal types] has been called the most sophisticated understanding of the past, it is, I think, an unstable level of historical understanding. It recognizes (or half-recognizes) what it cannot itself accommodate, and it cannot defend itself against being superseded by what is a genuine competitor, critical of it in its own terms, and thus capable of superseding it. (1999: 65)

Which is, namely, a past made up 'of historical events and conjunctions of historical events' (1999: 67–68).

Oakeshott's critique of 'ideal-type history' raises the question of why, on those occasions when he himself engaged in historical exposition, his analysis typically was at the level of ideal typification, the very approach that his philosophy of history deemed to have an intrinsically superior rival. I have no novel explanation to offer for this apparent discrepancy between theory and practice, but only the rather obvious one, which is that Oakeshott always launched his excursions into history with the aim of finding support and illustrations for his theoretical journeys, and thus he did not see fit to linger over the details of the scenery during such side trips, instead hurrying to resume his progress towards his ultimate destination as soon as he had collected such provisions as he needed from those secondary ports of call. As McIntyre (2004: 118) put it, 'Oakeshott's self-described historical essays are neither exclusively nor primarily historical, but consist of the construction of ideal types or characters...' designed to illuminate the past from the point of view of practice. Much the same can be said of this present work. It is not an historical enquiry proper, but an evidentially based examination of the efficacy of the concept of 'rationalism in politics', aimed at advancing our understanding of the concept of rationalism in politics. As Weber wrote, introducing a work of his own with a similar character:

> This point of view... is, further, by no means the only possible one from which the historical phenomena we are investigating can be analysed. Other standpoints would, for this as for every historical phenomenon, yield other characteristics as the essential ones. (Weber, 1992: 14)

However, despite how far our explorations fall short of representing a comprehensive, empirical examination of Oakeshott's claims, I believe that they are not thus rendered without interest. If, for instance, we should discover that his thesis does not help us to comprehend the history of the very instances, namely, the Roman and American republics, that Oakeshott himself offered as prominent examples of polities closely approximating his ideal types of pragmatic and rationalist politics, respectively, then that alone would present us with a good reason to question its more widespread applicability. On the other hand, should a closer look at these cases prove to support Oakeshott's analysis, it would demonstrate that, at least on occasion, his schema can be an aid to comprehending the real world, and that, contrary to those of his critics who argue that he has entirely misrepresented the nature of political reality — for instance, Eccleshall, who, as we will see, claims, contra Oakeshott, that all politics is intrinsically ideological politics — that there are at least some examples concerning which he has largely got it right. Peter Winch, who mostly agrees with Oakeshott's understanding of history, discusses ideal-type history, and asks what its use is. He answers that it 'may be helpful in calling one's attention to features of historical situations which one might otherwise have overlooked and in suggesting useful analogies' (1990: 126–127).

And this work aims only to achieve such modest goals.

Politics as the Crow Flies

The latter chapters of the present work will consist in examining how the historical development of two particular polities, one of which (Rome) Oakeshott offered as an exemplar of pragmatic politics, and the other of which (America) he presented as an exemplar of rationalist politics, can help us to understand better Oakeshott's political theorizing. However, in order to lay the groundwork for our empirical comparison, it will be useful to explore in more depth just what it is that Oakeshott meant by 'rationalism in politics', as well as the character of the alternative style of politics—that style which, although it never earned his unambiguous endorsement, he clearly considered to be, if not more satisfactory, then at least more in need of emphasis in our present circumstances than is its conceptual rival. In addition, in this chapter we will survey a contemporary example of rationalism in politics, to illustrate the continuing relevance of Oakeshott's work.

Was Oakeshott's critique merely an apology for conservatism?

It is worth noting, as a prelude to an exegesis of Oakeshott's critique of rationalism, primarily because this point often has been misunderstood or denied, that his critique was not composed with the aim of advancing or hindering the program of any particular ideology or party. As McIntyre wrote:

> Oakeshott's philosophy of political activity cannot be reduced to a branch of conservatism, liberalism, or postmodernism... [it] is a challenge... to all of the currently dominant schools of political theory and political practice. It questions their presuppositions and exposes as ambiguous, arbitrary, or confused all of the supposed certainties which they take for granted. (McIntyre, 2004: 4)

Oakeshott quite explicitly stated his conviction that rationalism is a primary ingredient in all of the major brands of modern politics, having 'come to colour the ideas, not merely of one, but of all political

persuasions, and to flow over every party line' (1991 [1962]: 5).[1]
Nevertheless, despite Oakeshott's declaration that his target is not any
specific segment of the current ideological spectrum, but rather a
(mistaken) understanding of how best to arrive at one's own, preferred
policy program that is shared by all currently popular political
postures, his thesis frequently has been dismissed as a partisan apology
for the status quo, one that serves the interests of the existent ruling
class.[2] That those thus pigeonholing Oakeshott misapprehend him is
evidenced by his criticism of a political theorist who might seem to be
his natural ally, F. A. Hayek. Oakeshott accuses Hayek of responding to
proposals for reordering and improving society according to a
'rational' plan, which Hayek's targets were advancing — proposals that
Hayek saw as both unworkable and destructive of the existing order —
with a rationalist system of his own designed to thwart their rationalist
schemes: 'This is, perhaps, the main significance of Hayek's *Road to
Serfdom* — not the cogency of his doctrine, but the fact that it is a
doctrine. A plan to resist all planning may be better than its opposite,
but it belongs to the same style of politics' (1991 [1962]: 26). Although
he is often seen as a fierce opponent of the 'substantive' activities of
modern government, such as health and welfare services, at one point
he explicitly declares,

> I am firmly convinced that if one of the two pre-eminent positions on
> the role of government [as regulatory or substantive] were to take over
> completely... we would find ourselves in a worse situation both
> practically and intellectually speaking. (2008: 105)[3]

To the extent he truthfully could be seen as an 'advocate' of the
regulatory role, it was because he thought that the current political
debate had forgotten its virtues.

It is no doubt true that Oakeshott, as the citizen of a modern state,
unavoidably affected by its activities and decrees, and as an individual
with practical interests, rather than a ghostly 'pure' theorist, obviously

---

[1] Indeed, despite his reputation as a conservative, Oakeshott at one point
praises philosophy as being 'radically subversive'! (See Oakeshott 1993a: 141)
And I am aware of at least one radical environmentalist's invocation of
Oakeshott as an ally; see Bowers (2005).

[2] A number of such criticisms of Oakeshott will be examined in the third
chapter.

[3] And Raynor notes, 'In fact, [Oakeshott's] most recent writings include a
sustained critique of prevailing conservative modes of justification, especially
in America' (1985: 316).

had his own beliefs about the proper scope of governmental activity and preferred some policy directions to others. Nevertheless, I suggest that he was largely successful in separating his views on contemporary political issues from his theoretical exploration of the essential characteristics common to all forms of rationalist politics, whatever their ideological affiliation. The malady he sought to isolate and whose symptoms he hoped to explain in 'Rationalism in Politics' and related works does not uniquely afflict any one party or produce an outstanding cluster of exemplary cases in any particular portion of the ideological spectrum.

The rationalist 'founders'

If Oakeshott was not, as some unsympathetic readers have contended, merely spinning a plausible apologetics for 'reactionary' policies, then what *was* the target of his critique? We gave an overview of his characterization of 'the rationalist' in the Introduction. With that preliminary description in hand, let us begin our deeper exploration of this matter by briefly looking at the work of two thinkers whom Oakeshott described as 'the dominating figures in the early history of [the rationalist] project, Bacon and Descartes...' (1991 [1962]: 18–19).

Oakeshott argued that, for Bacon, the already notable advances constituting the 'scientific revolution', while laudable, nevertheless pointed to 'something of supreme importance [that was] lacking... a consciously formulated technique of research, an art of interpretation, a method whose rules had been written down' (1991 [1962]: 18). Bacon sought to remedy that lacuna; as Oakeshott sums up his project:

> The art of research which Bacon recommends has three main characteristics. First, it is a set of rules; it is a true technique in that it can be formulated as a precise set of directions which can be learned by heart. Second, it is a set of rules whose application is purely mechanical; it is a true technique because it does not require for its use any knowledge or intelligence not given in the technique itself... Third, it is a set of rules of universal application; it is a true technique in that it is an instrument of inquiry indifferent to the subject-matter of the inquiry. (1991 [1962]: 19–20)

An example from one of Bacon's major works illustrates just how far rationalism held sway over his thought. Towards the close of *The New Atlantis*, there is a remarkable passage in which Bacon essentially foresees the invention of industrial agriculture, bioengineering, light shows, sound systems, microscopy, and manned flight. Bacon then describes the 'Father of Salomon's House' (the New Atlantean institute for science), which, for our purposes, is perhaps the most illustrative portion of this work, since all of these futuristic wonders are achieved by a scientific culture that is planned to a level of detail that foresees exactly how many scholars it is appropriate to assign to a list of equally foreseen, predetermined tasks:

> These are (my son) the riches of Salomon's House.
>
> For the several employments and offices of our fellows; we have twelve that sail into foreign countries, under the names of other nations, (for our own we conceal); who bring us the books, and abstracts, and patterns of experiments of all other parts. These we call Merchants of Light.
>
> We have three that collect the experiments which are in all books. These we call Depredators.
>
> We have three that collect the experiments of all mechanical arts; and also of liberal sciences; and also of practices which are not brought into arts. These we call Mystery-men.
>
> We have three that try new experiments, such as themselves think good. These we call Pioneers or Miners.
>
> We have three that draw the experiments of the former four into titles and tables, to give the better light for the drawing of observations and axioms out of them. These we call Compilers.
>
> We have three that bend themselves, looking into the experiments of their fellows, and cast about how to draw out of them things of use and practise for man's life, and knowledge as well for works as for plain demonstration of causes, means of natural divinations, and the easy and clear discovery of the virtues and parts of bodies. These we call Dowry-men or Benefactors.
>
> Then after divers meetings and consults of our whole number to consider of the former labours and collections, we have three that take care, out of them, to direct new experiments, of a higher light, more penetrating into nature than the former. These we call Lamps.
>
> We have three others that do execute the experiments so directed, and report them. These we call Inoculators.
>
> Lastly, we have three that raise the former discoveries by experiments into greater observations, axioms, and aphorisms. These we call Interpreters of Nature. (Bacon, 1937: 488–489)

Oakeshott contended that Bacon's contribution to rationalism 'may be summed up… as the sovereignty of technique… technique and some material for it to work upon are all that matters' (1991 [1962]: 20–21).

Descartes, like Bacon, 'also perceived the lack of a consciously and precisely formulated technique of inquiry… For Descartes, no less than for Bacon, the aim is certainty', the achievement of which required 'an intellectual purge' (1991 [1962]: 21). Descartes claimed that, this purge having been achieved, we would, not surprisingly, find everyone in a state of absolute equality: 'Rather, it provides evidence that the power of judging rightly and of distinguishing the true from the false… is naturally equal in all men' (1993: 1).

Descartes was cautious enough to add caveats to his program, such as declaring, for instance, 'Thus my purpose here is not to teach the method that everyone ought to follow in order to conduct his reason correctly, but merely to show how I have tried to conduct mine' (1993: 2). But Descartes's modesty here was not embraced by his epigones; as Oakeshott put it, 'the Rationalist character may be seen springing from the exaggeration of Bacon's hopes and the neglect of the scepticism of Descartes: modern Rationalism is what commonplace minds made out of the inspiration of men of discrimination and genius' (1991 [1962]: 22).

For Descartes, tradition is a barrier to the exercise of reason, with no intrinsic value:

> I learned not to believe too firmly in what only custom and example had persuaded me to accept as true; and, in this way, I freed myself, little by little, from many of those errors which obscure the natural light of the mind, and make us less capable of listening to reason. (Descartes, 1960: 43)

Descartes attempts to justify his rejection of any guidance from tradition with analogies:

> Thus we see how a building, the construction of which has been undertaken and completed by a single architect, is usually superior in beauty and regularity to those that many have tried to restore by making use of old walls which had been built for other purposes. So, too, those old places which, beginning as villages, have developed in the course of time into great towns, are generally so ill-proportioned in comparison with those an engineer can design at will in an orderly fashion that, even though the buildings taken severally often display as much art as in other places, or even more, yet the disorder is such with a large house here and a small one there, and the streets all tortuous and uneven, that the whole place seems to be the product of chance rather than the design of men who use their reason… Or, to take a purely human instance, I believe that Sparta flourished so well, not because of the excellence of its laws taken one by one, for some were extremely strange and even morally repugnant, but because, being all the invention of one man, they all tended towards the same end. (Descartes, 1960: 44–45)

The confusion to which Descartes falls prey here should be apparent: the fact that buildings designed by a single architect exhibit a pleasing unity lacking in 'design by committee' says nothing about Descartes's aim of rejecting all tradition in constructing his philosophical system. A more accurate analogy to Descartes's project would be the case of a novice architect who claimed that, because his mind was empty of all the wisdom accumulated by the experience of hundreds of generations of architects, he was in a better position to construct a sound building than his rivals who were 'encumbered' by all of that tradition. As the architect Christopher Alexander argues, all successful buildings are built on 'design patterns' drawn from experience. The difference between a solo architect and a committee is not whether or not they make use of such patterns, as they both will, but that the lone architect is more free to assemble them according to a coherent pattern she perceives, rather than having to compromise with similar visions possessed by others.[4]

When Descartes turns his attention to social theory, we find him again being much better than his epigones:

> That is why I could in no way approve those cloudy and unquiet spirits who, being called neither by birth nor fortune to the handling of public affairs, are forever reforming the State in imagination; and, if I thought that there was the least thing in what I have written to bring me under suspicion of such folly, I should deeply regret its publication. (Descartes, 1960: 47)

But while Descartes was loath to extend his rationalist techniques to attempting to plan an entire social order, his descendants would not share his scruples.

So what was this method Descartes proposed? He stated its 'first rule' as follows:

> The first rule was to accept as true nothing that I did not know to be evidently so: that is to say, to avoid carefully precipitancy and prejudice, and to apply my judgements [sic] to nothing but that which showed itself so clearly and distinctly to my mind that I should never have occasion to doubt it. (Descartes, 1960: 50)

But Descartes fails to realize that what is 'clear and distinct' to someone inhabiting one tradition of thought may appear as obvious nonsense to someone reared in a different tradition.[5] For instance, the advantage of choosing moderation in his personal conduct appears

---

[4] See Alexander (1979).

[5] See MacIntyre (1988) for an extended demonstration of this point.

clear to him: 'Again, among several generally approved opinions, I always chose the more moderate ones, as being the easier to put into practice and the more likely to be the better ones, since all excess is usually bad' (1960: 54). But if he had not been reared in a tradition steeped in Aristotle, how clear would this have been? Descartes extends his principle from metaphysics to physics:

> I also showed what the laws of nature were; and, without basing my argument on anything but the infinite perfections of God, I endeavoured to prove all those laws of which there could be any doubt, and to show that they were such that, even if God had created many worlds, there could not be one in which the same laws were not observed. (Descartes, 1960: 69–70)

Of course, today, most of the 'laws' that Descartes thought could not have been otherwise, such as his laws of motion, are known to be false. Later rationalists would commit similar errors on the level of society-wide planning; unfortunately, as Oakeshott noted:

> [P]olitics is a field of activity peculiarly subject to the lure of this 'rational' ideal. If you start being merely 'intelligent' about a boiler or an electrical generator you are likely to pulled up short by an explosion; but in politics all that happens is war and chaos, which you do not immediately connect with your error. (1991 [1962]: 113–114)

A further examination of the rationalist character

With the above examples of rationalist thought in hand, let us explore Oakeshott's critique more deeply. As he saw it, perhaps the most salient feature of the rationalist approach is the faith that every essential aspect of any human practice can be conveyed adequately by means of a 'guidebook' comprising explicitly stated rules, formalized technical procedures, and general, abstract principles. Such a belief implies that internalizing the 'correct' theoretical model of some subject is all that is required to achieve successful performances in that domain; indeed, it implies that in attending to any features of a practice, such as experienced participants' rules of thumb or tacit understandings about how to proceed, any features other than the theoretical principles that purportedly capture the essence of the activity in question, merely erect superstitious barriers thwarting the rational reformation of performances of that activity. What is necessary to be 'rational' is to approach any activity with a *tabula rasa* upon which the correct technique for that activity can be cleanly inscribed; as Oakeshott put it, in this view, rational conduct involves 'a certain emptying of the mind, a conscious effort to get rid of preconceptions' (1991 [1962]: 101).

Quite to the contrary of that understanding of the relationship between technical guidelines and tacit knowledge, Oakeshott argues that the rationalist, in awarding theory primacy over practice, has gotten things exactly backwards. Theoretical understanding, he contends, is always a by-product of practical know-how, and never its progenitor. In fact, he sees the parasitical dependence of theory upon practice as being so unavoidable that not only is the rationalist incapable of successful performances guided solely by a theoretical model of the activity to be performed, he is not even able to stick to his purported guidelines while performing the activity poorly; instead, he inevitably will fall back on some familiar but unacknowledged existing practice in trying to realize his abstract schema.[6]

Oakeshott's contention, that the rationalist ideal of conduct guided entirely by explicitly adopted and provably justified 'principles' is absurd because it is impossible to achieve, is a close kin of Wittgenstein's insight that every attempt to follow correctly a set of formalized rules necessarily is grounded upon informal customs and practices that determine what it *means* to follow a rule 'correctly'. The formal rules cannot also embody their own 'correct' interpretation because any effort to incorporate that interpretation into the first-level rules would create a set of 'meta-rules', themselves requiring meta-meta-rules to guide the interpretation of the meta-rules, and so on, in an infinite regress.[7] As MacIntyre put this point:

> What can never be done is to reduce what has had to be learned in order to excel at such a type of [concrete] activity to the application of rules. There will of course at any particular stage in the historical development of such a form of activity be a stock of maxims which are used to characterize what is taken at that stage to be the best practice so far. But knowing how to apply these maxims is itself a capacity which cannot be specified by further rules, and the greatest achievements in each area at each stage always exhibit a freedom to violate the present established maxims, so that achievement proceeds both by rule-keeping and by rule-breaking. And there are never any rules to prescribe when it is the one rather than the other that we must do if we are to pursue excellence. (MacIntyre, 1988: 31)

---

[6] There are important relations between Oakeshott's views on theory and practice and Aristotle's, which will be discussed in the next chapter, after we have looked at *On Human Conduct*. And that will lead us on to Onora O'Neill as well.

[7] See Wittgenstein (1994: 86-107).

A number of notable practitioners of some science or craft have also noted the primacy of practice over theory. For instance, the chemist Michael Polanyi, commenting on the importance of tacit knowledge in the successful practice of any science, wrote:

> Again, while *the articulate contents of science* are successfully taught all over the world in hundreds of new universities, *the unspecifiable art of scientific research* has not yet penetrated to many of these... Without the opportunity offered to young scientists to serve an apprenticeship in Europe, and without the migration of European scientists to the new countries, research centres overseas could hardly ever have made much headway. (Polanyi, 1962: 53)

Similarly, the stone artist Dan Snow wrote, 'How the stone is readied, or "banked", for shaping, the degree of force, and the number and placement of blows are all variables in a process that only experience teaches' (2001: 63). Oliver Sacks discusses how the loss of access to tacit knowledge can leave post-encephalitic patients *literally* unable to move (1990: 63). Or consider Temple Grandin, the leading designer of animal processing facilities in the United States, who attributes her success to being 'detail-oriented', and claims that most people cannot see the problems she sees because they are too 'abstractified' (2005: 26–27).

And even in a field dealing largely with algorithms, there are no algorithms guaranteeing successful performances! As software engineer Jon Bentley wrote:

> Good programmers are a little bit lazy: they sit back and wait for an insight rather than rushing forward with their first idea. That must, of course, be balanced with the initiative to code at the proper time. The real skill, though, is knowing the proper time. That judgment comes only with the experience of solving problems and reflecting on their solutions. (1986: 17)

If thinkers like Oakeshott, the later Hayek,[8] Wittgenstein, Polanyi, and MacIntyre are correct in this regard, then the most important aspects of an accomplished practitioner's skill in any craft cannot be conveyed to a neophyte through explicit, technical instructions, but instead must be learned tacitly, during a period of intimate apprenticeship. All compilations of the formal rules purported to

---

[8] See, for instance, Hayek (1973: 5): '[C]ertain widely held scientific as well as political views are dependent on a particular conception of the formation of social institutions, which I shall call "constructivist rationalism" — a conception which assumes that all social institutions are, and ought to be, a product of deliberate design.'

underlie successful engagements in an activity must merely present an abstract abridgement of the concrete and formally unspecifiable knowledge possessed by the true master, who may offer an explicit set of precepts as a rough, surface map of his deep sea of experience-born proficiency, useful so that the beginner does not feel hopelessly lost when first venturing into those waters, or perhaps justified as navigation buoys indicating a general direction in which the beginner can steer her studies. But, however useful such a chart may be for gaining some initial orientation as to the outlines of the body of water one has set out to explore, it is no substitute for an intimate, personal knowledge of its currents, reefs, tides, and other idiosyncrasies.

It is worth digressing for a moment to remark on the curiosity that Oakeshott himself, in his very construction of his ideal type of the rationalist, is engaged in an enterprise of abstraction in some ways similar to those comprising the rationalism he aims to rebuke. At first glance, that observation might appear to have uncovered a telling inconsistency in his critique: how can it be sound if its formulation relies on the very sort of schematization of reality that it criticizes? However, I suggest that objection is not as forceful as it initially seems to be, for Oakeshott never proposed that he was describing anything other than an abstraction, or that the rationalist character ever is realized in the world in a pristine form—indeed, as noted above, he held that it was not even possible to realize fully the rationalist ideal. Rather, Oakeshott is drawing our attention to, by theoretically isolating, an aspect of post-Enlightenment thought that he sees as pervasive, highly significant, and largely unprecedented. (On the last point, he does not suggest that modern rationalism miraculously emerged without antecedent from a vacuum; he wrote that '[n]o doubt its surface reflects the light of rationalisms of a distant past' but, nevertheless, 'in its depths there is a quality exclusively its own' (1991 [1962]: 5).

Oakeshott himself described the use of such ideal types in political theory as follows:

At first sight it might appear that, so far from representing political activity (actual or imaginary), doctrines of this kind are nothing but misrepresentations of the experience from which they spring. But this, I think, is not all there is to be said of them. It is true that, in a doctrine of this kind, political activity appears in a greatly abridged and simplified form... Nevertheless, a doctrine of this kind has an explanatory value, which springs precisely from its being a reductio ad absurdum of a political experience. By representing as actual what is, in experience, only potential, by reducing individuals to types, by simplifying the outline and approximating the details to one another... a political doctrine may reveal the nature of a political experience in the same way as the over-emphasis of caricature reveals the potentialities of a face and a parody the potentialities of a style. (1993a: 148)

Therefore, the critique of Oakeshott as contradicting his own thesis even by stating it loses its force. But to return to our analysis of the ideal type itself, the rationalist who is applying his method to, say, cooking, is oblivious to the years that the skilled chef has spent establishing intimate relationships with his ingredients and tools, and tries to get by in the kitchen solely with what he can glean from a cookbook. As a result, he botches most of the dishes he attempts. However, Oakeshott suggested, his repeated failures typically do not lead him to suspect that his fundamental method of proceeding might be faulty. Instead, each disappointment only spurs the rationalist to search for a new, improved, and even more 'rational' book of recipes. Despite that modus operandi being no more workable in political activity than it is in cooking, Oakeshott contends that it is in the arena of contemporary politics where rationalist ideas have had their greatest impact:

> But what, at first sight, is remarkable, is that politics should have been earlier and more fully engulfed by the tidal wave [of rationalism] than any other human activity. The hold of Rationalism upon most departments of life has varied in its firmness during the last four centuries but in politics it has steadily increased and is stronger now than at any earlier time. (1991 [1962]: 25)

Here arises another bone of contention: The place of pre-eminence that Oakeshott assigns to rationalist influence in modern political life may appear to be at odds with his assertion that the rationalist can never actually realize his full program, but will always, in fact, wind up acting more or less along lines indicated by some tradition. Moreover, as Franco noted:

> The epistemological aspect of Oakeshott's critique of rationalist politics has puzzled many commentators. If, in the end, all politics are necessarily traditionalist, if ideological politics are simply impossible, there would seem to be no reason for preferring one style of politics to another; rationalist politics, although theoretically naïve, would seem to pose no great danger and therefore not need to be criticized. (2004: 93)

However, Oakeshott's assertion that the rationalist never really can proceed according to her avowed principles does not mean that her attempt to adhere to them will be inconsequential, but only that it will not succeed. An analogy may be helpful here: A person undertaking an effort to fly by vigorously flapping his arms whenever he walks surely will fail to reach his end, but, in the endeavor, he will succeed in making his perambulations much more tiring, awkward, and comical. As Collingwood wrote, 'A person may think he is a poached egg; that will not make him one: but it will affect his conduct, and for the worse' (1924: 206). That is the point Franco was making in noting that 'an erroneous theory can have pernicious practical consequences' (2004: 93). Since the pronouncements of the rationalist disparage current practices, customs, and morals,[9] insofar as they do not follow from his rational deliberations about how his society *ought* to be ordered, they will erode the spontaneous ease of the communal life that those traditions nourished, while offering in its stead only the artificial routines and regulations of a 'rational' bureaucracy, or worse. Oakeshott offered this example: 'First, we do our best to destroy parental authority (because of its alleged abuse), then we sentimentally deplore scarcity of "good homes", and we end by creating substitutes which complete the work of destruction' (1991 [1962]: 41). Traditional ways are undermined further by the rationalist fantasy that social perfection is a realistic goal, so that any practice promoting social order, however workable it might have proved in the past, will be condemned as an atavistic relic standing in the path of progress for failing to have brought about utopia.

It does not follow, from Oakeshott's view of the rationalist project as ruinously misguided, that all traditional practices are sacrosanct, or even that they all are laudable. Traditions are like living organisms: both can suffer illnesses and other disabilities; both ought to and usually do learn and adapt in response to their external circumstances and internal tensions; or, failing to do so, both soon cease to exist. But those adaptations, if they are to successfully meet the challenges presented by novel situations, must not promote the deterioration of the very organic order they purport to be serving. An appreciation for such evolutionary adaptation does not entail denying that intellectual criticism of the present social order has a genuine and vital role to play in that process. The political theorist can serve to diagnose and treat ills

---

[9] Hayek quotes a marvelous example of this attitude being voiced by Keynes: 'We entirely repudiated a personal liability on us to obey general rules. We claimed the right to judge every individual case on its merits, and the wisdom, experience, and self-control to do so successfully. This was a very important part of our faith, violently and aggressively held, and for the outer world it was our most obvious and dangerous characteristic. We repudiated entirely customary morals, conventions, and traditional wisdom' (1973: 26).

in his polity much as a physician does with those ills he detects in his patients. But, as Oakeshott noted, 'to cure is not to transform, it is not to turn the patient into a different sort of being; it is to restore to him such health as he is naturally capable of enjoying' (2006: 114). Because the rationalist physician attempts to transform rather than merely heal his charge, his treatments are likely to do far more harm than good.

Unfortunately, the 'rationalist chef's' counterpart in social reform similarly is inclined to interpret the social maladies produced by his projects not as evidencing any problem with his modus operandi but, quite to the contrary, as signalling the need for an even more energetic and thorough implementation of rationalist social engineering. The engineering metaphor itself encourages the planners to regard the rest of the citizenry as parts of a machine, cogs to be readjusted and rearranged as called for by each new blueprint, each drawn up to fix the problems generated by its predecessor. Since most people are disinclined to acquiesce to a life in which they are constrained to behave as an externally controlled mechanical device, the breakdown of each new, rationalist design for society is made even more probable.

An example of rationalism in a modern, liberal democracy

As mentioned in the Introduction, even a reader sympathetic to Oakeshott's case against rationalism in politics may suspect that it applies mostly to the extremes of social engineering seen during the middle decades of the twentieth century, such as were found in Mao's China, Stalin's Soviet Union, or Hitler's Germany, and, as such, is no longer particularly relevant. Therefore, I believe it will be useful to briefly examine a real-world example of the sorry effects of the rationalist mentality in a liberal democracy, drawn from the works of the famed analyst of urban life, Jane Jacobs. Her detailed analysis of healthy urban neighborhoods is based on her close observation of them, not on armchair theorizing.

Unlike Jacobs, mid-twentieth-century urban planners, possessed by the rationalist mindset, looked at city tenements and saw only un-designed chaos. Jacobs explicitly recognized the rationalist mindset of those she criticized:

[T]he practitioners and teachers of this discipline (if such it can be called) have ignored the study of success and failure in real life, have been incurious about the reasons for unexpected success, and are guided instead by principles derived from the behavior and appearance

of towns, suburbs, tuberculosis sanatoria, fairs, and imaginary dream
cities — from anything but cities themselves. (Jacobs, 1992: 6)

(Jacobs also saw that the rationalist planner, despite his pretension of
working only from first principles, in reality, as Oakeshott contended,
unconsciously draws upon some tradition or other in devising his
schemes. Jacobs's point here is that these planners turned to
inappropriate traditions, since they refused to admit that they were
working from a tradition at all.) As the planners saw things, the
residents of tenement neighborhoods were subjected to the noisy
activities of industry and commerce, disturbing their peace. Their
children, living in densely built-up districts, were forced to play *on the
sidewalks*! What these people lacked was fresh air, sunshine, green
spaces, and quiet. (The planners inadvertently tried to create a likeness
of their own wealthy, suburban lives in the context of poor
neighborhoods, completely ignoring the differences that made
suburban life workable, such as greater wealth, ubiquitous ownership
of automobiles, lower population densities, more homogeneous
populations, the relative absence of strangers passing through the
neighborhood, and so on.)

Therefore, these planners claimed, the 'obvious' solution to the
discomforts of ghetto life was to tear down these 'slums' en masse, and
in their place erect purely residential complexes, consisting of high
rises separated by wide swaths of grass and trees — in other words, the
giant American housing projects of the 1950s and '60s. As Jacobs noted,
the rationalist planners, blind to the concrete reality of tenement life,
failed to realize that the mix of businesses and residences increased the
safety of the residents by providing 'eyes on the street' — the
neighborhood shopkeeper, who knew all the residents, was out
sweeping his sidewalk early in the morning; the workers going to and
from their jobs meant a steady stream of pedestrians; and even the
neighborhood bar meant that the streets were not deserted until the
wee hours of the morning. Parents transporting their children to and
from school would appear on the street. Mothers with preschool
children would head to the parks, workers would come out to eat lunch
in them, and shoppers would come and go from area stores. The
children playing on the sidewalks could easily be monitored by all of
these people, many of whom knew them, as well as their parents,
leaning out the second-story window to shout, 'Johnny, cut that
nonsense out!'

By contrast, the new, 'rational' housing projects were empty of life
around the buildings for most of the day. The basketball courts and the

lovely green parks were unsupervised because there was no one around. The mother, now living up in her thirtieth-floor, modern apartment, was completely unable to watch over her children's play if she let them go down to those 'recreational' spaces. Here again, in the design of these high-rise buildings, the planners could not actually act as good rationalists and shed all tradition; instead, they 'designed in an imitation of upper-class standards for apartment living...' while ignoring the fact that the residents lacked 'upper-class cash for doormen and elevator men', the paid security men who made the upper-class apartment building safe (Jacobs, 1992: 42). As a result, the corridors and stairwells of these buildings became like unwatched and deserted streets, meaning that they were lawless and dangerous places. That danger isolated law-abiding residents even more, so that parents concerned for their children's safety and character refused to allow them to go out of their apartment except when absolutely necessary, meaning that they received no benefit at all from the pleasant green spaces that the planners had thought would be their salvation. Discussing a single street in East Harlem, with a 'modern, rational' public housing project on one side and 'chaotic' tenement life on the other, Jacobs wrote:

> On the old-city side, which was full of public places and the sidewalk loitering so deplored by Utopian minders of other people's leisure, the children were being kept well in hand. On the project side of the street across the way, the children, who had a fire hydrant open beside their play area, were behaving destructively... (Jacobs, 1992: 57)

The result is well-known: the community ties of the bulldozed tenements were shattered, the spaces around the high rises became the domain of drug dealers and muggers, and the rationally designed inner cities of the late '60s exploded with crime and waves of riots. This outcome, while not planned, was very much the unintended outcome of deliberate, rationalist planning:

> There is nothing economically or socially inevitable about either the decay of old cities or the fresh-minted decadence of the new unurban urbanization. On the contrary, no other aspect of our economy and society has been more purposefully manipulated for a full quarter of a century. (Jacobs, 1992: 7)

The effects of rationalism in the nations of Nazi Germany, Soviet Russia, Pol Pot's Cambodia, and Communist China, to cite a few prominent examples, were even more extreme, of course, leading to the deaths of millions upon millions of people in the twentieth century. But I offer the above example from Jacobs because I think it is important to see the relevance of Oakeshott's work in a more familiar and less obviously rationalist setting.

Jacobs's work is also relevant as an illustration of the fact that rejecting rationalism is not equivalent to defending entrenched privilege, opposing all 'progressive programmes', or being a political reactionary. Jacobs is in favor of planning done with the real needs of real cities in mind; for instance, she argues that lot usages 'too big' for a neighborhood, such as a huge department store dominating a block in an area otherwise devoted to a mix of residences, small shops, and light industries, should be banned. Neither is she against all social programs aimed at helping the poor. Instead, she is arguing that programs that ignore the factors that actually make the life of the urban poor workable, and instead destroy their communities in an attempt to realize the fantasy of turning their neighborhoods into grassy, tree-filled suburbs, do much more harm than good. And while Jacobs held that certain planning schemes may at least assist the creation of the spontaneous urban order she admires, she firmly rejected the idea that all that is needed is a new, improved form of master plan: '[The] cultivation [of city order] cannot be institutionalized' (1992: 56).

But if rationalism fails, what is the alternative?

What is the character of 'anti-rationalist' politics?

In 'Rationalism in Politics', Oakeshott primarily critiques the rationalist conceit, rather than describing the contrasting approach, which he obviously holds in higher esteem, in any detail. Nevertheless, we can glean something of its character from that essay, and can fill in our sketch even further by considering other of his works, as we will do in the next chapter. And the attempt to assemble such a portrait clearly is germane for any evaluation of Oakeshott's thesis, for, however accurate his catalogue of the shortcomings of rationalist politics, it remains senseless to reject rationalism if it turns out to be the only game in town.

The question of how to designate the alternative to rationalism, so as to best indicate what Oakeshott endorses here, is not answered as easily as its fundamental place in his thought might suggest it should be. Initially, based upon a reading of 'Rationalism in Politics' and related essays from around the same period of his intellectual journey, 'traditionalism' recommends itself as aptly capturing the essence of 'anti-rationalist politics'. The problem with this label is that, in later works, Oakeshott explicitly rejects it as offering a misleading indication of what he understands to be the approach preferable to rationalism. In an essay responding to criticism of *On Human Conduct*, he states, 'I have become much more strict with the word "practice"… and I have abandoned "tradition" as inadequate to express what I want to express' (1976: 364).

Given that *On Human Conduct* offers the first published statement of this shift in Oakeshott's view on this matter, it is tempting to substitute the term 'civil association', which constitutes one of the main topics of that work, for 'traditionalism' as the best designation for the approach with which rationalism is being contrasted. By 'civil association' Oakeshott means a form of relationship between individuals in which their bonds are constituted not by attempts to satisfy substantive desires or goals through their interactions (a condition he designates as 'enterprise association'), but by their mutual recognition of an obligation to heed certain precepts (often formalized as 'laws') in conducting their pursuit of their individual ends, ends left unspecified by the conditions of civil association itself. But while there certainly are important parallels between the pairs 'rationalist politics'/'anti-rationalist politics' and 'enterprise association'/'civil association', the first and second terms of the former pair do not map exactly onto those of the latter one. In particular, as I will argue later in this work, the founders of the American republic displayed a significantly rationalist bent while attempting to create a polity that they intended to function much along the lines of a civil association as depicted by Oakeshott. Therefore, while the concept of civil association is linked to that of anti-rationalist politics, insofar as its pursuit intrinsically excludes any effort by the state intentionally to replace the traditions, practices, mores, and customs of its citizens with some rationally devised alternatives, that connection does not preclude the very real possibility of the intended form of a civil association itself being planned in a rationalist spirit. (Of course, if Oakeshott is correct, such a plan never will achieve its aim, but that does not mean that the attempt to implement it is inconsequential.) As such, 'civil association' does not serve as an adequate designation for the style of politics Oakeshott is opposing to rationalism.

What, then, should we call 'anti-rationalist politics', if we hope to avoid the repeated use of such an awkward and purely negative designation? In light of the distinction Oakeshott draws in *On Human Conduct*, the very work in which he first rejects his earlier use of 'tradition' to convey his conception of the alternative to the rationalist style, between the conduct of practical affairs and that of theorizing, I propose to call that alternative 'practical' or 'pragmatic' politics. This term suggests an approach that, while not rejecting the counsel offered by rational analysis of current practice, and thus not immune to modification through reflection, remains grounded in the concrete circumstances and earlier experiences of the participants in a polity, and resists the temptation to reject the ambiguities and uncertainties of the practical world by embracing some theoretical abstraction of political life that boasts it can provide definitive resolutions, incontrovertibly justified through their deduction from first principles, to any and all political issues. As Oakeshott describes him, the rationalist finds 'the intricacy of the world of time and contingency so unmanageable that he is bewitched by the offer of a quick escape into the bogus eternity of an ideology' (1991 [1962]: 34); the disciple of practical politics, to the contrary, does not flinch in the face of that intricacy, accepting it as an inherent and unremediable feature of the world of practice.

So, let us adopt 'practical politics' as naming the style opposed to rationalism, at least until a better suggestion is offered, and proceed to examine its character in more detail, briefly in this section, and at greater length in our historical study of the Roman republic, whose chapters contain the real answer to the question, 'What is the character of practical politics?' which is 'look and see'. While this term is the best I have been able to come up with, it does suffer from an unfortunate ambiguity: the 'practical' in 'practical politics' naturally enough might be thought to stand in opposition to what is 'impractical', so that 'practical politics' would mean 'politics restricting itself to what is readily achievable'. While it is true that what is meant here by 'practical politics' *will* tend to focus on what is actually achievable, 'practical politics' in our sense should be understood primarily in contrast to 'theoretical politics' — as an instance of Aristotle's distinction between *phronesis* and *theoria* — and only secondarily to 'impractical politics'. Furthermore, practical politics, as noted above, does not exclude the possibility or importance of an intellectual critique of current practice playing a salutary role in political life, as an antidote to dull complacency or a corrective to unjust institutions whose long establishment in a culture can serve to occlude their undesirability. But even while recognizing the value of reflectively guided modifications of established ways, the adherent of practical politics understands that in a healthy polity even innovations must be 'intimated', as Oakeshott likes to put it, to be natural developments of already existing practices. It is the practical experience of actually engaging in some activity that creates the possibility of improving one's future performances by reflecting upon past performances; abstract thought is incapable of giving birth to a novel mode of practice with no genealogical roots in any previously existing form of concrete activity. In pursuing practical politics, the most common and the most readily approved response to some novel situation facing a polity will involve seeking among the already familiar and time-tested practices and institutions, for the one(s) that can be modified most naturally to meet the new challenge.

Conclusion

Oakeshott saw the crucial mistake of the rationalist approach, in politics as elsewhere, in the attempt to substitute abstract principles for concrete knowledge of the particular circumstances of time and place in guiding practical activities. The rationalist is not endorsing a particular, possible way of engaging in practical action; he is beholden to a theory of practice that is mistaken, and cannot be engaged in at all. But his attempt is not harmless, for the fixation on abstractions renders actual conduct hampered by rationalist ideals awkward and stumbling, as if one were trying to run while at the same time analyzing each stride for conformity to ideal mechanical efficiency. Let us now see how the character of Oakeshott's critique of rationalism developed during the course of his intellectual career, so as to achieve an even deeper understanding of that critique.

Chapter 2

The Development of Oakeshott's Critique of Rationalism

Having examined Oakeshott's alternative to rationalist politics, it will now behoove us to explore how his own understanding of rationalism developed over time, by searching for various facets of his understanding of rationalism displayed by other works of his, even those in which the topic is peripheral to their primary concern. While 'Rationalism in Politics' and 'Rational Conduct' represent the two primary places in which Oakeshott addressed the topic of modern rationalism, the subject threads its way, sometimes more prominently, sometimes less so, through the bulk of his work. Indeed, as discussed above, Oakeshott himself contends that *On Human Conduct* contains an important modification to a central conception in those earlier essays. We next will proceed with our survey of the most relevant of those works in chronological fashion, beginning with his first major publication, *Experience and Its Modes*.

Experience and Its Modes

Published in 1933, this book is primarily a bold and, by its time, quite unfashionable defense of philosophical idealism by the young Oakeshott. Although the relationship of idealist philosophy to rationalism is beyond the scope of this project, the narrower case for the modality of human knowledge that Oakeshott incorporates into his main thesis provides much of the philosophical background for his later arguments for the inability of theory to act as the master of practice, so we will examine that in some detail.

In this work, Oakeshott contends that philosophy alone represents an attempt to grapple with 'experience without reservation or arrest'

(1933: 4), a view he would later modify but never entirely abandon.[1] Other forms of human knowledge, such as science, history, and practice, are inherently incomplete approaches to understanding experience, as they are founded upon certain unquestioned presuppositions that are formulative for their particular 'world of ideas'. Such inherent conditionality renders those 'modes' of experience not only ultimately unsatisfactory as methods for grasping the 'totality of experience', but also categorically distinct, since each mode is constituted by its own peculiar presuppositions, meaning that no mode is in a position to direct the progress of understanding in any of the others. Especially relevant, for our purposes, is Oakeshott's contention that science has no authority over practice, a view that indicts the rationalists' dream of reorganizing and correcting the 'irrational' world of practice, grounded in tradition, by applying abstract, scientific principles to everyday conduct as being guilty of categorical irrelevance. Science, per Oakeshott, is an 'attempt to find… a world of definite and demonstrable experience, one free from merely personal associations and independent of the idiosyncrasies of particular observers, an absolutely impersonal and stable world' (1933: 169–170). As a consequence of its founding postulates, the 'concepts [of science] do not, in any sense, refer to the world of practice, to the world given in sensation [and therefore,] the generalizations which express their necessary relations cannot be taken to imply that any event or occurrence will invariably take place. The concepts do not refer to events; and the generalizations are not in respect of events' (1933: 183).[2]

The world of practice, on the other hand, is experience viewed precisely in terms of how a current state of affairs might be transformed into a future state seen as more satisfactory *in the eyes of a specific agent*. As such, 'a scientific idea must be transformed, taken out of the world of scientific experience, before it can establish itself in the world of practice' (1933: 265). For example, an engineer in his work cannot simply use the laws of physics as they are provided to him by physicists; in trying to solve a practical problem like designing a satisfactory bridge, he must reformulate those laws in terms of concepts alien to physics, as he seeks not universal laws, but to determine, for

---

[1] In defense of the contention that Oakeshott's later works modify his early idealism without overturning it, see, for instance, Nardin (2001: 48–53) or Franco (2004); for a dissenting view, arguing that Oakeshott should be understood to have left the idealism of his youth behind, see Gerencser (2000).

[2] For a recent picture of the relationship between scientific laws and ordinary events that is supportive of Oakeshott's, see Cartwright (1983).

instance, 'Will *this particular* bridge, built as designed at *this particular* location, provide an adequate safety margin for *this particular* predicted amount of traffic while meeting *this particular* cost constraint?' All of those specifics, the incorporation of which is crucial for any successful solution to the engineer's problem, are categorically excluded from properly scientific laws. In light of the divergent aims characterizing the modes of science and of practice, the scientist is no more in a position to dictate the course of practical affairs according to his theoretical conclusions than is the practical person in a position to direct scientific research according to her personal ambitions. The relevance of this early conclusion of Oakeshott's to his later essays on rationalism is, I think, obvious, especially once it is recognized, as argued above, that the proper contrast class to rational politics is not traditional politics but practical politics.

The Politics of Faith and the Politics of Scepticism

Although not published until 1996, *The Politics of Faith and the Politics of Scepticism* was composed at roughly the same time as 'Rationalism in Politics'.[3] In this work, Oakeshott presented a conceptual spectrum of political attitudes running from total faith to complete scepticism, and argued that it offered one useful framework for organizing the complex reality of modern, European political experience. Once again, as with the dichotomy of 'rationalist politics' and 'practical politics' discussed earlier, it is important to recognize that Oakeshott was proposing ideal types lying at the extremities of a range of attitudes, abstractions that he suggested may prove fruitful aids to political understanding, even while he recognized that neither any actual polity nor even any actual political thinker will instantiate either extreme in its theoretical purity. As he pointed out early in the work presently under consideration:

> Nevertheless, in every heterogeneous and complex activity of governing there are extremes. Normally, the internal movement does not reach them; indeed, so far from being attracted to them it is usually repelled. But in the end it is these poles, which, defining the limits of characteristic movement, protect the identity of the manner of governing. (1996: 11)

---

[3] The editor of the posthumously published version, Timothy Fuller, remarks, 'Why Oakeshott chose to leave this (and many other writings) unpublished… is a mystery' (1996: ix).

In other words, he is contemplating actual approaches to politics in terms of the extent to which they exhibit the characteristics of one or the other of these polar ideals, in the hope that the exercise will make the concrete cases more intelligible. Early on in *The Politics of Faith and the Politics of Scepticism*, Oakeshott makes a point of distinguishing the disputed territory of which his contrasting ideal types of 'faith' and 'scepticism' represent the far reaches from another aspect of government that he sees as a quite separate matter, an important distinction because, he contends, these two orthogonal issues often are confused as being one. He is not, he informs his reader, concerned with the question, 'Who shall rule and by what authority?' (1996: 3). That question asks, what is the basis, if any such basis indeed exists, for justifying the authority of the state, and under what conditions, if any, are its subjects obligated to recognize a state's claim to their willing obedience? A multitude of grounds for the justice or desirability of the existence of a single, sovereign power have been offered, including the divine right of monarchs to rule; the conformity of social hierarchy with the cosmic order; the need of humanity, in its fallen state, to have its sinful impulses forcibly held in check; the rational requirement that every individual accept an implicit 'social contract' rescuing him from the horror of living in a brutish war of all against all; the moral claims of the 'general will', as embodied in the state, over the selfish whims of the ego; the role of the state as the historically necessary vehicle through which the proletariat will realize a socialist utopia, and so on. However, although some of those answers may incline those who embrace them more towards one end or the other of the spectrum running from faith to scepticism, none of them logically restricts its adherents to any particular region of that scale. The contrast between the politics of faith and the politics of scepticism is not drawn from a perspective as to what makes a state legitimate, but is a portrait of the range of possible answers to the question, 'What shall government (composed and authorized in whatever manner one thinks proper) do?' (Oakeshott, 1996: 3)

Where any thinker's views fall in that range of possible answers, Oakeshott contends, significantly depends on the degree to which they judge the current state of human nature as a given condition simply to be accepted and dealt with as we find it, as opposed to its being a contingent product of existing social arrangements, and therefore, amenable to open-ended improvement through the adoption of better institutions and policies. At one extreme, he proposes, the politics of faith springs from the conviction that 'human perfection is to be achieved by human effort', and its 'achievement... depends upon our own unrelaxed efforts, and that if those efforts are unrelaxed, perfection will appear' (1996: 23).[4] While the politics of faith shares that conviction with all varieties of utopian thought, what distinguishes it as the *politics* of faith from efforts to reach a utopia through, for instance, the widespread adoption of specific spiritual practices or by a process of individual, psychological transformation, is its belief that government action represents the true path for reaching that posited state of perfection.

In the politics of scepticism, on the other hand, 'there is absent... any idea whatsoever of government as the agent of human improvement and perfection'. Indeed, 'the idea of human perfection is for [the sceptic] absurd' (1996: 28). Instead, the sceptic sees 'order as a great and difficult achievement never beyond the reach of decay and dissolution' (1996: 32), so that a government will have all it can do merely to maintain it.

Initially, it might appear that this is only a variant of the commonplace depiction of political views as occupying a particular position on a scale running from the far left (radical communism) to the extreme right (with rigid social stratification or perhaps the embrace of all market outcomes). Indeed, John Horton saw it much that way:

> The book articulates a distinction between two 'styles' of the activity of governing—'the politics of faith' and 'the politics of scepticism'. This distinction is clearly related to others he deploys elsewhere, most obviously between rationalism and conservatism, collectivism and individualism and enterprise and civil association. On the one hand, the left as we might say, we have the politics of faith, rationalism, collectivism and enterprise association and on the other, the right, the politics of scepticism, conservatism, individualism and civil association. The terms in each of these sets are certainly not equivalent, but they form two broad families, each loosely linked within a binary structure that is characteristic of Oakeshott's thought. (Horton, 2005: 25)

However, while Horton's contention is not without some merit, in that it notes a tendency for individuals approaching these various poles to cluster as he indicates, Oakeshott's schema, examined more carefully, resists any such neat mapping. Some advocates of unfettered capitalism, typically seen as being well towards the right of the political

---

[4] Compare this with Voegelin on 'gnosticism': Voegelin argues that, far from seeing the 'end times' as a purely spiritual symbol, as, for instance, a traditional Christian like Augustine did, '[t]he Gnostic revolutionary... interprets the coming of the realm as an event that requires his military cooperation' (1987: 145).

spectrum, nevertheless will appear as representatives of the party of faith when viewed from the perspective from which Oakeshott has chosen to paint his subject, should they regard a full embrace of laissez-faire policies as being not merely the best available method for coping with the unavoidable difficulties inherent in the human condition, but as providing the road to a utopian society in which those difficulties are vanquished. (Ayn Rand—see her 1957 novel *Atlas Shrugged*, for instance—comes to mind as a good example of this possibility.) At the same time, many other political thinkers, usually located far to the left using the conventional gauge, may be included in the party of scepticism under Oakeshott's classificatory criteria, if they conceive of socialism not as heralding the dawn of the kingdom of heaven upon the earth, but as simply the most practical system for making an imperfect, messy world as palatable as is possible.

Similarly, a superficial critic of Oakeshott might be tempted to equate the terms of this dichotomy with the polar pair presented in his analysis of rationalism, so that rational politics = the politics of faith, and practical politics = the politics of scepticism, and thus accuse Oakeshott of merely saying the same thing over again while trying to disguise his repetitiveness by shifting his vocabulary.[5] However, as elegantly symmetrical as that correspondence may appear at first glance, the genuine relationship between the two conceptual schemes is not that simple: the opposition between rationalism and practice regards how a government might plausibly proceed in fulfilling its appointed functions, whatever those functions are deemed to include, while that between faith and scepticism is a matter of what sort of functions government should properly undertake. Nevertheless, as indicated above, the inkling that the members of Oakeshott's pairs of polarities can be matched up in some nontrivial fashion is not baseless, because there exists a genuine affinity between rationalism and the politics of faith, just as there does between practical politics and the politics of scepticism. It seems quite plausible that the personal predilections leading one to embrace the utopian vision also will incline one towards the position that utopia can be reached by following a rationally devised, theoretically guided itinerary, especially since achieving the lofty aims of one's undertaking may appear to demand the most rigorous planning. Similarly, a sceptical view on the inherent limits to what may be accomplished through political action fits

---

[5] Spitz (1976) made just such an accusation in his review of *On Human Conduct*, while Corey (2006) also equates rationalism and the politics of faith, albeit in a more laudatory tone.

comfortably with a presumption in favor of time-honored political practices and institutions, since a reluctance to abandon what worked in the past impedes the adoption of untested new schemes for the government to attempt steering social conduct along a better course.

However, while the above considerations suggest that the coexistence of the practical style of politics with political scepticism and that of rationalism with the politics of faith will be common, nevertheless those pairings are contingent rather than necessary: there is nothing inherently contradictory about believing that the traditions of one's own society providentially happen to be the best means for achieving human perfection, nor is it on its face incoherent to devise a rationalist scheme aimed at restricting the activities of government to those deemed proper by the sceptic. (As mentioned earlier in this chapter, Oakeshott presented Hayek's *The Road to Serfdom* as an example of this latter possibility.) Indeed, I will argue that the two polities we will examine in the greatest depth later in this work largely exhibit the reversal of the naturally assumed association of rationalism with the politics of faith and traditionalism with the politics of scepticism, although, being real historical entities rather than ideal constructs, they display only a rough correspondence to the pure, theoretical types presented here. The Roman republic provides our empirical support for the possibility of a pragmatic approach to the politics of faith. The Romans, for many centuries, looked to their traditions as offering the best guidance in responding to novel political situations. Nevertheless, as Oakeshott put it, they saw 'the events and the fortunes of [their] remarkable people [as being] endowed with a universal significance by being made to compose a work of art—a drama, or a story whose moral was always being made explicit in events' (2006: 208). The Romans believed that they were 'blessed by the gods... their destiny to rule the world and impose a civilization and an orderliness upon its barbarisms' (2006: 213), placing the general tenor of their political life clearly on the 'faith' side of the scale.

In American politics, on the other hand, while such a belief in a unique national destiny has made regular appearances, the more dominant influence upon the efforts of those framing the constitutional foundations of the new nation was the sceptical concern to ensure that the nascent government would not do more harm than good by exceeding its proper limits, and thereby threatening its citizens' inalienable rights to 'life, liberty and pursuit of happiness'. However, the American founders pursued that sceptical aim by attempting rationally to devise a system of government whose very structure would prove to be a bulwark against the threat of tyranny. They hoped to safeguard their dream of enduring republican liberty from the vicissitudes of historical change by surrounding it with institutional mechanisms engineered to shelter it from the capricious whims of *fortuna*.[6]

It is also worth noting that, even for someone who recognizes that Oakeshott's dichotomy of faith/scepticism cannot be neatly mapped onto his dichotomy of rationalism/pragmatism, it still might be suggested that the former does map neatly onto his differentiation of enterprise association and civil association, with the politics of faith equated to a view of the state as an enterprise association, and the politics of scepticism aligned with an endorsement of the state as a civil association.[7] However, while once again, I see such a mapping as initially plausible and as perhaps indicative of a general affinity between the pairs of ideal types, that those poles are not equivalent can be demonstrated by means of a counterexample: Murray Rothbard, whose work will be discussed in more detail in Chapter 4, came down on the side of civil association, or organizing society solely in terms of general laws, so strongly that he viewed granting a single entity (the state) coercive powers to collect taxes to enforce those laws as immoral. Nevertheless, Rothbard's political writings clearly fall well on the 'faith' side of the faith/scepticism divide, since he, in contrast to Oakeshott, painted a utopian picture of how social life would proceed should all traces of enterprise association be expunged from politics. [8]

Thus, as I see it, the conceptual framework Oakeshott erected by contrasting the politics of faith with the politics of scepticism provides a complementary but distinctive perspective to that offered in his work on rationalism, as well as to his schemata of civil versus enterprise association. Although the primary focus of this work will be to explore

---

[6] See Pocock (1975) on the importance of the concept of *fortuna* in the history of republican thought.

[7] Worthington offers a theoretical argument for the association of the politics of faith with an enterprise conception of the state: 'In short, the politics of faith divines the authority to govern from an idea of perfection that lies beyond [civil] association. Civil association is viewed not as an on-going practice but as an expendable resource whose only value is to be exploited for future perfection and improvement. In reducing the authority of civil rules to considerations of their desirability enterprise association has, once again, prevailed over civil association' (2005: 118). While Worthington is correct in noting this as a predilection, his observation does not foreclose the possibility of pursuing an ideal state of civil association with the attitude of the politics of faith, as noted below in the case of Rothbard.

[8] See, for instance, Rothbard (1998).

the applicability of his theory of rationalism to the world of actual polities, I also, where appropriate, will occasionally call upon this alternative schema to shed further light upon some topic relevant to my project.

Morality and Politics in Modern Europe

As in the previous case, we are dealing here with material composed long before it was published. This book appeared in 1993, but is based upon a series of lectures that Oakeshott delivered at Harvard University in 1958. Thus, the ideas presented are those Oakeshott was entertaining roughly midway between his authoring of 'Rationalism in Politics' and the development of his thought culminating in *On Human Conduct*, the work considered in the next section.

As in previous works, and, as we will see, in those subsequent, Oakeshott again posits a dichotomy in manners of political acting and thinking; and it is one related to, but different from, his other dichotomies. In writing the present portion of this work, I found myself taken by the image of Oakeshott as a sort of 'political-thought jeweler', holding up the history of Western political theory and practice before the light of his craft, but turning the gem this way and that, first examining the facets it displayed when held at one angle, then at another, hoping to comprehend the gem as a concrete whole by understanding each of these facets in turn.[9] In any case, the facets here illuminated are the history of modern European politics seen as a dialectical confrontation between the politics of individualism and the politics of collectivism.

Oakeshott contends that in the course of the breakdown of the communal world of the Middle Ages, there arose a new moral disposition, 'the disposition to make choices for oneself to the maximum possible extent, choices concerning activities, occupations, beliefs, opinions, duties and responsibilities... [and] to approve of this sort of conduct... as conduct proper to a human being' (1993b: 21). Naturally enough, as Oakeshott sees it, the individuals who embraced this disposition sought to have their morality reflected in the political arrangements under which they would conduct their affairs, leading to an understanding that:

---

[9] In fact, in the essay 'The Concept of Government in Modern Europe', Oakeshott presents yet another dichotomy in which to conceive political activity, that between 'substantive' and 'regulatory' activities (2008: 99).

The office of government is not to impose other beliefs and activities upon its subjects, not to tutor or to educate them, not to make them better or happier in a way other than that which they have chosen for themselves, not to direct them, lead them or manage them; the office of government is merely to rule... The image of the ruler is not that of the manager but that of the umpire whose business it is to administer the rules of a game in which he does not himself participate. (1993b: 49)

This, of course, describes the classical liberal view of the state, as propounded by numerous thinkers such as Locke, Kant, Adam Smith, Burke, Bastiat, many of the American founders, and so on.

But the morality of individualism was not alone on the stage of modern European history. Many people, as Oakeshott saw it, were ill-equipped to meet the challenge of living as such autonomous individuals, whether by disposition or material circumstances. The communal character of life in the Middle Ages had not vanished from memory, and they longed for the security and sense of belonging it had offered. However, in the wake of the Protestant reformation, the scientific revolution, and the emergence of the morality of individualism, the simple, unreflective embrace of communal life that had characterized the medieval world was no longer an option. As Oakeshott put it, 'this "common good"... is not "given" (as it was in the communal life of a medieval village, for example): it has to be chosen and established. It entails a criticism and a modification of the multiplicity of activities and beliefs which are afoot' (1993b: 90). This meant that the morality of collectivism had to be explicitly worked out as a response to those altered circumstances. The attempt to revive what had existed as a traditional way of life, once that way of life had passed, required a traditionalist ideology. (The phenomenon of a dying tradition being transformed into a traditionalist ideology will reappear later in this work, particularly regarding the appearance of a traditionalist party, the *optimates*, in the waning years of the Roman republic.) And naturally, just as the morality of individualism has a style of politics that is its natural expression, so, too, does the morality of collectivism.

So what characterizes this second style?

By the politics of collectivism I mean an understanding of government in which its proper office is believed to be the imposition upon its subjects of a single pattern of conduct, organizing all their activities in such a manner that they conform to this pattern. It understands governing as creating a 'community' by determining a 'common good' and enforcing conformity to it. (1993b: 89)

Now, yet again we find a dichotomy that bears some similarity to others that Oakeshott has proposed or will propose. The politics of collectivism clearly resembles both rationalist politics and the politics of faith, while the politics of individualism is akin to both pragmatic politics and the politics of scepticism. But, once again, an attempt to regard them as merely alternative names for the same phenomena won't do, because the politics of individualism is also susceptible to the pull of rationalism, as Oakeshott recognized:

> Writers in this idiom, in order to make their position impregnable, have been accustomed to construct a foundation far in excess of what is required to carry the superstructure. They have invoked metaphysical theories of personality, they have appealed to principles of natural law, they have elaborated theories of human nature in general… in short, the vice of those who have elaborated the historic versions of the political theory of individualism is that they have tended to encourage us to expect too much from their reflections. (1993b: 85)

In particular, as we will see in the case of a thinker like Rothbard, these writers have sometimes dreamed of creating a 'pure' politics of individualism, untainted by any whiff of collectivism. But these tendencies, as Oakeshott rightly sees them, are only abstractions that cannot exist in their pure forms.

On Human Conduct

As mentioned above, in *On Human Conduct*, published in 1975, Oakeshott presents yet two more pairs of dichotomous ideal types, the first of which is that of the practitioner and the theorist; indeed, his previously cited remark, made while responding to critics of this book, that he had abandoned his earlier use of 'tradition' as an apt term for the style of politics he opposed to rationalism, was the basis for our adopting 'practical politics' as superior to the perhaps more common 'traditional politics' for designating that style.

Oakeshott opens this work with a lengthy meditation on the nature of theorizing. As he concludes that section, he segues into the discussion of the practice/theory dichotomy by noting the debt his analysis of theorizing owes to Plato's examination of the same topic, especially to the metaphor of the cave presented in *The Republic*. In light of the similarity of their views, Oakeshott continued, 'it may be instructive to notice [our] divergencies' (1975: 27). And indeed it may.

As Oakeshott understood Plato, the latter's cave dwellers represent those individuals whose conceptual horizon is bound within the world of practical affairs. Plato was correct, in Oakeshott's view, in holding that, because such individuals fail to recognize the intrinsically conditional nature of the practical understanding of reality, instead mistakenly accepting it as the only possible mode of comprehending experience so that, however clever and adept they become at dealing with the practical world, they have, in effect, imprisoned themselves within its confines (i.e., within Plato's cave). As Corey wrote of Oakeshott's understanding of the conditional nature of practical experience, 'Nowhere in practice is there uninterrupted progress or final achievement... If human life were to consist wholly in engagement in practical affairs, then it would seem to be a depressing predicament' (2006: 39). And Plato also was accurate in regarding the understanding of the theorist, in that it represents at least a recognition of those limitations, as being, in a sense, a higher form of knowledge than that gained by the solely practical thinker.

However, Oakeshott argued, 'distracted by his exclusive concern with the engagement of theoretical understanding and with the manifest shortcomings of [the cave-dwellers' world]... [Plato] is disposed to write [the latter] off as nescience. This, I think, is a mistake' (1975: 27). That the practical understanding of the world is inherently limited does not imply that what it yields it is not really knowledge at all; rather, the proper conclusion is that practical understanding offers only a conditional form of knowledge—but conditional knowledge is nevertheless knowledge, and not mere ignorance. Moreover, quite crucially for Oakeshott, the abstract superiority of theoretical knowledge over its practical counterpart in no way means that the former can replace the latter in dealing with the practical world, which is, after all, precisely the conditional realm for which practical understanding is the appropriate species of knowledge. While it is true that discovering 'a platform of understanding is conditional and to become acquainted with its proximate conditions is a notable step in the engagement of understanding', such a discovery 'is not like exposing a fraud [, since] shadows are not forgeries' (1975: 28).

Given that genuine knowledge of the realm of the shadows is a real and hard-won achievement, the 'pure' theorist goes gravely astray if he erroneously employs his theoretical insights as grounds for issuing directives to accomplished practitioners, ridiculously trying to 'set them straight' on matters with which the theorist has no familiarity. Oakeshott wryly noted:

> The cave-dwellers, upon first encountering the theorist after his return
> to the world of the shadows [very well might be impressed] when he

tells them that what they had always thought of as 'a horse' is not what they suppose it to be... but is, on the contrary, a modification of the attributes of God [, and they will] applaud his performance even where they cannot quite follow it. [The cave-dwellers can appreciate the exotic pronouncements of the theorist, as long as he confines those pronouncements to their genuine field of applicability.] But if he were to tell them that, in virtue of his more profound understanding of the nature of horses, he is a more expert horse-man, horse-chandler, or stable boy than they (in their ignorance) could ever hope to be, and when it becomes clear that his new learning has lost him the ability to tell one end of a horse from the other... [then] before long the more perceptive of the cave-dwellers [will] begin to suspect that, after all, he [is] not an interesting theorist but a fuddled and pretentious 'theoretician' who should be sent on his travels again, or accommodated in a quiet home. (1975: 30)

The preceding passage from *On Human Conduct* provides a fresh perspective from which we can contemplate the character of the rationalist and perceive how it is that he has gone astray. Here, the modern rationalist is understood as an imperialist 'theoretician' who is repeating Plato's ancient misstep. Furthermore, Oakeshott now offers a more sympathetic picture of the rationalist than did his earlier, more polemical essays—the reader can appreciate how easy it is to fall into the error of rationalism, since the theorist really has broken through to a higher form of knowledge, and it is quite understandable that, elated by his achievement, he mistakenly concludes that theory ought to be the unquestioned master of practice, failing to realize that the fundamentally different presuppositions of theoretical and practical thought render theoretical findings categorically irrelevant to practical matters, unless they are translated from their native idiom into that of practice.[10] But while this model of rationalism significantly enriches the one put forward in the earlier essays, and will significantly guide our terminology in the present work, nothing it contains stands in contradiction to the central thesis of those essays.

The second important theme found in *On Human Conduct* that is relevant to our purposes is the distinction Oakeshott therein draws between 'civil association' and 'enterprise association'. As he explained these concepts, in an enterprise association, individuals are related by their agreement to cooperate in pursuing some substantive end—for

---

[10] Here we can see that, despite the fact that Oakeshott's thought evolved over the decades, there is still a basic continuity present: his idea that practical activity is based upon distinctive presuppositions dates back over four decades before the work we are considering, to his very first book, *Experience and Its Modes*.

example, both the owners and employees of Microsoft hope to make money by selling computer software, and they mutually embrace the plan put forward by Microsoft's management aimed at furthering that end. (Of course, this posited unity of ends applies only to the ideal enterprise association—any real enterprise will incorporate shirkers and dissidents working contrary to the commonly held goals of the association.) In contrast, members of a civil association have no such single aim in common; instead, they are related in their recognition of a body of law that delimits the acceptable means that may be employed by any of its members in the course of their pursuit of their own diverse ends. Different strands of European political thought have characterized the state as either primarily an enterprise or primarily a civil association, and Oakeshott sees these competing characterizations as a major source of the confused nature of the modern European state, so that the actual course of Western political life has been a wavering path heading alternately, more or less erratically, towards one or the other of those envisioned ideals. Oakeshott's sympathies clearly lie with those who conceive the state as properly being a civil association, which he regarded as the most civilized conception of the role of the state; for instance, he contends that a compulsory enterprise association—for example, a state attempting to achieve an aim such as 'a drug-free society'—necessarily cuts 'the link between belief and conduct which constitutes moral agency' (1975: 170).

This particular dichotomy of Oakeshott's is germane to our theme for several reasons. First of all, a major component of his admiration for the Roman republic was his belief that it was a paradigmatic example of 'the rule of law'—of civil association.[11] Additionally, there is clearly, in Oakeshott's theoretical edifice, a natural affinity between rationalist politics and the 'enterprise association' understanding of the state, and, similarly, an affinity between pragmatic politics and a 'civil association' understanding of the state. Despite this natural linking of these pairs of ideal types, I suggest that, once again, they are not tied by a relationship of necessity. It is possible, as our empirical studies will demonstrate, to seek to create a polity largely conforming to the ideal type of 'civil association' by rationalist means; and, furthermore, as we will see, this is a fairly accurate description of what the American founders sought to do—while they oriented their nation-building efforts around a political vision closely approaching Oakeshott's ideal type of civil association, they sought to realize that end through rationalist means. On the other hand, the Romans sometimes explicitly

---

[11] See Oakeshott (1999).

saw themselves as a sort of enterprise association, namely, one organized around the purpose of bringing Roman civilization, and most specifically Roman civil order, to all of the known world, even while pursuing that end by following the intimations of their traditions.

Aristotle on practice versus theory

Given our recent encounter with Oakeshott's reading of the allegory of the cave from *The Republic*, this seems an opportune place to leave our historical survey of Oakeshott's works and consider the similarity of his critique to that of Aristotle. Now, there is an interesting critical debate about the extent to which Aristotle 'broke' with Plato rather than merely continued to develop his teacher's thoughts in a direction in which they had already been moving. MacIntyre, for instance, argues that many of Aristotle's supposed disagreements with Plato are already implicit in the latter's later work.[12] There is also a debate as to what extent Plato intended *The Republic* as a serious political proposal. But neither of these debates need concern us here; for our purposes, it is enough that Plato wrote a political tract that contains at least an element of rationalism, and that Aristotle criticized that position. So let us look at Aristotle's critique of Plato and see how it compares to Oakeshott's.

Unlike Plato, who, at least in *The Republic*, holds forth theoretical knowledge as the only form of real knowledge and denigrates practice as 'nescience', as Oakeshott puts it, Aristotle regards both theoretical and practical understanding as valid: the former is about universals and gives us necessary truths, while the latter has more to do with particulars than universals, and its truths are less certain: 'Scientific knowledge is supposition about universals, things that are by necessity... Prudence [practical understanding], by contrast, is about human concerns, about things open to deliberation' (1999: 90–91). Furthermore, practical understanding is especially concerned with the concrete, rather than the abstract:

> Nor is prudence about universals only. It must also acquire knowledge of particulars, since it is concerned with action and action is about particulars. That is why in other areas also some people who lack knowledge but have experience are better in action than others who have knowledge. (1999: 92)

---

[12] See MacIntyre, 1988: 88–96.

This difference in focus is made apparent in terms of the greater life experience required to become proficient at a practical versus a theoretical skill:

> Indeed [to understand the difficulty and importance of experience] we might consider why a child can become accomplished in mathematics, but not in wisdom or natural science. Surely it is because mathematical objects are reached through abstraction, whereas in these other cases the principles are reached from experience. (1999: 93)

The above, in fact, points to a good definition of what constitutes rationalism in politics: A rationalist tries, by creating an abstract world of political 'principles' (e.g., the libertarian 'nonaggression principle') to make politics, a practical activity requiring experience, into a theoretical activity that even a bright child can become adept at through textbook learning. As Oakeshott would have it, a rationalist ideology provides a 'cheat sheet' for those lacking political experience. However, this creation of an ideology rests on a confusion:

> It is apparent that prudence is not scientific knowledge; for, as we said, it concerns the last thing [i.e., the particular], since this is what is achievable in action. Hence it is opposite to understanding. For understanding is about the [first] terms, [those] that have no account of them; but prudence is about the last thing, an object of perception, not of scientific knowledge. (1999: 93)

By mistakenly equating political prudence with scientific knowledge, the rationalist has made a crippling error. Not that he can actually conduct politics as a sort of theoretical activity: in fact, he will again and again fall back upon disguised practical reasoning in forming his supposedly theoretical conclusions.

Deveroux's commentary on the relation of theory to practice in Aristotle reveals its relationship to Oakeshott's ideas on rationalism quite clearly. Deveroux notes,

> Practical wisdom, as Aristotle understands it, is analogous not to medicine but to medical skill; it is practical both in aim and in efficacy, and it is self-sufficient in the same way as medical skill: the practically wise person has what he needs to achieve his aims' (Deveroux, 1986: 494)

While abstractions can certainly enter helpfully into the deliberations of the skilled practitioner, they do so not as 'laws' or 'theorems', as they would in a theoretical discipline, but as rules of thumb:

> Matters of health and conduct [and, by extension from conduct, politics as well] 'have no fixity', and therefore it would be futile to attempt to

formulate precise statements about how we should act in various situations. One must speak 'in outline' and 'not precisely'... Such statements will at best be useful as rules of thumb; the experienced agent or doctor will be guided not so much by them as by his judgment of what is 'appropriate to the occasion. (Deveroux, 1986: 494–495)

So, another formulation of rationalism we might draw from Aristotle is: The rationalist is someone who, lacking in experience, tries to turn such rules of thumb into hard-and-fast 'principles' that will provide him with an unambiguous guide to proceeding in politics that will compensate for the uncertainty caused by his lack of experience in the area.

O'Neill on abstraction versus idealization

Onora O'Neill makes a distinction between abstraction *simpliciter*, which she finds 'theoretically and practically unavoidable, and often ethically important' (1996: 40), and idealization, which is a form of abstraction that 'ascribes predicates—often seen as enhanced, "ideal" predicates—that are false of the case in hand, and so denies predicates that are true of that case' (1996: 41).[13] She notes that 'idealizations are... dangerous in practical reasoning, because it aims at guidance rather than explanation'. If the world fails to live up to the idealization being employed, 'the world rather than the reasoning may be judged at fault' (1996: 42).

Boucher has contended that:

Oakeshott's distinction between abridgement and abstraction may be illuminated by O'Neill's more recent, but similar, distinction between abstraction and idealization... What O'Neill calls idealization, Oakeshott calls abridgement. Rationalists typically abridge a tradition to the point of caricature. The very features that O'Neill identifies in the post-Enlightenment as characteristic of idealization are the features that Oakeshott identifies as characteristic of rationalism in politics. (Boucher, 2005b: 93)

The value of this analogy lies in the crucial distinction it highlights between the use a rationalist makes of his abstractions and that of someone like Oakeshott, who is, after all, as critics have noted, dealing in abstractions such as 'rationalism'! The difference is that the rationalist *believes* his abstractions; that is, he forgets that they are

[13] O'Neill's distinction is quite similar to the one made by Aristotle, Abelard, Aquinas, and others, between nonprecisive and precisive abstractions.

partial views of reality and comes to believe they have somehow captured its essence. His abstractions are thus turned into O'Neill's idealizations, as he is led to deny, if not the very existence of the factors he is leaving out, then at least their relevance. When we turn our attention to particular rationalist thinkers we will note that their error generally lies not in what they choose to focus on, be it property rights, equality, prosperity, utility, and so forth, but in their idealization of that chosen principle into a place of unique importance for judging political conduct, so as to deny any relevance to the neglected factors. And this idealization is not an accidental feature of the rationalist style; in the attempt to employ principles of practical reasoning, not as the rules of thumb they really are, but as the axioms of a deductive system, Oakeshott pointed out that it is necessary to idealize one such principle into the status of the master axiom, to avoid being thrust back into the world of contingency by 'diverse and potentially conflicting axioms' (1991 [1962]: 84).

However, I think it is also important not to push this analogy between Oakeshott's and O'Neill's distinctions too far. For the British idealists and, by inheritance, for Oakeshott, abstraction *itself* was problematic, whether or not it was, as O'Neill would have it, 'idealized'. Certainly, an abstraction that falsifies a situation is worse than one that merely leaves details out, but, as Oakeshott wrote, as abstractions both represent a 'partial and defective point of view' (1933: 79).

Collingwood stated that, for idealist thought:

> The concept is not something outside the world of sensuous experience: it is the very structure and order of that world itself... This is the point of view of concrete thought... To abstract is to consider separately things that are inseparable: to think of the universal, for instance, without reflecting that it is merely the universal of its particulars, and to assume that one can isolate it in thought and study it in this isolation. This assumption is an error. One cannot abstract without falsifying. (Collingwood, 1924: 159–160)

Or, per Bernard Bosanquet, 'the fullest universal of character and consciousness will embody itself in the finest and most specialized and unrepeatable responses to environment' (1927: 105–106).

That does not mean we must not engage in abstraction; in fact, as O'Neill notes, we cannot avoid doing so. Rather, it is a warning not to take our abstractions too seriously, and to bring to bear multiple abstractions, as Oakeshott has done in theorizing politics, on a problem.

Conclusion

Oakeshott's entire corpus enriches, but does not contradict, the understanding of rationalism put forward in the main essays in which he set out his understanding of the phenomenon. We will apply insights from that body of work to see what light they might shed on the course of the Roman and the American republics. But, before launching that investigation, it will behoove us to consider some criticisms of Oakeshott, as well as more closely connecting his ideas to our empirical studies by exploring what they have to say about contemporary constitutional theory; and so, on to our next two chapters.

Chapter 3

Misunderstanding Oakeshott

Having explored the nature of Oakeshott's critique of rationalism and how it evolved over time, it is now appropriate that we spend some time surveying some of the most notable criticisms of Oakeshott's views. While this would perhaps be of interest as an academic exercise in its own right, the primary role of this survey in the present work will be to provide us with a set of theoretical questions, questions that will direct our forthcoming empirical investigations, and that we may hope those investigations can go some way towards answering.

Some typical criticisms

We will begin this chapter by examining a number of common critiques of Oakeshott's views by topic, both asking how Oakeshott did answer or might have answered these criticisms, and looking ahead to what light our empirical work may cast upon these debates. We will close this chapter by looking at a political theorist, not directly critical of Oakeshott, whose writings nevertheless can be used as foils against which to set his ideas. (Certain other famous critiques of Oakeshott's work, such as that of D. D. Raphael, will be taken up in subsequent chapters, as they particularly bear upon some material in that chapter.)

Traditionalism as an apology for the status quo

It was clear to most readers of 'Rationalism in Politics' that, despite Oakeshott's disavowal that he was engaged in 'mere' political advocacy, and despite the irrelevance of political theory to political practice that he posited, he nevertheless regarded the 'traditional' style of politics as clearly preferable to its rationalist alternative. That Oakeshott had not yet modified 'traditional' to 'practical' (or the lack of awareness that he *had* done so after 1975) led some critics to accuse him of advocating a blind, thoughtless adherence to tradition, endorsing existing institutions simply because, well, there they are, without regard for their justice or their efficacy. For instance, Bernard Crick wrote:

> Britain has the distinction of possessing some academic doctrinaire anti-doctrinaires to whom all theoretical knowledge of society is either a fallacy – 'rationalism', or else a threat to the working of those unconscious intimations and habits on which true political depends, etc., etc. Even when they choose to earn their living as students of politics they spend their time, in fact, mixing frivolity with malice, trying to retard or sabotage the advance of knowledge. For they are quite sure – and quite right – that knowledge leads to reform... (Crick, 1992: 191)[1]

Although I contend that Crick has misread Oakeshott, his mistake is understandable in light of the fact that even some sympathetic reviewers of Oakeshott, such as Chandran Kukathas, characterized his views in a similar fashion: 'Rationalism, for Oakeshott, identifies that attitude or cast of mind that elevates the intellect or reason above tradition or practice' (1993: 339). (To be fair to Kukathas, subsequent passages in the very review containing that quote exhibit an awareness that Oakeshott was not opposed to rational thought as such.) However, Oakeshott made it quite explicit, but unfortunately mostly in private letters and little publicized reviews, that he considered rationalism as fundamentally *irrational*, and tradition and practice as intelligent.[2] For instance, he wrote, in a private letter to Karl Popper:

> First, of course, when I argue against rationalism, I do not argue against reason. Rationalism in my sense is, among other things, thoroughly unreasonable. That reason has a place in politics, I have no doubt at all, but what I mean by rationalism is the doctrine that nothing else has a place in politics and this is a very common view. The place of reason, in politics & in life, is not to take the place of habits of behaviour, but to act as the critic of habits of behaviour, keeping them from superstition etc. (1948: par. 3)[3]

---

[1] Crick specifically names Oakeshott as a prime example of this sort of academic on the page after the one containing the above passage.

[2] This point will bring us back to *Experience and Its Modes*, as we shall see in the section on Hayek at the end of this chapter.

[3] Popper responded to Oakeshott by largely agreeing with him, but sounding a caveat similar to that of other critics of Oakeshott examined in this chapter: 'But I am against the spirit of non-intervention and wait-and-see, and perhaps even complacency, to use a strong and perhaps not quite just term, which speaks

Similarly, in reviewing a book by Hans J. Morgenthau in 1947, Oakeshott wrote:

> What he really has in mind is not this, but a belief about the nature and scope of rational understanding which, on the one hand, confines it to the promulgation of abstract general propositions and, on the other hand, extends its relevance to the whole of human life – a doctrine which may be called 'rationalism'. And there is as much difference between rational enquiry and 'rationalism' as there is between scientific enquiry and 'scientism', and it is a difference of the same kind. (1993: 99)

And it is certainly not the case, as Crick contends, that Oakeshott saw all social theory as either a 'fallacy' or a 'threat'; Oakeshott, as we have seen in our review of *On Human Conduct* in the previous chapter, regarded theoretical understanding as superior, in a meaningful sense, to practical understanding, and what he cautioned against was not the mere existence of theory, but the temptation, to which too many theorists have succumbed, to try to dictate or direct practice on a purely theoretical basis. Nor did Oakeshott oppose 'reform' in general, but only reform efforts made heedless, by rationalist hubris, of the wisdom contained in traditional practices.

Other commentators upon Oakeshott, such as Archer, saw that a charge like Crick's above was misguided even without the benefit of reading auxiliary or later works which refute it more explicitly: '[The essays in *Rationalism in Politics*] do not represent an attack on rational thought or an appeal to irrationality. Rather, they dispute that all knowledge is technical knowledge' (1979: 153). Furthermore, as we have seen above, Oakeshott's modification of his views in *On Human Conduct*, replacing 'tradition' with 'practice' as the opposing style to rationalism, is even less open to the charge Crick levels at him. Crick's criticism is particularly surprising in that, in the very same work we find the quote cited above, he provides his own attack on rationalism, complaining of the 'technological view' of a society run by '[e]ngineer[s who] will try to reduce all education to technique and training... [with the aim to] transform society into something radically more efficient and effective' (1992: 95).

---

from the second passage quoted (p. 153) and others. *It is this spirit, which by way of a reaction to it, has created most of the symptoms you call by the name rationalism'* (1948: par. 5). And he goes on to note *'Even Burkeanism* (if this word is possible) *is not exempt from becoming Utopian'* (1948: par. 8). The role of 'utopian' traditionalism in fostering the Roman revolution will be examined in more depth in Chapter 6.

Traditionalism as denigrating the role of rational reflection

Crick's charge is closely related to the criticism that Oakeshott has seriously undervalued the importance of rational reflection, not only as a valid means to improve upon existing practices, but also as having been crucial in bringing about social forms later regarded as 'traditional'. For example, Haddock contended:

> But when Oakeshott opposes ideological politics to customary politics in such a way that there can be no middle term, I think he goes astray. The implication of customary habitual behavior is that it is completely unreflective. But even though most of our days are spent going through regular motions without a second thought, that does not mean that we could not account for our behavior if occasion arose. Habitual behavior is implicitly rule-governed and most of us could make the implicit rule explicit if we were asked to justify ourselves. The fact that voting behavior is to large extent habitual does not mean that people could not give some sort of account of what they were doing. And because Oakeshott overemphasizes habit in moral political activity he denies himself an insight into the constitution of tradition. Politics as an intentional activity is no less traditional for being intentional. Its purposiveness is a fundamental factor in the creation of tradition. (Haddock, 1974: 427)

Unfortunately, Haddock penned this passage just a year before Oakeshott decisively refuted the charge that when he mentioned 'habit' there was any implication of 'behavior is that it is completely unreflective', as illustrated in the following passages: 'Social being must be recognized as one of the engagements of reflective consciousness, and not as itself "the determinant of reflective consciousness"' (1975: 96–97). The 'social being' behaving in a traditional fashion is a creation of agency, and not vice versa: 'The contention that the substantive performance of an agent is to be theorized in terms of his "social being" makes sense only when "social being" is understood as his self-recognition in being related to others in some particular respect...' (1975: 98). And it is the actions of individuals that create social practices: 'Practices... are footprints left behind by agents responding to their emergent situations...' (1975: 100).

In point of fact, Haddock himself later seems to recognize that traditions are not devoid of reason for Oakeshott, writing:

> Reasoning goes on within traditions of understanding. Any conception of practical reason worth its salt would have to start from the complex

of received understandings that we may be said to be working within, yet with scope for adjustment to contingencies as they arise. We are thus both situated and thinking on our feet. And our thinking may be done well or ill. (Haddock, 2005: 10)

Archer voiced a similar worry concerning Oakeshott's case against rationalism: '[A] problem involves Oakeshott's belief that all theories are merely derived from activities. This rules out the possibility of inventive thought' (1979: 156). However, Oakeshott does not rule out inventiveness; rather, he argues that it always arises within the context of an existing practice, instead of from a blank slate upon which are inscribed first principles. Even in his first works on rationalism he recognizes that traditions evolve. How can they do so if not by inventive acts? We might consider a musical composer's creative acts as offering a useful analogy here; musical inventiveness always occurs within *some* tradition of composition. Even 'avant-garde' works have roots in previous musical forms. And the quotes from *On Human Conduct* cited above in discussing Haddock's criticism of Oakeshott make this point even more strongly; social being is not 'the determinant of reflective consciousness', clearly allowing scope for inventive thought.

Peter Winch lodges a protest about Oakeshott's view of human activity similar to Archer's second objection. He admits that Oakeshott agrees with his own understanding that '[p]rinciples, precepts, definitions, formulae – all derive their sense from the context of human social activity in which they are applied'. But he accuses Oakeshott of going too far in thinking that 'it follows from this that most human behaviour can be adequately described in terms of the notion of habit or custom and that neither the notion of a rule nor that of reflectiveness is essential to it' (1990: 45).

But Oakeshott, in his reply to Raphael, made it clear that he did not view customary behavior in such a fashion:

> The view I ventured to suggest was that explaining conduct… is a different activity from recommending that a certain action should be performed or from approving or disapproving of an action which has been performed. This, of course, does not mean that reasoning is foreign to practical discourse; it means only that the reasoning will be of a different sort from explanatory reasoning… (2008: 181)

The rules Winch discusses can be used to explain action, but (most?) often are not the genuine basis for decision-making. Furthermore, as MacIntyre noted, Winch's criterion of rule-following, which is that there is a right way and a wrong way of doing the thing in question, does not seem to apply to many conscious actions; as MacIntyre asks, 'Is there a wrong way of going for a walk?' (1973: 21)

Winch attempts to buttress his argument by pointing to an alleged categorical distinction between human action and animal behavior. We cannot, he contended, regard animals as 'following rules' in their behavior as we do with humans, except in that we read their performances through the lens of humans' interest in training their animal charges to behave in a certain fashion:

> It is only the dog's relation to human beings which makes it intelligible to speak of his having mastered a trick; what this way of speaking amounts to could not be elucidated by any description, however detailed, of canine behaviour in complete isolation from human beings. (Winch, 1990: 57)

And, invoking Pavlov's famous experiments, he asserts that they demonstrate that 'the dog has been *conditioned* to respond in a certain way' (1990: 58), instead of displaying anything like human understanding of the situation it confronts. However, Winch seems to be interpreting animal behavior by means of a mechanistic framework that is not justified by the evidence, but is instead assumed as an a priori truth. As Michael Polanyi notes, regarding Pavlov's experiments,

> the dog does not jump and snap at the bell as if it were food, nor does a red light cause the kind of muscular contraction which results from an electric shock... This entitles us to say, in contrast to Pavlov's description of the process, that in sign-learning the animal is taught to expect an event by recognizing a sign foretelling the event. (Polanyi, 1962: 72)

And more recent work in semiotics supports Polanyi's view; for instance, the semiotician Thomas Sebeok declared, 'The phenomenon that distinguishes life forms from inanimate objects is semiosis' (2001: 3).

Winch goes on to accuse Oakeshott of self-contradiction:

> But human history is not just an account of changing habits: it is the story of how men have tried to carry over what they regard as important in their modes of behaviour in to the new situations which they have had to face... Oakeshott's attitude to reflectiveness is, as a matter of fact, incompatible with a very important point which he makes early on in the discussion. He says that the moral life is 'conduct to which there is an alternative'. Now though it is true that this 'alternative' need not be consciously before the agent's mind it must be something which *could* be brought before his mind... at least he must be

able to *understand* what it would have been like to act differently. (Winch, 1990: 61)

But again, once it is understood that Oakeshott readily acknowledges the importance of reflective thought in the development of habits and customs, the appearance of incompatibility between his endorsement of traditional practices as a guide for human conduct and his understanding of morality as inherently supposing alternatives to any morally laudatory choice disappears.

If we step back and consider the criticisms of Oakeshott's work we have examined in this section, we can detect the presence in them of a central theme, which might be captured as follows: 'It is true that human activities *begin* in the kind of habitual behavior that Oakeshott describes. But humanity has become more rational over time; as our knowledge and self-awareness have increased, so has our desire to order social life per rationally developed rules, as well as our ability to do so.'

In other words, while a more primitive mentality dealt largely with the specifics of its circumstances without formulating the universal, abstract principles that provide the ultimate means of comprehending human life, modern, 'scientific' man has advanced past such a stage of development, and is increasingly able to achieve the deeper understanding of reality that his ancestors lacked. But R. G. Collingwood devised an ingenious answer to such a line of reasoning, which, although he was working in the context of theology, applies just as readily to politics. Examining the idea that the Supreme Being ought to be guided in its actions by abstract, universally valid rules, he contends that, quite to the contrary, such abstractions are only of use to beings unable to fully grasp the concrete details of reality: 'For a perfectly moral being, one who really appreciated duty as such, these maxims and laws would recede into the background and disappear; such a being simply ignores and does not act on them at all, but acts merely on his intuition of duty' (1994: 206). Or consider Bosanquet, writing in a similar vein:

And we must have read Plato's *Philebus* and Aristotle's *Ethics* to very little purpose if we do not understand that, in principle, the fullest universal of character and consciousness will embody itself in the finest and most specialized and unrepeatable responses to environment; and that life, and especially its intensified forms as morality or knowledge, do not consist in observing general rules, but in reacting adequately, with logical, that is, with fine and creative adjustment to the ever- varying complexities of situations. Precision, measurableness, and universal law, these are in the moral act, but they are features of the solution of problems by constructive organization, and not of obedience to abstract rule, and the same thing is relatively true of the adjustments and arrangements of a highly unified society. (Bosanquet, 1927: 105–106)

Increasing the sophistication of practical understanding is not a matter of making it more theoretical, but of making the practical world 'more of a world'.

Is pragmatic politics sufficient when serious reform is called for?

However, criticism such as Crick's and Haddock's does point to a genuine problem that Oakeshott perhaps ought to have addressed somewhere in his work on rationalism, which is whether the process of making incremental changes to existing institutions and practices by pursuing the 'intimations' they contain, as he seems to recommend, is adequate to address situations where one or more of a society's traditional features serve to perpetuate some gross injustice such as the continuing oppression of one faction or class by another. A caricature of Oakeshott's actual views may depict him as a reactionary willing to endure any institution, however morally questionable, so long as it had an ancient pedigree, but that caricature does not do him justice. Oakeshott, I suggest, found it likely that any deeply lived tradition of practical activity will contain within itself the resources necessary for a self-reflective critique of its current performances, and believed that only reform driven by such immanent considerations can offer a realistic possibility of improving upon an existing practice. For example, it was not necessary to scuttle the entire liberal social order existing in Britain at the beginning of the nineteenth century in order to abolish slavery; to the contrary, reflection on the very ideas grounding that order was sufficient to expose the inconsistency between its high regard for individual liberty and the continued presence within it of enslaved individuals. And, as we will see when we look at the status of women at the time of the American founding, if a tradition does not contain the resources to address some injustice, then reform just is not agenda. As Tseng put it, 'Oakeshott's point is not that every tradition must be excellent, but that it is so comprehensive that every political crisis "always appears within a tradition of political activity; and 'salvation' comes from the unimpaired resources of the tradition itself"' (2003: 160). This will raise the question, in later chapters, as to why the Roman republic's traditional resources were not enough to save it.

While Archer, as noted above, appreciates that Oakeshott is not denigrating truly rational thought more than do some other critics, nevertheless he detected a flaw in Oakeshott's attack on rationalism:

> Oakeshott destroys the rationalist in the same way that Popper destroys the historicist. He first creates the monster at the opposite pole of opinion from his own ideas. The product (or figment) of his imagination is then dismantled with ease. Oakeshott draws a picture of the rationalist who holds his view to the point of lunacy, and so destroys rationalism. The question is not whether or not the monster exists. Even if the world is rife with lunatic rationalists, many milder creatures are tarred with the same brush by Oakeshott... [W]hen we look at Oakeshott's list of the progenies of rationalism, we find it includes a planned society, the 1944 Education Act in Britain, and votes for women. R. A. Butler and Stalin are thrown together in the same category as Hitler, Napoleon, and the members of the gradualist British Labour Party. One wonders if such a category is too wide. (Archer, 1979: 153–154)

This objection is, I think, less easy to categorize as a mere misunderstanding than those discussed previously. We will pause to examine its force at various points in our empirical investigations of Rome and America, to see if Archer has scored a hit. Specifically, we will ask to what extent Oakeshott's portrayals of the character of the Roman republic as an exemplar of 'practical politics' and of the founding of the United States as an essentially rationalist enterprise are themselves caricatures, rather than largely accurate, if necessarily idealized, sketches of those two polities. Still, it is already worthwhile to point out, once again, that Oakeshott recognized he was trading in ideal types, which only fit any particular case more or less. I believe he would have had little difficulty in assenting to the proposition that 'the 1944 Education Act in Britain' was not *as* rationalist as, say, Mao's Cultural Revolution. But what he was attempting to elucidate is that both episodes partook of a common mindset, even if one did so much more moderately than the other, just as both the weekend drinker and the hard-core alcoholic share a desire for intoxication, albeit to significantly different degrees.

'Non-ideological politics' as covertly ideological

Other critics of Oakeshott, in a complaint similar to the one just discussed, have dismissed his rejection of ideological politics as a disingenuous ploy designed to exempt his own ideology, which such critics often classify as some form of reactionary conservatism, from the requirement that it defend itself on a level playing field against its ideological rivals. For instance, Eccleshall contends that anyone involved in politics at all is an ideologue by necessity, and that thinkers, such as Oakeshott, who claim they are above ideology exhibit at 'its silliest, and usually within a British context... the suggestion that conservatives are not ideologues at all, which at face value implies that they are incapable of coherent thinking about the nature of a sound polity' (2001: 74).

As we shall see, conservatives can be ideologues; Oakeshott pointedly said that his critique of rationalism applied to every part of the political spectrum, as we noted in Chapter 1 — we shall give an example of this in a couple of paragraphs. However, Eccleshall has failed to grasp Oakeshott's distinction between rationally contemplating some form of activity with the aim of improving one's own or others' performance in that field and the attempt to direct practical activity by means of abstract principles supposedly arrived at by reasoning unsullied with the taint of received ideas. To offer an analogy, Eccleshall supposes that all coherent thought about cooking must take the form of a culinary dogma from which any 'valid' recipes can be deduced. Contrary to Eccleshall's equation of ideology with coherent thought, a great deal of Oakeshott's work is an attempt to think seriously about political activity and what constitutes a sound polity, and one conclusion of that thinking is that ideology is the equivalent of culinary dogma and not of the knowledge of a skilled chef. In examining the period of Roman history known as 'the Roman revolution', in a later chapter, we will reinforce this theoretical distinction with the concrete example of the activities of the '*Optimates*', arguing that when the Roman reliance on tradition was turned into an ideology of traditionalism, the outcome was quite the opposite of what the *Optimates* intended.

In the same collection of essays, the volume's editor, Freeden, wrote:

> Oakeshott recognized this function of abridgement as part of the technique of ideology, but for him this was the falsification of political activity. There is no need to take that bleak view of ideology as a limited and artificial device. Any discourse becomes intelligible only by means of 'artificial' checks on its significatory potential. If a constructed ideological harmony with the capacity for cultural survival emerges, it becomes an asset for any society, enhancing its communicative capacity, adumbrating boundaries among alternative ideological patterns and thus offering the ideological choices that eschew the post-structural approach. Indeed, through the insights of hermeneutics one may endow the phenomenon of ideology with the stimulating function of

introducing unceasing ideational richness and vitality into the political
thinking of groups and societies. (Freeden, 2001: 10)

But Oakeshott, as we shall see, had no problem with an ideology as
a communicative device. The problem arose, for him, when it was
thought that such a communicative device could spit out automatic
answers to political conundrums. Freeden added:

> Some ideologies are theory-averse. That is not to say that they have no
> conceptual apparatus. Far from it, they often possess intricate but
> unintended, even unconscious, patterns of thought, but their promoters
> prefer to interpret themselves as based on concrete experience,
> permitting existing human conduct to express itself through customs,
> rules and, as Oakeshott avowed, performances. (Freeden, 2001: 205)

Of course, Oakeshott, as an idealist, was quite aware that concrete
experience possesses 'intricate... patterns of thought'! It was the claim
to superiority, by the rationalist, of *abstract* thought over practical
reasoning to which he objected. Andrew Vincent voiced an objection to
Oakeshott's views similar to Freeden's:

> One of the many problems with [Oakeshott's] line of argument is its
> intrinsic reflexivity. It is clear that both practical reason and knowledge
> are conceptually structured. They are drawn rationally distinct from
> theoretical reason. Practical reason provides a coherent principle of
> interpretation and a prescription for action. Therefore, is Oakeshott's
> view on tradition and practice an abridgement of tradition? We find
> Oakeshott speaking in clear intelligible terms about something
> (tradition), which is supposed to be rationally inchoate. It seems that
> Oakeshott himself poses the reflexive problem by acclaiming his own
> position as virtually an Archimedean standpoint on the nature of theory
> and philosophy. What, for example, is the nature of Oakeshott's linked
> distinctions between technical and practical knowledge, rationalism and
> tradition, the conservative disposition and ideological thought? Are
> these distinctions 'traditionally situated' or 'abridgements of tradition'?
> In other words, is Oakeshott just a covert conservative ideologist
> artfully trading on philosophy? (Vincent, 2004: 153)

But Oakeshott made it clear just why he viewed ideology as a
potential perversion of political practice, as if answering Freeden and
Vincent in advance:

> As explanation, then, a political doctrine of this kind [an ideology] has a
> characteristic and limited value; it is an undeniable attempt to make
> politics intelligible. It springs from a reflective enterprise which is
> neither to be despised nor overrated. But when, as so often happens, it is
> converted to the service of political activity and is given the task of
> guiding policy, its very virtues prevent it from supplying what is
> expected of it... the degree of subversiveness in the reflective enterprise

which terminates in a political doctrine is such as to make the doctrine a necessarily false guide in political activity. We should expect, then, enlightenment of a certain sort, but no practical guidance from this kind of explanatory reflections on politics. (1993: 149)

By the way, it is interesting that, despite the criticism Oakeshott's view of ideology has drawn from several fellow political theorists, it is largely supported by the sociological literature on the subject.[4]

Benjamin R. Barber, in his paper 'Conserving Politics', focuses his attention on *On Human Conduct*. He saw the book as a long-called-for attempt on Oakeshott's part to 'dig in, stake out an explicit, theoretical territory and stand fast in its systematic defence; the easy victories of partial criticisms are to be supplanted by the far more challenging test of developing a coherent, systematic theory' (1976: 450). And he thinks Oakeshott has performed this task quite admirably: '*On Human Conduct* is indeed then a stupendous putting together of parts...' (1976: 455).

But Barber's genuine and deep admiration for the book does not mean he agrees with its main political conclusions – far from it. Barber contended that 'the private realm (state of nature) has none of civility's moral modesty: its cardinal virtues, however, are force and fraud' (1976: 459). There are two lacunae in this one sentence. The first is equating the private realm with the Hobbesian state of nature, as if nonstate actors cannot develop private law. However, as Friedman (1989), Stringham (2003), Leeson (2007), and others have ably shown, this is simply not empirically true. Second, Barber designates 'force and fraud' as the 'cardinal virtues' of the private realm, leaving out virtues such as 'voluntary exchange', 'honest dealings', 'good reputation', and so on. Here, he ignores Shaftesbury's critique of Hobbes, in which he pointed out that sociality must have preceded, not followed upon, the creation of the state.[5] Certainly the private realm may include force and fraud, and many have found the best justification for the existence of the state to be the prevention of such private vices. But to claim that those crimes are the 'cardinal virtues' of spontaneous, unsupervised human interaction is surely a gross mischaracterization of the more typical modes of social intercourse.

Barber contended that 'abjuring consideration of possible *legitimate* public ends does not guarantee to individuals the safe pursuit of individual, private goals, it merely guarantees that collective goods will

---

[4] See Geertz (1973: 203–205) for a summary of this literature; note particularly the discussion of the 'morale' function of ideology.

[5] On this point, see Grean (1967: 138–142).

be pursued that are *illegitimate*, unconsidered and coercive to boot' (1976: 459). The charge ignores Oakeshott's argument that the pursuit of concrete aims through a compulsory association is inherently illegitimate;[6] it also ignores the coercive nature of state-produced collective goods (which is regrettable even if such coercion may be justified in some cases, as we all would, presumably, prefer that our fellows voluntarily contribute their share of support for those goods); and it ignores the voluntary nature of collective goods producers such as charities, simply assuming that nonstate production of collective goods is illegitimate – but surely, if a number of environmental groups work together to reduce CO_2 emissions by, say, persuading people to drive less, there is nothing illegitimate about that activity! Barber continued, 'Americans will not suffer governmental national planning, a process in which they might participate; as a consequence, they suffer corporate national planning, a process in which they cannot participate and which is still more injurious to their autonomy and individuality' (1976: 459). One has to wonder if one is looking at a difference without a distinction here: to the extent that corporations can engage in 'national planning', they do so by lobbying the state to plan in their interests; in other words, they can do so only to the extent that 'governmental national planning' is accepted. No corporation can 'plan' the national economy except by co-opting public policies already intending to plan that economy. Furthermore, per public choice theory, this is exactly the result we should expect in state planning: the planners' efforts are directed not by some virtuous democratic dialogue of the sort Barber seems to fantasize as taking place, but by powerful lobbying interests that use the planning apparatus to their own advantage.[7]

While the criticisms of Oakeshott addressed above generally indict him for being insufficiently appreciative of the virtues of Enlightenment rationalism, we now turn to a critic, Walter Mead, who, perhaps surprisingly, accuses Oakeshott of having 'unbridled faith in the reliability of Enlightenment rationality' (2005: 41). Mead's paper attempts to contrast Oakeshott's lack of a 'deep or extended' (2005: 37)

---

[6] As Oakeshott puts it in *On Human Conduct*, 'For him to be associated in the performance of joint actions contingently related to a common purpose and not to have chosen his situation for himself and to be unable to extricate himself from it by revoking this choice, would be to have severed the link between belief and conduct which constitutes moral agency' (1975: 158).

[7] See, for instance, Buchanan and Tullock, 1965 [1962].

understanding of the limits of rationalism with Michael Polanyi's superior grasp of those limits. Mead contends that Oakeshott:

> ...[u]nabashedly embraces an essentially Enlightenment type of rationalism, aspires to a kind of Hegelian perspective that would allow for a totally comprehensive, clear, and certain understanding of the entire 'world of experience', offers an understanding of values as essentially relative—the circumstantial 'prejudices' of tradition, denies any meaning to the concept of 'transcendence', and advances an essentially Hobbesian/Humean perspective that human motivation is explainable in terms no loftier than the pursuit of 'desire', 'delight', and 'satisfaction'. (Mead, 2005: 37)

Every single one of Mead's accusations directed at Oakeshott is incorrect, as will be evidenced below. However, it is perhaps even more disturbing that Mead seemingly attempts to put words in Oakeshott's mouth: in (mis)characterizing Oakeshott's understanding of ethics, he puts the word 'prejudices' in quotes, implying that Oakeshott at some point referred to ethical principles as mere 'prejudices'—yet I have never found any instance of Oakeshott doing so, nor does Mead cite any examples.

Mead's contention that Oakeshott 'unabashedly embraces an essentially Enlightenment type of rationalism' runs directly counter to the opinion of Oakeshott himself and both Oakeshott's admirers and the bulk of his critics, who see him as a fierce opponent of Enlightenment rationalism. Faced with such an extraordinary claim, this reader of Mead immediately turned to his footnotes to see how Mead deals with the supposition that Oakeshott's essays 'Rationalism in Politics' and 'Rational Conduct' represent some of the sharpest rebukes of Enlightenment rationalism penned in the twentieth century—only to find that Mead never references either essay at all!

In an effort to refute the idea that Oakeshott may have moved more towards a 'Polanyian' position of recognizing the importance of 'tacit knowledge' in human understanding, Mead wrote:

> But we must not read too much into Oakeshott's employment of these 'Polanyian' terms... The thought that, in his reference to 'intimations', (above) Oakeshott may have attained the imaginative and intuitive 'reach' implied in Polanyi's use of the term disperses when we hear him say, 'We never look *away from* a given world to another world, but always *at* a given world to discover the unity it implies.' (Mead, 2005: 38)

It's not clear to me how Mead's quotation from Oakeshott bears on the issue of rationalism, but what is more puzzling is that Mead appears to be rejecting the idea that the later Oakeshott became more appreciative of 'Polanyian' ideas as his career progressed by citing a quotation from *Oakeshott's very first book*!

Mead makes several other elementary blunders in his exegesis of Oakeshott. For example, he claimed that

> [i]n both *Experience* and *Liberal Learning*, speaking specifically respectively about modes and fields of teaching/learning, he identifies four of these: 'science', 'history', 'poetry' (in which he includes all the visual, audio, and dramatic arts), and 'practice' (in which he includes politics, economics, sociology, and psychology). (Mead, 2005: 40)

Yet Oakeshott did not include poetry as a mode in his first book, a lacunae he apologizes for in his later writings, and economics is explicitly called to task for containing 'a miscellany of scientific, historical and practical idea and arguments' (1933: 220), although he also describes the possibility of a purely scientific economics.

Mead's apparent lack of familiarity with Oakeshott's full corpus is further displayed when he writes, 'Where Polanyi speaks of open boundaries, Oakeshott speaks only of closed boundaries [between disciplines]' (2005: 41), showing no awareness that, in Oakeshott's essay, 'The Voice of Poetry in the Conversation of Mankind', he explicitly 'opens up' those boundaries (1991 [1962]).

Mead proposes that Oakeshott 'regards "practice" as the "most important" of the fields of inquiry' (2005: 42), without giving any reference as to just where Oakeshott so thoroughly contradicts his contention that modal forms of experience have no hierarchical relationship. Furthermore, his contention that 'Oakeshott, by contrast, firmly denies any hierarchical characteristics in his system' not only contradicts the above statement, but also the fact that Oakeshott, at least in his first book, explicitly contends that *philosophy* (not practice) is a superior form of understanding to the modes. But then, to further confound the reader, Mead recognizes just that point, writing:

> In *Experience*, he makes it clear that philosophy is not to be viewed as one of the modes of experience. It represents totally comprehensive and wholly coherent understanding (what Oakeshott calls 'concrete' knowledge), knowledge that has no conditionality (specific goal to attain), or boundaries. It is, in other words, Absolute knowledge. (Mead, 2005: 42)

The above quotation may help explain Mead's view of Oakeshott as an Enlightenment rationalist. His confusion stems, I think, from mistaking Oakeshott's view of the essential aim of philosophical thought—that it *strives* for unconditional understanding—with a foreign claim that philosophers actually attain such 'Absolute knowledge'. The distinction can be easily understood in considering the condition of any practical performance; a musician setting out to play a Bach sonata likely will aim to play it 'perfectly', while her actual performance will, no doubt, fall short of achieving that goal.

Mead goes on to contend:

> Oakeshott understands moral values and meaning from a Hobbesian perspective. They are mere servants of the task appropriate to the world of practice. The purpose of ethics (a sub-field within practice) is to optimize society's meeting of individual appetites and desires by assigning to human beings some quality of innate worth and, from this, deriving rules to keep people from harming each other or otherwise interfering in their pursuit of their desires. (Mead, 2005: 43)

But the reason Oakeshott admires Hobbes, as McIntyre put it, is that '[f]or Oakeshott, Hobbes is the first philosopher to provide a satisfactory account of the morality of individualism and of the state as a *non-purposive* civil association under the rule of law' (2004: 8, emphasis mine). And Mead's ascription to Oakeshott of an 'optimizing' role for morality is directly contradicted by statements of Oakeshott's such as: 'In short, a morality may be identified as a practice without any extrinsic purpose; it is concerned with good and bad conduct, and not with performances in respect of their outcomes' (1975: 62).

Due to these numerous misreadings of Oakeshott contained in Mead's paper, I think it is difficult to credit his contrarian view of Oakeshott as a thinker who 'unabashedly embraces an essentially Enlightenment type of rationalism' (2005: 37) as anything more than a inadequate understanding of the thinker under his gaze.

F. A. Hayek: 'Why I am not a conservative'

We will next turn our attention to F. A. Hayek, who naturally might be thought of as an 'ally' of Oakeshott, as his position seems to be largely in sympathy with Oakeshott's understanding of the malady affecting modern political life, but whose work offers some implicit criticisms of his views. Given this relationship, we can employ Hayek's ideas as foils to Oakeshott's own.[8] Hayek saw himself as a modern representative of

---

[8] A curious side note here is that both Hayek and Voegelin spent many of their formative intellectual years as attendees of the inter-war 'Mises circle' colloquiums in Vienna, events led by Ludwig von Mises, whose work I have related to Oakeshott's elsewhere — see Callahan, 2005.

what is sometimes called 'classical liberalism', going so far as to term himself an 'Old Whig' (1960: 409), and critiqued conservatism from that perspective.

Hayek and Oakeshott had a curious intellectual relationship. They are not infrequently paired (or, perhaps, along with Michael Polanyi, 'triptyched') as major twentieth-century critics of rationalism. They also have in common long periods of employment at the London School of Economics (Hayek from 1931 to 1950, and Oakeshott from 1950 to 1969), as well as prominent places, which perhaps neither desired, in the pantheon of modern conservative heroes. Nevertheless, the only reference by Oakeshott to Hayek's work published during Oakeshott's life was his somewhat dismissive summary of *The Road to Serfdom*, which was referenced in the first section of the present chapter. However, Oakeshott, in a review not published until after his death, called Hayek's *Constitution of Liberty* 'a long and solid work, impressive in its candour and the patience with which each point is elaborated and in the clear picture which emerges... never boring or irrelevant... well-arranged... forceful. It may be said to accomplish its purpose with a good deal to spare' (2004: 301) – quite a change from his remarks on *The Road to Serfdom*! Hayek noted *On Human Conduct* as an important work in the introduction to *Law, Legislation and Liberty* (1979: xii), but he basically only references Oakeshott there to say that he lacks the time to address his ideas in any depth. The only other reference to Oakeshott I have located in Hayek's work is in his essay 'The Confusion of Language in Political Thought', where he notes the similarity of his differentiation of spontaneous orders versus organizations to Oakeshott's between *nomocracy* and *telocracy* (which was to develop into the distinction between civil association and enterprise association made in *On Human Conduct*) (1978: 89).

Given this paucity of efforts on the part of either of these thinkers to relate his own understanding of politics to that of the other, we are, I suggest, justified in attempting to reconstruct how Hayek might have differentiated his own position from that of Oakeshott by examining his corpus for places where implicit criticism of Oakeshott plausibly can be read into the text. In particular, I will focus here on Hayek's essay entitled 'Why I Am Not a Conservative', which was published as a postscript to his book *The Constitution of Liberty*.

Hayek opened this essay by acknowledging the genuine virtue he detects in the conservative political disposition, writing, 'Conservatism proper is a legitimate, probably necessary, and certainly widespread attitude of opposition to drastic change. It has, since the French

Revolution, for a century and a half played an important role in European politics' (1960: 397). Even so, his admiration for conservatism was qualified. He continued:

> Let me now state what seems to me the decisive objection to any conservatism which deserves to be called such. It is that by its very nature it cannot offer an alternative to the direction in which we are moving. It may succeed by its resistance to current tendencies in slowing down undesirable developments, but, since it does not indicate another direction, it cannot prevent their continuance. It has, for this reason, invariably been the fate of conservatism to be dragged along a path not of its own choosing. The tug of war between conservatives and progressives can only affect the speed, not the direction, of contemporary developments. But, though there is a need for a 'brake on the vehicle of progress', I personally cannot be content with simply helping to apply the brake. (Hayek, 1960: 398)

In a passage that quite credibly could be read as being directed against political approaches such as the one Oakeshott, at times, seems to endorse, Hayek contended:

> This brings me to the first point on which the conservative and the liberal dispositions differ radically. As has often been acknowledged by conservative writers, one of the fundamental traits of the conservative attitude is a fear of change, a timid distrust of the new as such, while the liberal position is based on courage and confidence, on a preparedness to let change run its course even if we cannot predict where it will lead. There would not be much to object to if the conservatives merely disliked too rapid change in institutions and public policy; here the case for caution and slow process is indeed strong. But the conservatives are inclined to use the powers of government to prevent change or to limit its rate to whatever appeals to the more timid mind. (Hayek, 1960: 400)

Hayek, in the above passage, has indicated a crucial problem confronting Oakeshottian political theory, and one that, as I noted earlier, it seems to me that Oakeshott ought to have addressed in greater depth, namely, whether Oakeshott's endorsement of looking to the 'intimations' of existing practices for guiding political change can avoid taking on the role of a mere sycophant providing intellectual cover for whatever power structure is currently in place, and can cope with situations in which some egregious injustice appears to call out for possibly radical redress. In raising that issue previously, I suggested some resources that might be available within Oakeshott's system of thought for rebutting the charge that it merely hangs a superficially attractive veneer over structures that essentially function to sustain the unwarranted privileges of whatever elite faction currently happens to control the reins of power. (That charge, for instance, I take to be at the core of Crick's attack on 'doctrinaire anti-doctrinaires'.) In the course of pursuing our empirical case studies in the subsequent chapters of the present work, we will revisit this topic whenever our findings seem to have bearing on the question of whether or not Oakeshott's conceptual framework is sufficiently supple to be stretched far enough to grapple with this difficulty. At present I will merely point back to the claim made, earlier in this chapter, that Oakeshott suspected that the only viable route to genuine, beneficial reform in politics lay within rather than beyond the resources a tradition offers to those living it.

The final charge of Hayek's contra conservatism that I will consider is what he saw as conservatives' reflexive aversion to new ideas:

> I have already referred to the differences between conservatism and liberalism in the purely intellectual field, but I must return to them because the characteristic conservative attitude here not only is a serious weakness of conservatism but tends to harm any cause which allies itself with it. Conservatives feel instinctively that it is new ideas more than anything else that cause change. But, from its point of view rightly, conservatism fears new ideas because it has no distinctive principles of its own to oppose them; and, by its distrust of theory and its lack of imagination concerning anything except that which experience has already proved, it deprives itself of the weapons needed in the struggle of ideas. Unlike liberalism, with its fundamental belief in the long-range power of ideas, conservatism is bound by the stock of ideas inherited at a given time. (Hayek, 1960: 404)

Once again, Hayek's brief against conservatism contains an implicit challenge to Oakeshott's views: are the latter's 'intimations' drawn from existing practice adequate weapons with which to oppose the power of enticing ideological visions of a more perfect social order? And, once again, we will seek out whatever light our historical explorations may shed on this matter, while noting that Oakeshott was not averse to 'principles', but only to regarding them as unambiguous guides to conduct.

Kenneth Minogue summed up the difference between Hayek and Oakeshott, from a perspective sympathetic to the views of the latter, as follows:

> How might we formulate the difference between Hayek and Oakeshott? Let me suggest that it might be done in terms of levels of scepticism. At the least sceptical level, the socialist actually believes that revolutionary upheaval, or some plan of social engineering, can save the world. The twentieth century was full of such moths who found the flames of abstraction irresistible, and many perished as a result. We are far from having done away with their successors. Against this kind of thing, Hayek's sceptical account of an economy as a 'discovery procedure' was

an exhilarating illumination of what socialist melodramas of oppression had obscured. A society whose power was dispersed among all its individuals was the epitome of freedom. It was also, as Hayek perhaps at times overemphasized, the epitome of prosperity. At the level of proposals to engineer society so as to remove the disharmonies of inequality, Hayek's scepticism was in good working order. It was not, however, a scepticism about abstract proposals in general, and it was on this point that the Oakeshott-Hayek disagreement emerged. Oakeshott's scepticism is a philosophical distancing from any form of human folly. He interprets the Hobbesian account of Christianity in particular as dealing (as he puts it) with 'the local and transitory mischief in which the universal predicament of mankind appeared' in his time. Hayek is too close to the mischief to recognize the universal predicament. (Minogue, 2002)

While I find Minogue's analysis largely on target, two caveats should be mentioned. First of all, Hayek's thought grew closer to Oakeshott's over time, to the extent that his three-volume work from the 1970s, *Law, Legislation and Liberty*, often reads like an expansion of Oakeshott's essays on rationalism, and posits a key distinction between 'spontaneous orders' and 'organizations' that closely parallels Oakeshott's between 'civil' and 'enterprise' associations, as noted above. However, even at this stage of his thought, Hayek was still, despite his critique of what he calls 'constructivist rationalism', proposing abstract rules to fix the problem. As Rowland wrote:

> On the one hand, Hayek appears to evaluate institutions according to whether they are the products of spontaneous evolution; liberty and order, he suggests, are a product of such evolutionary processes. On the other hand, his development of a model constitution appears to demonstrate his willingness to engage in rational design, exactly the process his traditionalism argues against. (Rowland, 1988: 222)

Furthermore, there are important differences lurking beneath the surface similarity of Oakeshott's and Hayek's understanding of rationalism, connected, I think, to Oakeshott's idealism. At first glance, Hayek, by the time he is writing *Law, Legislation and Liberty*, sometimes seems to be echoing Oakeshott's views from 'Rationalism in Politics', for instance, when he writes:

> The first view holds that human institutions will serve human purposes only if they have been deliberately designed for these purposes, often also that the fact that an institution exists is evidence of its having been created for a purpose, and always that we should so re-design society and its institutions that all our actions will be wholly guided by known purposes. To most people these propositions seem almost self-evident and to constitute a attitude alone worthy of a thinking being. Yet the belief underlying them, that we all owe all beneficial institutions to

design, and that only such design has made or can make them useful for our purposes, is largely false. (Hayek, 1973: 8–9)

Or this:

> Yet the basic assumption underlying the belief that man has achieved mastery of his surroundings mainly through his capacity for logical deduction from explicit premises is factually false, and any attempt to confine his actions to what could thus be justified would deprive him of many of the most effective means to success that have been available to him. It is simply not true that our actions owe their effectiveness solely or chiefly to the knowledge which we can state in words and which can therefore constitute the explicit premises of a syllogism. (Hayek, 1973: 11)

But then Hayek writes something like, 'That freedom can be preserved only if it is treated as a supreme principle which must not be sacrificed for particular advantages was fully understood by the leading liberal thinkers of the nineteenth century...' (1973: 72), and one realizes there is something significantly different going on here.

The key to understanding how, starting from a similar critique of rationalism, Hayek arrives at such a different position from Oakeshott lies, I think, in the fact that Oakeshott is an idealist while Hayek is not. For Hayek, what is opposed to abstract thought is not concrete thought, but instinct, mechanism, or emotion. Writing of Hegel's statement that 'the view which clings to abstraction is liberalism, over which the concrete always prevails...' Hayek contends, 'he truly described the fact that we are not yet mature enough to submit for any length of time to strict discipline of reason and allow our emotions to constantly break through its restraints' (1973: 33). However, he fails to understand that for Hegel, as for most of the idealists who followed him, concrete thought was the pinnacle of reason, and not a fall from it. (Recall the quote from Bosanquet presented earlier in this chapter.) Hayek mistakes the relationships that make up his 'Great Society' as abstract because the *theory* of such relationships is highly abstract; but those relationships themselves are concrete: *this* businessman buys *this* amount of concrete from *this* vendor to be delivered at *this* time and *this* place. Trying to intelligently decide policies on a case-by-case basis will only result in irrational, emotional interventions that eventually will lead us down 'the road to serfdom'; only a dogmatic insistence on classical liberal principles can preserve freedom.[9]

---

[9] For instance: 'A successful defence of freedom must therefore be dogmatic and make no concessions to expediency...' (1973: 61).

However, even if we are philosophically inclined to side with Oakeshott, we may wonder, given that rationalism, as Oakeshott himself noted, has 'come to colour the ideas, not merely of one, but of all political persuasions, and to flow over every party line' (1991 [1962]: 5), if there is any hope of 'going back' to a prerationalistic state of affairs, and ask: if there isn't, then is Hayek's 'rationalist anti-rationalism' a more realistic antidote to our ills than is Oakeshott's perhaps nostalgic longing for a political discourse purged of the rationalist toxins? As MacIntyre pointed out:

> Those who respond to periods of rapid and disruptive change by appealing for a retention of or a return to the ways of the past, to the customary, to the traditional, always have to reckon with the fact that in a established customary social order those who follow its ways do not have and do not need good reasons for doing so. The question of what constitutes a *good reason for action* is thrust upon them only when they are already confronted by alternatives, and characteristically the first uses of practical reasoning will be to justify pursuit of some good not to be achieved by following the customary routines of the normal day, month, and year. It is only later when these routines have more largely and more radically disrupted that the question of whether it was not in fact better to follow the older ways unreflectively can be raised, and when the conservative offers his contemporaries good reasons for returning to an earlier relatively unreflective mode of social life, his very modes of advocacy provide evidence that what he recommends is no longer possible. (MacIntyre, 1988: 54)[10]

Was Oakeshott's work an instance of the phenomenon MacIntyre describes above? Is the mere fact that he was compelled to articulate an 'anti-rationalist' theory a sign that it was already too late to attempt a restoration of the traditions he admired? Is it true, as Hegel claimed, 'When philosophy paints its gray on gray, then has a form of life grown old, and with gray on gray it cannot be rejuvenated, but only known; the Owl of Minerva first takes flight with twilight closing in?' (1896) We will attempt to address those questions, too, as we engage with our historical cases.

---

[10] Or, as Watkins wrote, 'A politician in the highly vocal, argumentative, Western political world cannot be [taciturn]. Having to answer questions and meet criticisms he is *inevitably* a rationaliser, and his rationalisations obviously invite critical scrutiny. It is really *non*-ideological politics which have become impossible in the West, because a process of critical awareness cannot reverse itself' (1952: 336)

Conclusion

In brief, it is clear that many of the criticisms of Oakeshott are well wide of the mark. This is probably due, for one thing, to Oakeshott's own way of putting his ideas, the difficult features of which include an exact but somewhat esoteric writing style, a lack of references to contemporary lines of thought in the areas he addressed, and a reluctance to explain where he felt he had gone wrong when he changed his mind. Another factor is that Oakeshott's ideas diverged from the mainstream to an extent that made it difficult to grasp just how different they were, as, for instance, when critics read his invocation of tradition in explaining how we proceed in politics as an endorsement of a traditionalist ideology (since for them *all* politics was ideological politics), rather than as an explanation of how we *always* really do proceed.[11] Clearing up these confusions has been an important preliminary to our case studies.

---

[11] As Raynor put this, '[Oakeshott's] account of political activity as "the pursuit of intimations" is not a recommendation that we all become "traditionalists", but a description of what we actually succeed in doing in conduct' (1985: 320).

Chapter 4

Constitutionalism and Oakeshott

The present chapter has both a primary and a secondary purpose. First, it will serve as a bridge between the more theoretical chapters preceding it and the more historically oriented ones that follow it. In particular, the question of whether a rationally designed constitution can perform the tasks its advocates claim will be examined here; this will serve to relate the theoretical issues discussed earlier to a more concrete question, and connect them to the problem of constitutional design, which will serve as a crucial differentia in our analysis of the Roman and the American republics. The American founders saw the rational design of a written constitution as the antidote to the ills that brought down the Roman republic, which had no written constitution, so this chapter introduces a background from which to evaluate the success of their enterprise. It is for this reason that the introduction referred to this chapter as the 'linchpin' in this work.

Second, given that Oakeshott wrote 'Rationalism in Politics' well over 50 years ago, it is worth examining (further than we did in Chapter 1) whether or not his critique is still relevant to contemporary political theory. While his ideal types may be coherent, do they refer to empirical reality or, as Weber would have put it, do they possess 'causal adequacy'? It might be suspected that, insofar as he aimed his polemics at the grand utopian schemes still popular at that time, such as communism and fascism, his essay has little to say to us today, when such political utopianism generally has fallen into disrepute. However, rationalism can appear in both more grandiose and more modest forms, and its spirit, at least in its more modest incarnations, has hardly been absent from today's political discourse. As Minogue wrote, arguing for the continuing importance of Oakeshott's ideas: 'The twentieth century was full of such moths who found the flames of abstraction irresistible, and many perished as a result. We are far from having done away with their successors' (2002: par. 32). The present work opened by suggesting that the confidence placed in a written constitution as at least a partial solution to the civil strife in Iraq, following the Anglo-American invasion of 2003, is a symptom of a continuing spirit of rationalism infecting modern political thinking. In Chapter 1, I also presented recent urban planning efforts as examples of less extreme rationalism than that of, say, Pol Pot killing all of the intellectuals. Here, we will explore the persistence of the rationalist disposition in recent political theory.[1]

Constitutionalism

A particularly salient instance of what I take to be the continuing influence of rationalism on political theorizing is the great importance placed upon constitutional design in the works of many contemporary political thinkers, displayed in practice in the case of Iraq that opened the present work, and important in the European Union today. Indeed, the modern faith in constitutionalism is so great that a group of thinkers in the late 1940s met to draft a 'world constitution' as a solution to the threat of atomic war, and all of the many new countries established since that time have routinely adopted a written constitution.[2] I suggest that the chief impetus motivating this focus is the rationalist notion that a properly designed, rationally derived set of guidelines setting out a framework that must be respected by all legitimate political actions can trump any contingent circumstances that might hinder the realization of an acceptable, liberal democratic polity, such as the artificial composition of the nation in question arising from largely arbitrary colonial boundaries, the existence of

---

[1] It is notable, in light of my earlier contention (echoing that of Oakeshott) that the critique of rationalist politics is not merely 'reactionary politics' in new clothing and that several of the rationalist political theorists discussed below are from the 'right' side of the political spectrum. I suggest that Oakeshott would have shared my evaluation of these thinkers—see his remarks on Hayek's *Road to Serfdom* quoted previously—and that this offers further evidence that the 'rationalist malady' is not merely a phenomenon affecting the left, and that the diagnosis of this disorder is not a covert defense of right-wing policies.

[2] See Hutchins *et al.*, 1948. Sounding a contrary note is Levinson, who speculates that the '"death of constitutionalism" may be the central event of our time' (1988: 52). His important study is largely compatible with the conclusions of the present work; however, although he may be correct about the theoretical health of constitutionalism, if so, the news of its impending demise has been slow to spread.

fiercely antagonistic factions within the newly formed state, or the lack of any tradition of broad participation in politics and experience with self-governance at the level of the nation-state on the part of the general population. A central theme of this and the subsequent chapters of the present work is whether or not this faith in the efficacy of a 'sound constitution' to overcome such difficulties is well grounded; perhaps the character of any actual polity will be determined foremost by the attitudes towards governance prevailing amongst its populace as a result of their historical experiences of rulership and their customary beliefs about the proper or natural form of social organization. In particular, the respective histories of the Roman and the American republics suggest that possession of a written constitution is not always of primary importance in determining the success of any polity: the Roman republic worked well for more than three centuries despite having no written constitution, while the practice of politics in the American republic, almost as soon as it was founded, began to deviate from the formal constitution that was supposed to rigidly dictate the guidelines to which practice must conform. What is more, as we shall see, American political practice *needed* to set aside the idea that all political actions must strictly adhere to the written letter of the Constitution in order for the fledgling republic to survive and prosper. And the attempt to make explicit the principles that had guided the Roman republic successfully before the Roman revolution, by setting them out as written directives with the force of law behind them, could not save that republic from dissolution. But, I do not wish to overstate this claim: first of all, only two cases will be examined in depth, which is hardly a conclusive survey; and second, I am not arguing that a well-written constitution is entirely otiose, but, rather, that it is at best the 'icing on the cake' for a polity based on a pretheoretical, commonly embraced, and viable conception of how social life should be structured, as it may serve as a focal symbol representing and clarifying the central norms underlying that political order. As Oakeshott put it, 'In certain circumstances an abridgement of this kind may be valuable; it gives sharpness of outline and precision to a political tradition which the occasion may make seem appropriate' (1991 [1962]: 55).

I suggest that the intense current interest in constitutional theory is driven, to a great extent, by the rationalist desire, central to modern liberalism, to delimit coherently and rationally defend, based on first principles, a domain of individual autonomy within which every citizen is immune from state interference. As demonstrated by Levinson, a constitution serves as a kind of substitute 'sacred text' for a political community lacking a unified cosmological view (1988: 9–53).

The basis of placing one's faith in this text is the belief that it will serve as the scriptural foundation for protecting a secular, liberal social order against attempts to undermine it. The performance of such rituals as requiring officeholders to take oaths to uphold the constitution[3] or, as Warren Burger, Chief Justice of the United States Supreme Court, recommended, 'Teach the [Constitution's] principles… to your children, speak of them in your home… write them on the doorplate of your home and upon your gates' (quoted in Levinson, 1988: 12, who noted Burger's echoing of Deuteronomy 6:7–9), it is hoped that the continued existence of a liberal polity can be safeguarded. Typically, the existence of such a founding document is understood as a primary criterion for asserting the legitimacy of the state it purports to establish, just as the existence of a sacred book grounds many religions. The authority of this founding constitution is regarded as categorically distinct from, and superior to, the multitude of more concrete directives that are issued by political actors in response to the transient circumstances that arise in the day-to-day governance of their polity. The constitution does not dictate or determine the content of those lower-level legal and administrative promulgations except in requiring that they be genuine instances of the abstract classes of state activities that it permits. The role such a constitution plays in guiding the actual performances of state agents is seen as similar to the relationship that a body of rules governing a sport has to any particular engagement in that game: the constitution of a state and the rule book for a sport alike set constraints on the range of actions legitimately open to those who purport to be participants in the activity in question, and provide penalties for those who fail to heed those limits, but they do not attempt to determine the 'play' of any particular 'contest'. In the view of constitutional optimists, the ultimate authority of the constitutional directives of any polity over the policy options available to political actors present formidable barriers likely to thwart the ambitions of any would-be tyrant and protect the basic rights of the citizens of that state from being trampled by power-hungry office holders. A well-designed constitution is supposed to offer a 'steady, unchanging, independent guide to which a society might resort [in a time of crisis]'.[4] Modern constitutionalism, in short, is an instance of the general rationalist tendency at work in modern political thought, as it understands deductively derived principles and abstract design to be the best basis for creating a flourishing polity.

---

[3] See Levinson (1988: 90–121).

[4] Oakeshott (1991 [1962]: 59). And he continues, 'But no such guide exists…'

However, at the core of the case for the ability of a written constitution to meet the lofty expectations of its advocates resides an apparent paradox: how can a constitution successfully restrict the scope of action of state agents when it is those very same agents who possess the ultimate authority to decide how its text should be interpreted and its dictates enforced? Furthermore, since the founding constitution of a polity necessarily was created in the absence of the constitutional constraints supposedly needed to ensure the just exercise of sovereign authority, the justice of its own generation is rendered doubtful. And, as discussed earlier in this work, Oakeshott has presented a strong indictment of all such attempts to design social arrangements from first principles, accusing them of neglecting the true relationship between theory and practice. As he sees it, good abstract rules are, at best, the distillation of sound practice, rather than being a superior substitute for the lived experience of good governance.

Political theorists of a constitutional bent have not been oblivious to the challenge with which the above considerations present them. One heavily travelled route taken in addressing the first problem relies upon some variation of the Polybian 'mixed constitution'. (The American founders were greatly influenced by this Polybian ideal, especially via the work of Montesquieu.) The aimed-for destination is characterized by having different governmental powers apportioned among several—most often three, in a bow to Aristotle's typology of constitutions according to whether rule was by 'the One', 'the Few', or 'the Many' (1995: 99–101)—distinct branches of government or estates of society, so that, should any one of those entities seek to exceed its constitutional bounds and achieve a tyrannical domination over the others, its partners in governing can act to restrain it. The goal of an ideally balanced republic offers an attractive resolution of the 'constitutional dilemma', but one relying upon preserving the genuine independence of the several organs of the state, so that they continue to act as rivalrous loci of political power. But what sort of obstacles can a constitution erect that plausibly will prevent the representatives of those institutions from effectively uniting to pursue common ends, given that the primary responsibility for maintaining the impregnability of those barriers rests with the very officials who may wish to undermine them? It appears that the intentions motivating the architectural design of the mixed constitution will be thwarted should a significant portion of the governmental agents, whose possibly excessive ambitions are supposedly checked by others occupying roles in distinct and competing institutions, come to regard their different institutional affiliations as primarily nominal divisions, offering no substantial impediment to their cooperating in the project of increasing the power of the state over its subjects.

Now, a believer in the efficacy of written constitutions readily may acknowledge that the problems of who will watch over the watchers and the dubious genesis of all existing constitutions plague existing attempts to provide a theoretical defense of constitutionalism—they are, perhaps, less likely to recognize the force of the third difficulty mentioned in the previous paragraph—but still attempt to respond to those issues by noting that they are of little practical significance. It is true, he might admit, that the process by which any particular constitution was constructed and then adopted might not have followed the principles of republican government and equal representation for all citizens, the very principles underpinning his own notion of political legitimacy, but of what use is crying over that spilled milk to us now? If today the great majority of citizens are satisfied with the political institutions that emerged from the efforts of the original, constitution-creating body, however questionable was its claim legitimately to possess the authority requisite to its undertaking, then why make the desire that the past should have been more perfect the enemy of the good today? And if today the constitution thus produced, whatever its theoretical shortcomings might be, in fact serves to ensure that any legitimate action by the state must respect certain basic rights possessed by its citizens, then purely speculative arguments as to why a constitution might fail to perform as intended could be dismissed as insignificant in practice, which would render Oakeshott's thesis on rationalism of little practical importance, at least as far as constitutional issues are concerned.

A work such as this one, consisting of an extensive examination of only two cases selected from the multitude of potentially relevant instances of existing and historical polities (although a few other examples are touched upon), is in no way comprehensive enough to yield an empirically compelling decision either for or against the efficacy of written constitutions. I make no pretense that it can offer anything more than suggestions as to some promising paths for further research. Furthermore, any comprehensive survey of the current state of constitutional theory would require several volumes as long as our present endeavor, and would represent an enormous digression from the topic we have at hand. Nevertheless, both because suggestions for future avenues of exploration are not without value, and also because, as mentioned above, invoking these live issues presents an opportunity to gauge the current relevance (or lack thereof) of Oakeshott's critique of rationalism and an opportunity for exploring his concept of rationalism in relation to actual 'case studies', I believe we are justified in briefly examining what bearing Oakeshott's thesis might have on theoretical aspects of modern constitutional theory. As such, the following discussion does not pretend to be an exhaustive survey of the vast literature on the theoretical basis of constitutionalism—instead, I will largely focus on a few examples of this literature that I hold out as representative.

The varieties of constitutions

In order to look at how Oakeshott's thesis relates to modern constitutionalism, it might be helpful to briefly survey the varieties of constitutionalism. It would be a mistake to view constitutionalism as a monolithic body of beliefs, or to suggest that all modern constitutions are mere clones of each other. K. C. Wheare, in his pioneering study *Modern Constitutions* (1966), classifies constitutions according to several different, central distinctions in their various structures, a classification scheme having bearing on just how much 'rationalism' a particular constitution should be seen to embody. A notable feature in Wheare's schema is that constitutions may be categorized by the degree to which they are 'unitary' or 'federal'. A unitary constitution grants supreme and unlimited authority over issues of governance to the national-level political institutions, even while, at that level, it still may posit a separation of powers amongst various national authorities. Regional governments are perhaps permitted to legislate on particular matters, but only at the indulgence of the national governing bodies, which always have the ability to override the decisions reached by local officials. Examples of unitary constitutions offered by Wheare include New Zealand and Ireland.

In contrast, federal constitutions aim to cordon off certain topics as being the exclusive domain of provincial policy, restricting the power of the national government over what are seen as properly more local concerns. Wheare's examples of this latter form include the United States, Switzerland, Australia, and West Germany. For our purposes, it is salutary to note that the attempt to direct the course of a polity according to a unitary constitution is a more rationalist approach than is federalism, since it allows less room for local politics to follow customary, practical wisdom, and attempts to impose a single, rational design on political activity at every level. In that the American founders chose a federalist design,[5] their efforts were less rationalist than if they had decided upon a unitary constitution, an important qualification of Oakeshott's view of that founding as a paradigm of rationalism.

A second way to divide constitutions is according to whether they are regarded as superior in authority to ordinary legislative decisions. Overwhelmingly, they are; the only example Wheare cites of the contrary case, in which a simple legislative act can override a constitutional directive, is that of New Zealand. And Wheare contends that this isolated case only exists because of the *de facto* reluctance of New Zealand's parliament to modify the constitution in such a fashion. However, in regimes where the constitution is regarded as the supreme authority, what often occurs, should that constitution appear to thwart some widely popular legislative measure, is that the measure passes and subsequently the constitution is reinterpreted so as to allow what was previously seen as an unconstitutional action. To the extent that a constitution is understood as laying down inviolable restrictions about the permissible scope of mundane legislation, it is more rationalist than one that does not purport to do so, as it presumes that its authors have a comprehensive grasp of what sorts of legislation might be appropriate in response to unpredictable future situations. In this regard, the U.S. Constitution receives a check mark on the 'more rationalist' side of the ledger; as we will see, certain of the founders, such as Jefferson, contended that even the least violation of constitutional boundaries created a breach through which the most egregious might pass unhindered.

Whether or not a constitution is made explicit in a written document is yet another important way to distinguish constitutions, one of particular import for us in comparing Rome and America. As in the previous case, it is one for which Wheare cites only a single polity as falling into one of his two categories: among modern nation-states, the sole instance he offers of one with an unwritten constitution is the United Kingdom.[6] He explains this anomaly as being the result of

---

[5] In that they truly did so — a chief complaint by the anti-federalists in the debates over ratification was that the proposed constitution was not really federalist at all. See, for instance, Brutus (1787) or Lee (1787).

[6] Wheare, in fact, rejects the term 'unwritten constitution' and writes that Britain has *no* constitution. Whatever the merits of Wheare's vocabulary, it has not caught on, and would make nonsense of all discussion of the 'Roman Constitution', so we will employ the more common terminology. Among modern nations, only Israel and New Zealand are widely regarded to also have 'uncodified' constitutions.

Britain's unique history. The English revolution of the 1640s, as Wheare sees it, attempted to create a formalized, written constitution for the British nation, but the unpalatable outcome of that episode, along with the relief from civil strife following the subsequent restoration of the monarchy, created a climate of national opinion unfavorable to radical tampering with the traditional, evolved arrangements structuring British political life, which came to be seen as better defenses of English liberty than were novel, rationalist inventions. Obviously, the present work will turn to the ancient world for another example of an unwritten constitutional order, when it examines the history of the Roman republic.

Our next classificatory criterion, the degree of difficulty facing efforts to amend an existing constitution, exhibits a much broader variation than did the previously described differentiae. The various, contemporarily realized requirements for altering constitutional strictures range from, at the least onerous extreme, a simple majority of votes by the national legislative body, to demands for supermajorities of various sizes, such as three-fifths, two-thirds, and three-quarters, the imposition of mandatory delays of various lengths of time between the formal advancement of a proposed amendment and the actual vote concerning its adoption, the necessity for concurrence from other bodies than the national legislature (such as in the United States, where three-fourths of the states must approve a proposed amendment), and even declarations that certain portions of a nation's constitution are not subject to amendment (as we will see, for instance, in examining the problematic Honduran constitution later in this work). Clearly, the more significant are the hurdles erected to limit amendments to a constitution, the more it displays the influence of rationalism; after all, if the founders correctly deduced the proper form to which concrete political life should mold itself, then attempts to modify that blueprint are largely just examples of weakness of the will in the face of trying circumstances, or perhaps corruption or the ascendancy of factional interests. In this regard, the American founders appear roughly in the middle of the range of possibilities, having made constitutional amendment difficult, but not having rendered any portion of the constitution unalterable.

While all of the above methods of classifying constitutions are relevant to the present work, for our purposes, perhaps the most interesting of Wheare's distinctions concerns how authoritative the members of a polity consider their constitution to be. He notes that in polities where the executive has traditionally wielded great power, or those in which the ideas embodied in the constitution are not widely accepted by the public, the restraints on state action supposedly guaranteed by that document are likely to have little force. For example, the 1936 constitution of the Soviet Union guaranteed that citizens had the right to freedom of assembly and meeting, freedom of speech, the inviolability of their homes from arbitrary state incursions, and the freedom to organize political demonstrations. Of course, these precepts meant little in practice, as the extant political culture of that nation had no tradition of expecting and asserting such rights. On the other hand, in a society where such rights are broadly held sacrosanct, they are likely to be respected whether or not they are formally asserted. Indeed, as Wheare noted, the classification of constitutions per the previous criteria rests importantly on the climate of opinion as well:

> The fact is that the ease or the frequency with which a constitution is amended depends not only on the legal provisions which prescribe the method of change but also on the predominant political and social groups in the community and the extent to which they are satisfied with or acquiesce in the organization and distribution of political power which the constitution prescribes. (Wheare, 1966: 17)

This contention forwarded by Wheare, one of the foremost researchers into constitutional reality in recent times, supports a central theme of the present work: a written constitution can offer, at best, a subsidiary support for the maintenance of some particular, desired manner of ordering a nation's political life, the continuation of which depends primarily on the importance that the citizenry assigns to preserving that form of government.

The case for constitutionalism

I have suggested that one consequence of the rationalists' predominance in political thought is that currently it is broadly held that the optimal method of restraining any moves by agents of the state aimed at exercising arbitrary power over the rest of the citizenry is to devise a written constitution delimiting the scope of their authority. Perhaps, in addition, the polity ought to create a 'bill of rights' enumerating certain liberties that the state must never deny its subjects. As Elster put it, 'Many writers have argued that political constitutions are devices for precommitment or self-binding, created by the body politic in order to protect itself against its own predictable tendency to make unwise decisions' (2000: 88). Or, per Wheare, 'a Constitution is thought of as an instrument by which government can be controlled.

Constitutions spring from a belief in limited government' (1966: 7). In this view, political actors are free to enact any law or pursue any policy within the confines of those constitutional boundaries, but the constitution confronts them with what might be called a body of 'meta-laws', which they are compelled to obey. To again cite Elster, 'In one interpretation, constitution-makers regard themselves as superior both to the corrupt or inefficient regime they are replacing and to the interest- and passion-ridden regimes that will replace them' (2000: 115).

When one of the foremost of contemporary republican theorists, Philip Pettit, wondered '[h]ow to make republican instrumentalities maximally non-manipulable [by those wishing to use them to achieve dominance over others]?' the solution he proposes is 'constitutionalism[, which consists of] legally established ways of constraining the will of the powerful'. He acknowledges that such constraints may operate 'even if [they] are not recorded in a formal constitution' (1997: 173). Clearly, however, in looking at the recent history of new states formed with external guidance by foreign advisors, the contemporary preference is strongly towards constitutional constraints on 'the will of the powerful' that are explicitly worked out in advance, based on rational considerations of the proper role of the state, and set out in a founding document. As noted earlier, the great importance placed, in the wake of the Anglo-American overthrow of the Hussein regime in Iraq, on having Iraqis draw up a written constitution, even as their society lacked any semblance of rudimentary civil order, offers a salient example. Apparently, factions who, the day before the constitution was ratified, were anxious to wipe each other out, would, upon reading the document, lay down their arms and launch into reasoned political debate within the new constitutional framework.

I only will explore a few notable instances of this confidence in the power of a written constitution to protect the general populace from the danger of becoming mere pawns serving to advance the interests of their rulers; the reader can easily find many others that fit this bill. To repeat: I make no effort here to be comprehensive, but only to set the stage for our subsequent empirical explorations, as well as to illustrate that Oakeshott's ideas are relevant in this contemporary debate. But my examples will, I believe, be sufficient for my purposes, without leading us too far astray from our primary theme.

Constitutions as embodying a priori
natural rights: Rothbard

The libertarian economist and political theorist Murray N. Rothbard, in
his work *The Ethics of Liberty*, argued that the rational guidance offered
by natural law is sufficient to pick out a uniquely justified
constitutional order, one based entirely on property rights, most
fundamentally the right to self-ownership. Citing Late Scholastic
philosophers as providing precedent for his conception of natural law,
he pointedly contended that recognizing the authority of that law over
issues of justice in no way depends on divine revelation or any specific
religious creed:

> The statement that there is an order of natural law, in short, leaves open
> the question of whether or not God created that order; and the assertion
> of the viability of man's reason to discover the natural order leaves open
> the question of whether or not that reason was given to man by God.
> The assertion of an order of natural laws discoverable by reason is, by
> itself, neither pro- nor anti-religious. (Rothbard, 1998: 4)

Rationally working out the implications of the basic precepts of this
natural law, in Rothbard's system, does not merely offer constraints
that any just legal system must respect, but instead yields concrete
answers to all questions regarding what constitutes a just law.
Consider, for instance, an article in which Rothbard ridiculed Frank
Meyer for advocating prudence as a virtue:

> Anyone who believes in the existence of a natural law discoverable
> through right reason (as Mr. Meyer and myself both do), *must* also
> believe that this natural law is self-consistent. Outside of the irrational
> world of the Hegelian dialectic, there can be no conflicting truths, nor
> contradictory but true propositions. And since the rights of man are
> deducible from natural law, these rights *cannot* conflict with one
> another. If one discovers a contradiction, one has also discovered an
> error in one's process of reasoning. We must not surrender reason at its
> most critical point by meekly accepting contradiction. We must go
> further to seek out the error and discard it. (Rothbard, 2005)

Rothbard's view that 'rights *cannot* conflict with one another' stands
in sharp contrast to the more commonsensical position taken by
Aristotle (who could hardly be deemed an opponent of reason!) that
the 'admitted goods' of a society must be weighed one against another
in practical political reasoning. Furthermore, in the course of his
attempt to derive an inclusive and deductively correct legal order from
a minimal set of rationally justified principles, Rothbard reaches some

startling conclusions.[7] For example, discussing what commonly would be regarded as cases of illicit police brutality, he proposed:

> Police may use such coercive methods [as beating and torturing suspects] *provided* that the suspect turns out to be guilty, *and* provided that the police are treated themselves as criminal suspects if the suspect is not proven guilty. For, in that case, the rule of no force against non-criminals would still apply. Suppose, for example, that police beat and torture a suspected murderer to find information... If the suspect turns out to be guilty, then the police should be exonerated, for then they have only ladled out to the murderer a parcel of what he deserves in return; his rights had already been forfeited by more than that extent. (Rothbard, 1998: 82)

In the interest of what he sees as a consistent adherence to the dictates of abstract reasoning, Rothbard gives no weight to the belief, held widely in our day, that torture is inherently wrong even if the target of the torture truly is guilty, no weight to the idea that allowing the practice of torture dehumanizes its practitioners, and is unconcerned with the readily apparent, practical downside of permitting police torture so long as the tortured party is ultimately convicted, which is that it gives legal authorities a strong motive to frame anyone they have tortured.

When Rothbard turned to the question of what legal responsibilities parents ought to have for their offspring, he wrote:

> In the free society, no man may be saddled with the legal obligation to do anything for another, since that would invade the former's rights; the only legal obligation one man has to another is to respect the other man's rights.
>
> Applying our theory to parents and children, this means that a parent does not have the right to aggress against his children, but also that the parent should not have a legal obligation to feed, clothe, or educate his children, since such obligations would entail positive acts coerced upon the parent and depriving the parent of his rights. The parent therefore may not murder or mutilate his child, and the law properly outlaws a parent from doing so. But the parent should also have the legal right not to feed the child, i.e., to allow it to die. (Rothbard, 1998: 100)

---

[7] Rothbard proceeds from essentially *one* principle: property rights are inviolable. As Oakeshott noted, this is a logical maneuver given Rothbard's goal: if one wants to transform political discourse from 'mere' persuasion to apodictic demonstration, 'it must escape from having to balance one single "admitted good" against another in deciding upon a response to a political situation, because this can never reach a demonstrative conclusion' (1991 [1962]: 83).

Thus, for Rothbard, the logical elegance of his legal theory trumps any arguments based on the moral reprehensibility of a parent idly watching her six-month-old child slowly starve to death in its crib, or based on long-standing legal proscriptions of such neglect. As we discussed in Chapter 2, in terms of rationalist political theorists in general, he has engaged in what O'Neill calls idealization: he has taken a valid concern in political reflection, that of property rights, and treated it as if it were the *only* valid concern, as if, for instance, the concern that the powerful ought not be allowed to abuse the weak means nothing.

Rothbard similarly rejects the legal validity of many, seemingly unproblematic, contracts. For instance, he holds that enforcing a contract in which party A promises to pay for the education of party B, even if there is no doubt that the obligation was undertaken freely and knowingly, and even if B has made significant investments and decisions based on A's pledge, represents an unjustified violation of A's rights. His defense of this position is that such a breach of faith involves no violation of property rights, since 'mere promises are not a transfer of property title' (1998: 133). And he contended that blackmail must be legally permissible in a just polity, since the victim has no exclusive right to control his reputation (1998: 124–126).

It may be difficult to imagine that a workable social order could be built upon a legal regime that allows the police to torture guilty suspects, parents to intentionally starve their helpless infants, solemn promises to be cast aside without penalty, and blackmailers to operate freely. What's more, we are entitled to wonder if seriously advocating that such a law code be adopted immediately and in its entirety, despite the absence of any experience suggesting its practicality, displays a cavalier and reckless disregard for the fact that the existing social arrangements, however far they may fall short of fulfilling one's idealized visions for society, possess at least the virtue of having demonstrated that they enable most of those whose affairs they guide to lead reasonably tolerable lives. But to Rothbard, it appears that such pragmatic apprehensions about his manifesto for radically transforming the fundamental governance of social life are merely irrational obstacles to the logically required acceptance of his political vision.

And Rothbard is not an instance of an idiosyncratic thinker whose ideas died with him; indeed, he has more disciples today than he did when he passed away (in 1995), and there are currently a number of think tanks in America and Europe dedicated to advancing his political program. To cite just a single example of the continuing rationalism of Rothbard's followers, Hans-Hermann Hoppe (1988) has attempted to argue that the mere fact that a person engages in argument deductively proves that, at the risk of self-contradiction, the arguer must accept the entire libertarian political program.

Constitutions as contracts I: Rawls

Perhaps the most cited work of twentieth-century political philosophy is John Rawls's *A Theory of Justice*.[8] Rawls's rationalism is less extreme than that of many of Oakeshott's contemporary targets — plausibly a result of the critiques of rationalism offered by Oakeshott, Hayek, Voegelin, and others. Nevertheless, as I hope to demonstrate, the rationalist spirit is still alive and well in Rawls's work.

Rawls launched the tome under examination here with the aim of creating 'a theory of justice that generalizes and carries to a higher level of abstraction the traditional conception of the social contract' (1999: 3) — in other words, the social contract, already an abstract, rationalist understanding of society, is to be made even more rationalist. And the conclusions of his abstract reasoning will give no quarter to practical or traditional quibbles: 'Being first virtues of human activities, truth and justice are uncompromising' (1999: 4). Rawls was not interested in workable arrangements, but in 'what a perfectly just society would be like' (1999: 8). Like a good rationalist, he held that only theory yields true knowledge: 'I shall assume that a deeper understanding can be gained in no other way [than ideal theory]' (1999: 8).

Theory is able to stand outside practice in the role of judge: 'A conception of social justice... is to be regarded as providing... a standard whereby the distributive aspects of the basic structure of society are to be assessed' (1999: 8). From the abstract position they occupy behind his 'veil of ignorance', where individuals have no concrete attributes except their 'rationality', 'a group of persons must decide once and for all what is to count among them as just and unjust' (1999: 11), a decision not to be reconsidered in light of subsequent experience. This grounding of social affairs is not 'an actual historical state of affairs [or] a primitive condition of culture [but] as a purely hypothetical situation characterized so as to lead to a certain conception of justice' (1999: 11). As MacIntyre noted, surely it goes a long way

---

[8] See, for instance, Schwitzgebel, 2006.

towards dismissing Rawls's concept of justice as irrelevant merely to point out '*we* are *never* behind such a veil of ignorance' (2007: 249).

The concrete details of the just polity, much as in Rothbard, are held to flow from its initial, abstract design:

> Justice as fairness begins, as I have said, with one of the most general of all choices which persons might make together, namely, with the choice of the first principles of a conception of justice which is to regulate all subsequent criticism and reform of institutions. Then, having chosen a conception of justice, we can suppose that they are to choose constitution and a legislature to enact laws, and so on, all in accordance with the principles of justice initially agreed upon. (Rawls, 1999: 12)

Rawls, in a nod to the case against rationalism, recognizes that his program cannot really be followed in any detail — 'I shall not, of course, actually work through this process' — but this hardly deters him, as he continues, 'Still, we may think of the interpretation of the original position that I shall present as the result of such a hypothetical course of reflection' (1999: 18).

When he turns his attention to institutions, we see that, once again for Rawls, abstract design is primary and concrete practice is generated from the theoretical framework:

> Now by an institution I shall understand a public system of rules which defines offices and positions with their rights and duties, powers and immunities, and the like. These rules specify certain forms of action as permissible, others as forbidden; and they provide for certain penalties and defenses, and so on, when violations occur... An institution may be thought of in two ways: first as a abstract object, that is, as a possible form of conduct expressed by a system of rules; and second, as the realization in the thought and conduct of certain persons at a certain time and place of the actions specified by these rules. (Rawls, 1999: 48)

In other words, concrete institutions are birthed by abstract rules, rather than the rules having been abstracted *from* the existing institutions, as Oakeshott would have it.

As I mentioned earlier, Rawls, unlike rationalists writing before the wave of critiques of their program that began appearing in the 1950s, is at least partially aware of the limits of the rationalist approach, and it is only fair to cite a passage where he acknowledged such limits: 'A conception of justice cannot be deduced from self-evident premises or conditions on principles; instead, its justification is a matter of the mutual support of many considerations, of everything fitting together in one coherent view' (1999: 19).

Nevertheless, passages like those on the previous page do not represent an embrace of abstinence from imbibing at the rationalist tap, but are more like occasional days of reduced intake scattered amongst many of serious drinking. I could cite many more examples such as the one offered above to defend this view. However, the purpose of addressing Rawls here has not been to offer an extended critique of his work, which, while possibly worth undertaking, would represent a serious digression from the main theme of this study. Therefore, I will provide just one more case of Rawls's rationalism, while trusting that the interested reader could discover further instances for herself.

My final example concerns Rawls's categorical rejection of any polity that does not extend the right to hold any political office to any sane, adult citizen. He wrote:

> For it may be possible to improve everyone's situation by assigning certain powers and benefits to positions despite the fact that certain groups are excluded from them. Although access is restricted, perhaps these offices can still attract superior talent and encourage better performance. But the principle of open positions forbids this. It expresses the conviction that if some places were not open on a basis fair to all, those kept out would be right in feeling unjustly treated even though they benefited from the greater efforts of those who were allowed to hold them. They would be justified in their complaint not only because they were excluded from certain external rewards of office but because they were barred from experiencing the realization of self which comes from a skillful and devoted exercise of social duties. (Rawls, 1999: 73)

The disconnect from reality here should be obvious. First of all, Oakeshott pointed out, the achievement of a stable and reasonably humane political order is no mean feat in and of itself. Should some people, fortunate enough to enjoy living in such an order, feel compelled to dismantle it simply because it fails to meet Rawls's abstract criteria of justice? Second, in the sort of modern, constitutional welfare state that Rawls obviously holds up as a near approach to his ideal, just what percentage of citizens actually are engaged in 'a skillful and devoted exercise of social duties'? Of course, in Rawls's abstraction, the answer is 'all of them'; the problem is precisely that he is entranced by his abstraction and fails to note that, in the real world, the answer is 'very few of them'.

The rationalist hubris underlying the 'principle of justice' declared above by Rawls might be illustrated by considering the case of Liechtenstein. In March of 2003, the electorate of that country approved, with a two-thirds majority, a new constitution that actually strengthened the power of the nation's hereditary monarch. The Council of Europe, proceeding, no doubt, on the basis of a rationalist conception of justice, condemned the result as antidemocratic, a condemnation of which Rawls, per the above passage, clearly would have approved. But Liechtenstein is prosperous, received top rankings from the survey 'Freedom in the World' for both civil liberties and political rights[9]—something that many democratic regimes, with open access to all offices, failed to achieve—and its citizens in general are, apparently, quite happy to have a hereditary monarch. Nevertheless, per Rawls, this seemingly benign situation is inherently 'unjust', and really ought to be remedied so that Liechtensteinians can enjoy the happy state of the residents of countries like, say, Rwanda or Sierra Leone, where there are no hereditary restrictions on holding any office. (Of course, I do not mean to imply that every democratic state inevitably becomes as chaotic and unpleasant to inhabit as have the two polities I have just mentioned. Rather, the point is that, once one surveys the real condition of real nations, Liechtenstein comes off pretty well, and it is not so obvious that open access to all offices is as absolute a political good as Rawls makes it out to be, but, instead, may be one of those 'admitted goods' to be balanced against others.)

Williams, in his critique of Rawls entitled 'Rawls and Pascal's Wager', notes that, as we have noted with other rationalists, Rawls cannot really free himself to take the lofty abstract view he sets out to take:

> There is nothing inherently wrong in falling back on Primary Goods at this point, and, granted the rules of the game, there is not much else that could be done. But it underlines the peculiarity of the game. Any actual concrete social outcome would include people who took different views of the ranking of the primary goods—indeed, it needs no very ambitiously deterministic theory to suppose that the view they took on that matter would itself be a characteristic of and a product of their society. Rawls' people can cash it all out in terms of Primary Goods even in the Original Position, and it is indeed built in right from the beginning that they have a preference for liberty over other goods. But this feature of the choice situation must bias the outcome. (Williams, 1981: 96)

In other words, Rawls gets the modern, social democratic state out of his system because he puts it in at the beginning. What would happen if he did not do that is apparent when we see what G. A. Cohen made of the difference principle. If social affairs must be rearranged

---

[9] See Freedom House, 2008.

wholesale according to first principles, then Cohen (2008) demonstrated, in an unintended reductio of *A Theory of Justice*, that Rawls has not gone nearly far enough: in fact, the difference principle calls for complete egalitarianism, and, in the process, the destruction of the entire economic structure of society.

Constitutions as contracts II: Buchanan and Tullock

The first thing I will note about *The Calculus of Consent*, a famed book that was instrumental in garnering one of its authors, Buchanan, the Nobel Prize in Economics, is its striking similarity to Rawls's *A Theory of Justice* as far as how a just, initial social contract can be established; both works see this as necessarily taking place from an impersonal, abstract position in which no one has any concrete social characteristics. Consider this passage from Buchanan and Tullock:

> For individual decisions on constitutional questions to be combined, some rules must be laid down; but, if so, who chooses these rules? And so on. We prefer to put this issue aside and to assume, without elaboration, that at the ultimate stage, which we shall call the constitutional, the rule of unanimity holds... Recall that we try only to analyze the calculus of the utility-maximizing individual who is confronted with the constitutional problem. Essential to the analysis the presumption that the individual is *uncertain* as to what his own precise role will be in any one of the whole chain of later collective choices that will actually have to be made. For this reason he is considered not to have a particular and distinguishable interest separate and apart from his fellows. This is not to suggest that he will act contrary to his own interests; but the individual will not find it advantageous to vote for rules that may promote sectional, class, or group interests because, by presupposition, he is unable to predict the role that he will be playing in the actual collective decision-making process at any particular time in the future. (Buchanan and Tullock, 1965 [1962]: 77–78)

This is remarkably like Rawls's 'veil of ignorance'. However, despite this similarity, Rawls is somewhat dismissive of Buchanan and Tullock's contribution to his project:

> It is important to distinguish the four-stage sequence and its conception of a constitutional convention from the kind of view of constitutional choice found in social theory and exemplified by... *The Calculus of Consent*... The aim [of my project] is to characterize a just constitution and not ascertain which sort of constitution would be adopted, or acquiesced in, under more or less realistic (though simplified) assumptions about political life, much less on individualistic

assumptions of the kind characteristic of economic theory. (Rawls, 1999: 173)

Now, there is a difference here, and it highlights a weakness in Buchanan and Tullock that is not present in Rawls—they consider 'politics' and 'economics' to be the 'prodigal offspring of political economy' (1965 [1962]: v), apparently not realizing that politics predates political economy as a science by some two millennia, and thereby truncating their analysis so that it ignores issues such as virtue and justice, which are the essence of classical political theory—but, nevertheless, there is a remarkable similarity in the rationalist style of approach to constitutional questions being adopted, most specifically in the adoption of the idea of the 'plain vanilla individual' rationally choosing a constitution in total ignorance of his societal role.

Gray trenchantly commented on this sort of contractarian as follows:

> Given such manifold singularities, what is the justification for modelling the person in a way that will inevitably screen out much of the variety of personal life? The answer, of course, is that unless the variety of personhood is ironed out, there will be no agreement on principles and so no upshot of contractarian deliberation. On the other hand, any abstraction from the particularities of persons already begs every important question in favor of liberalism. Behind the veil of ignorance, we are no longer ourselves, but ciphers, constructed expressly for the purpose of grounding liberal society. The derivation of liberal principles is then circular, since it works with the artificial persons of liberal theory and not with the varieties of personhood we find in the real world... The fact that an abstract or artificial person, screened by an imaginary veil of ignorance from that knowledge of his own life that is constitutive of any real person, would choose a specific set of moral or political principles, if he were able to choose anything at all, has no force for any real person. For any real person, only the values he in fact upholds, the projects and attachments he actually harbours, can generate reasons for action. (Gray, 1989: 250-251)

Having noted this similarity to Rawls, let us proceed to examine how the work presently under examination exhibits rationalist tendencies in its own, unique fashion. Buchanan and Tullock wrote, of their object of study: 'An imposed constitution that embodies the coerced agreement of some members of the social group is a wholly different institution from that which we propose to examine in this book' (1965 [1962]: 15). In other words, they were examining a sort of constitution that never has and never will exist. The purpose of this ideal constitution is to place rational restrictions on the scope of state activity:

It is precisely the recognition that the State may be used for such purposes which should prompt rational individuals to place constitutional restrictions on the use of the political process. Were it not for the properly grounded fear that political processes may be used for exploitative purposes, there would be little meaning and less purpose to constitutional restrictions. (Buchanan and Tullock, 1965 [1962]: 13)

The state itself is a tool of instrumental rationality, and, as such, subject to perfection through rational analysis:

Collective action is viewed as the actions of individuals when they choose to accomplish purposes collectively rather than individually, and the government is seen as nothing more than the set of processes, the machine, which allows such collection action to take place. This approach makes the State into something that is constructed by men, an artifact. Therefore, it is, by nature, subject to change, perfectible. (Buchanan and Tullock, 1965 [1962]: 13)

What restrictions ought to be imposed, and what the legitimate scope for state activity is, is to be set by rational, utility-maximizing individuals calculating where drawing that boundary will yield them the highest net benefits. All concern for the *justice* of constitutional arrangements is set aside for the sake of theoretical tractability:

We have assumed that the rational individual, when confronted with constitutional choice, will act so as to minimize his expected *costs of social interdependence*, which is equivalent to saying that he will act so as to maximize his expected 'utility from social interdependence'. (Buchanan and Tullock, 1965 [1962]: 49)

For Buchanan and Tullock, man is no longer the political animal, but is a (perhaps the supreme) utility-maximizing animal:

What are some of the implications of the analysis of individual choice of constitutional rules that has been developed? First of all, the analysis suggests that it is rational to *have a constitution*. By this is meant that it will be rational for the individual to choose more than one decision-making rule for collective choice-making under normal circumstances. (Buchanan and Tullock, 1965 [1962]: 81)

Buchanan and Tullock's work is considered a founding text of what has become known as Public Choice Theory. Crucial to their case for strong constitutional restrictions on political actors is the idea that, in ordinary legislative activity, powerful special interest groups can easily capture the legislative process, due to the great rewards they might earn by getting laws serving their interest passed. This tendency, as they saw it, could only be held in check by a robust constitution that strictly limited the extent to which government could intervene in the

interest of one group or another. Anthony de Jasay addressed the
Public Choice School's case for constitutionalism as follows:

> In public choice, winning groups get the best available payoffs and
> impose worse ones on the losers. However, for some reason or other,
> this ceases to be true where the payoffs are indirect and take the form of
> alternative constitutional rules, which are but gates giving access to
> direct payoffs... The contractarian-cum-public-choice school appears to
> hold that these persons and their respective groupings respond to
> incentives and maximize payoffs when shaping legislation and
> imposing policies, but not when shaping the constitution that is a
> determinant, both of what policies may be imposed and who is entitled
> to impose them. (de Jasay, 2002: 80)

I suggest that the reason the central public choice contention 'ceases
to be true' for Buchanan and Tullock in the constitutional setting is that
they have posited that constitution-making takes place behind a
Rawlsian 'veil of ignorance', where no one *knows* what his or her
interests are. But, of course, that construct is what O'Neill termed an
'idealization', since it supposes something that is necessarily false of
any real person, and no actual constitution could ever be established in
such a fashion, precisely because it is an idealization and not a real
situation in which any actual people could ever find themselves.

De Jasay, for the sake of argument, sets aside the question of the
legitimacy of the original constitutional process, but notes that even
granting constitutionalists that concession hardly alleviates the central
problem they must confront:

> An obvious down-to-earth objection to this is that momentous choices
> can and since time immemorial have been imposed by some people on
> others without benefit of agreed, formal rules. Let it be the case,
> however, that there is a benign constitution to begin with and the
> greedy gremlins who swarm around public choices had no hand in its
> making. Since, however, they know no taboos and are led by interests,
> what is to stop them from profanely starting to reshape the constitution
> the moment it provides them with the rule system for engineering
> agreement to non-unanimous choices?

> Public choice theory, if it were not imbued with the contractarian dream
> of redeeming the republic through prescription, would in good logic
> have to predict that an impartial constitution will first be changed to suit
> the broad winning coalition, and then be changed again to let
> progressively narrower coalitions despoil ever larger minorities... (de
> Jasay, 2002: 81)

However, contractarians may look to the existence of an
independent judicial branch, given the ultimate authority over

enforcing adherence to the principles embodied in the constitution, as providing an adequate defense against the potential betrayal of the founders' ideals by self-serving factional interests. De Jasay argued that such a faith is unwarranted:

> It is flying in the face of experience to suppose that judicial interpretation—be it informed by the best in legal scholarship and honesty—can for long disassociate itself from the political climate, the pressure of society's demands, and, most potent of all, the trend of articulate opinion. (de Jasay, 2002: 82)

If the logic of de Jasay's case is correct, as it seems to me it is, then it would appear that, if the people of a nation require a written constitution to protect them from potential domination by their government officials as they go about their ordinary administrative, legislative, or judicial activities, then they also must need a meta-constitution to defend their liberty against the potential depredations of those same officials when they are acting as the authoritative interpreters of the basic constitution, as well as a meta-meta-constitution to guarantee that the dictates of the meta-constitution are obeyed, and so on ad infinitum. As Tollison wrote:

> The design of better institutions starts with the design of better institutions to choose the rules we live under. The difficulty of this problem cannot be understated. Think of it this way. Suppose we convened a constitutional convention in the US? Who would participate? What would happen? What type of institutions would be selected? (Tollinson, 2009: 128)

De Jasay presented a further significant argument against the contractualist understanding of constitutions when he noted that no constitution is capable of interpreting or enforcing itself.[10] And, unlike the case of an ordinary contract between two parties, which assumes the prior existence of some legal framework including a third party that can be called upon to adjudicate compliance in the event of a dispute, a constitutional disagreement can never be resolved by turning to a higher authority, since the constitution itself has been deemed the supreme 'law of the land'. Therefore, whether or not some legal or institutional development ultimately will be considered constitutional will turn on the opinions of contemporary political actors, the very agents whose range of legitimate conduct the contractarians' constitution is supposed to constrain. As de Jasay saw it, if there is sufficient support for some policy, either in the general populace or

---

[10] Levinson (1988: 31-37) makes much the same point.

among a powerful group of the political elite, then a reading of the
constitution will be devised that renders that policy constitutional.
Barnett's argument (2004) that adopting the criterion of original intent
in interpreting a constitution will block efforts to read that document in
whatever way current political actors wish to read it has some truth to
it, but it is also somewhat circular: originalism is only likely to be
embraced by those who, like Barnett, would be happier with political
arrangements more in keeping with the constitutional authors'
intentions than they are with interpretive models that stress reading the
document in light of changing circumstances and political beliefs.
Furthermore, as Hardin and others have noted, and as Oakeshott's
theoretical reasoning argues, written constitutions always will prove
inadequate to deal with all of the contingencies faced by practical
politicians but unimagined by the constitution's authors. A final
objection to Barnett's reliance or 'originalist' interpretation is the fact
that there typically is no single, 'original' intent behind a constitutional
dictum at all: as we will see in the case of the American constitution,
the constitutional authors may have a variety of different visions of the
polity that their constitution is meant to establish, so that they wind up
agreeing on quite ambiguous wordings, each in the hope that his or her
own vision will triumph within the leeway that lack of clarity creates.
Hardin, as discussed in the next section of this chapter, also notes the
difficulties faced by a contractarian understanding of constitutions.

Constitutions as coordinating devices: Hardin

A leading contemporary constitutional theorist, Russell Hardin, rejects
the currently popular contractarian understanding of constitutions, as
represented above by Rawls, and by Buchanan and Tullock. In its place,
he proposes, offering an understanding somewhat more compatible
with Oakeshott's case against rationalism, that constitutions are
'coordination' devices, not contracts. He recognizes the force of
arguments such as de Jasay's against constitutional contractarianism,
since a constitution lacks the third-party enforcer characteristic of
meaningful, potentially effective contracts. In the absence of such an
external arbiter, he contends, 'A constitution, if it is to work in bringing
about and maintaining social order, must be self-enforcing' (1999: 89).
Much like a social convention to drive on a particular side of the road, a
successful constitution must incorporate incentives for individual
actors to adhere to it of their own accord.

Hardin admits that unwritten and informal conventions can play much the same role that motivates his advocacy of formal constitutions, namely, fostering the existence of beneficial social coordination. Thus he is led to ask, 'So why a written constitution?' His answer is:

> Obviously in order to hasten the establishment of relevant conventions and direct them in certain ways rather than others by getting people to commit themselves immediately rather than bumbling through to a result, a result that might have been the rise of a tyrant by force. (Hardin, 1999: 134–135)

Per Hardin, those living under an existing constitutional order need never have agreed to abide by its dictates for it to function successfully; they only have to acquiesce to the order it generates. Hardin acknowledges that his view does not endow 'legitimate' constitutions with the normative authority that many theorists argue they have, but only justifies them as possessing a practical value. However, he argues that practical efficacy is both sufficient to justify workable constitutional arrangements and the best defense genuinely available for them. A constitution will succeed to the extent that the great majority of individuals living under its precepts perceive accepting the status quo to be in their self-interest when weighed against bearing the high cost of rebelling against it. They very well may prefer that a quite different constitution were in place, but find themselves in a situation similar to that of a British immigrant to the United States, who might prefer strongly that Americans would drive on the left as in his homeland, but nevertheless accepts the custom of his new land rather than self-destructively defying it.

Hardin's understanding of the character of constitutions thus avoids the paradoxes inherent in the contractualist view. Furthermore, he bolsters his case by offering episodes from constitutional history that strongly suggest that it captures the essential role of actual constitutions in the societies to which they lend structure. No known constitution ever was adopted through the universal consent underpinning the normative claims of some contractarians; 'we cannot plausibly believe there has been anything vaguely like contractual consent to undergird our governments and we doubt that there could be' (1999: 149).

Hardin rejects the recent attempt by contractarians to patch over the absence of any real-world constitutional contract with the notion of a 'reasonable' social contract with which we all ought to agree. If one believes, as few contemporary political theorists do, that it is possible to deductively ascertain a single, 'correct' way to organize political life – a prominent exception is the 'natural rights' theorists, among which Rothbard was discussed above — then a 'social contract' is superfluous, as that optimal arrangement simply should be put in place, whether it is assented to or not. On the other hand, if a contractarian rejects the existence of such an objectively optimal political system, then they lack a sound basis for dismissing as 'unreasonable' those who refuse to embrace their proposed social order, and, therefore, their case for employing coercion to compel acquiescence is undermined.

In reality, Hardin argues, a constitution will be able to create a (relatively) stable polity when it serves to coordinate the actions of the individuals within its domain well enough that they are better off consenting to its authority than not, even if the vast bulk of them never agreed to adopt it and would prefer another political order but for the cost of overthrowing the existing one. He offers as an example the U.S. Constitution, which certainly was not agreed to by either contemporary American women or slaves, as both groups were disenfranchised, but still worked to hold the nation together for many decades, since it coordinated 'urban commercial interests and agrarian plantation interests, both of whom needed open, national markets' (1999: 29). And he sees the difficulties that have arisen in the attempts by many ex-communist nations to transition to liberal regimes as stemming largely from the lack of a way to coordinate the interests of two crucial groups: the employees of the old, nationalized industries, who wish to preserve their status, and those who stand to benefit from economic liberalization (1999: 195–202).

Hardin presents a compelling theoretical and empirical case for his thesis. However, if it is sound, it raises the question, 'Why bother with devising a formal constitution at all?' Instead, why not strive for a polity that is open and flexible enough to permit self-enforcing, spontaneous orders to emerge gradually? After all, per Hardin, it is only self-enforcing constitutional arrangements that will succeed anyway. The process of drawing up a written constitution is inevitably divisive until it reaches its resolution, and the effort, if misguided, runs the risk of setting up legal obstacles to the appearance of a genuinely coordinating order.

Moreover, Hardin recognizes that even his exemplar of a workable constitution, that of the United States, has not proceeded per the designers' intentions. The constitution of 1789 'solved' nonexistent problems, such as the imagined conflict between the interests of small and large states: 'There still has not been any significant conflict between small and large states as such since the ratification of the

Constitution... [perhaps] this widely perceived conflict was of little or no concern' (1999: 121). He admitted that 'neither the commercial nor the plantation agrarian interests knew enough to guess at the spectacular economic changes they might have wanted to control if only they had known enough to do so', and that, 'in the actual life of a constitution, contingent factors are enormously important' (1999: 131). He recognizes that the contested election of 1800 highlighted 'a flaw in the Constitution, whose designers had not anticipated the invention and use of political parties to control elections' (1999: 137). (We will discuss this election at some length in Chapter 8.) Although he defends written constitutions for the promise they hold out in achieving coordination, he concedes that 'whether we can coordinate is largely a matter of luck' (1999: 139). A written constitution chiefly, in his view, creates institutional structures that ought to constrain future political choices, 'but the structure and eventually the actions of institutions are substantially unintended consequences, the result of growth and not the outcome of popular choice or even any systematic choice at all' (1999: 154).

Hardin even suggested that the U.S. Constitution, as written, was not viable: 'Washington's prestige enabled a government of jealous and antagonistic men to collaborate for eight fundamentally important and difficult years to set the U.S. Constitution into institutional forms that then could survive' (1999: 226). In fact, '[t]he ostensibly written U.S. Constitution is only different in degree from the ostensibly unwritten British constitution' (1999: 246).

Hardin (1999: 290) presents the following table:

TABLE 4.1 Liberalism, constitutionalism, and democracy in the United States of America

1789–c.1850	Political and economic liberalism, constitutionalism, democracy
c. 1850–77	Breakdown of coordination on constitutionalism and democracy
1877–1937	Political and economic liberalism, constitutionalism, partial democracy
1937–	Political and economic liberalism, partial constitutionalism, democracy

In other words, constitutionalism itself, let alone strict adherence to the U.S. Constitution as written, has, by itself, only partially or negligibly described the American political system in about half the years since 1789.

In short, Hardin recognizes that the U.S. Constitution 'solved' nonexistent problems, that it contained fundamental flaws, that its authors could not foresee how the economic development of the new country would render some of their concerns irrelevant, that subsequent, contingent political circumstances often played a larger role in how their constitution actually came to be interpreted than did the founders' 'original intent', and that these 'deviations' from the designed order were not the result of some nefarious attempt to subvert the original constitution, but rather the inevitable outcome of trying to put that rationalist design into practice.

Hardin's specific caveats significantly weaken, even if they do not totally negate, his more abstract argument for written constitutions. On the one hand, if a written constitution merely makes explicit a contemporaneously accepted set of political conventions, and will evolve in step with those conventions, then it serves little more purpose than does a manual setting out the 'rules of thumb' abstracted from the current state of the art for any other human endeavor — quite possibly a helpful aid to practice, but certainly not of primary importance for the successful conduct of the activity in question. On the other hand, if a written constitution attempts to fundamentally reshape a social order, the importance of contingent factors and unintended consequences, noted by Hardin, seem to doom such an effort to failure. As Voegelin wrote:

> The ruler does not legitimate his position by the constitution, but the constitution derives its legal validity from the function of regulating the implementation of the idea... and it is a matter of an insight that is unfortunately misunderstood all too often when any board of directors that itself has no political or executive qualities issues a written constitution and expects that the piece of writing will function as the constitution of the society... If the social reality presupposed by the constitution exists, then the written constitution functions; if it does not exist, then de facto modes of conduct will result that deviate very strikingly from what is foreseen in the written project. (Voegelin, 2000: 195)

As noted before in this work, this relative insignificance of the specifics of a written constitution is what we would expect if Oakeshott's critique of rationalism is on target. Per Oakeshott, rational precepts for conducting some activity can only be derived sensibly from the experience of actually engaging in that activity, and cannot be formulated in advance as rules guiding our conduct in that domain.

In actual practice, we always proceed, as Hardin put it, by 'bumbling through to a result', a result we are incapable of determining in advance of pursuing the activity. If Oakeshott is correct, that does not render written constitutions meaningless — they still may play a role in steering the outcome of future, practical decision-making in a direction indicated by the abstract principles they embody — as Hardin has it, they may serve as 'coordination devices' — but the importance often currently assigned to the specifics of a written constitution for the subsequent evolution of a polity appears to be greatly exaggerated.

The fact that Hardin, in attempting to make a case for a written constitution, still admits the primacy of public opinion and ideological tides in determining the nature of a nation's politics offers, I suggest, further evidence that the current confidence in the efficacy of written, rationally constructed constitutions in promoting good governance is overblown. As mentioned above, in the process of evaluating Oakeshott's critique of rationalism in politics, we will explore that possibility in more depth by means of historical examples seeking in them evidence as to whether, in practice, attempting to set out the limits of state power in advance has any significant effect on what the state thus established actually winds up doing, and whether the actions of state actors operating under a written constitution appear, in fact, to be any more constrained than those of their counterparts lacking such a document, as in, for instance, modern Britain or ancient Rome.

Chapter 5

The Roman Republic as Pragmatic Polity

The first of our case studies will examine the ancient Roman republic, a polity that never adopted anything resembling a modern, formal constitution. Instead, the Romans of the republican era discovered the overarching guidelines for their day-to-day political decisions in their own traditions, consulting *mos maiorum*, the way of the ancestors, in much the same way that a modern citizen of the United States might consult the First Amendment when faced with a question about the permissibility of some form of speech regulation. Our choice of Rome as one of our case studies is motivated, in part, by the sharp contrast it offers to the prevalent, contemporary rhetoric concerning the proper way to address political issues, which suggests that deference to long-established customs is largely an obstacle to arriving at a rational resolution in such matters, and that a written constitution is almost a *sine qua non* of a legitimate polity. (For instance, in our introduction, we remarked upon the great importance the invading powers attached to the adoption of a written constitution in Iraq, even at a time when the people of that country were in a state of virtual civil war.)

Our selection of the Roman republic further is justified by the fact that the American founders were obsessed with the history of that polity, as that history was presented in the sources available to them, seeing in Rome both a model, since its republic endured and flourished for many centuries, and an ominous warning, as the Roman republic ultimately succumbed to the forces of autocracy and the vicissitudes of *fortuna*. In fact, it is arguably the case, a case for which I will provide evidence in the chapters of this thesis on the United States, that a primary concern driving the drafters of the U.S. Constitution was to safeguard their nascent republic against the dangers that had proven fatal to its illustrious predecessor.

Finally, the inclusion of the Roman republic in our survey is apt because of its place in Oakeshott's writings. He displayed great fondness for what he saw as the Roman approach to politics, writing, for instance: 'I think it is hardly an exaggeration to say that the Romans are the only European people to show a genuine genius for government and politics' (2006: 176). What's more, he invoked Rome as an exemplary instance of an actual state closely conforming to his ideal type of a practical polity:

> It was the politics of a people whose inventive powers were devoted, *not* to risky political experiments or dazzling speculative adventures, but to interpreting and responding to the situations into which their impulses or fortunes led them. The 'rationalistic' disposition of the Greeks (or, at least, of the Athenians) was almost wholly absent from Roman politics. (2006: 177)

He also saw the Roman republic as an exemplar of governance by the rule of law, which he greatly admired: 'And above all we owe [the conception of the state as the rule of law], not to the theorists, but to the two peoples who, above all others, have shown a genius for ruling: the Romans and the Normans' (1999: 178). As discussed in Chapter 2 of the present work, Oakeshott's dichotomies of 'civil association' (an association governed by the rule of law) versus 'enterprise association' (an association formed for the pursuit of concrete ends) and 'rationalist politics' versus 'pragmatic politics' do not present two sets of contrasted instances standing in a one-to-one correspondence with each other. Nevertheless, there does exist a nonarbitrary connection between an understanding of the state as fundamentally a civil association and a pragmatic orientation towards politics, since embracing the idea that the state ought to operate according to the rule of law rather than by specific commands inherently restrains the ability of political actors to pursue rationalist projects. As such, the fact that Oakeshott cited the Romans as exemplary in this regard further renders them a suitable subject for our attention.

Did the Roman republic have the pragmatic character Oakeshott attributed to it?

In our examination of the Roman republic in this chapter we will concentrate on the centuries from the republic's founding up until the period generally known as 'the Roman revolution', and then deal with the events of that revolution in the following chapter. (This chronological divide will not be held inviolable—episodes from one of these periods may be discussed in the chapter focusing on the other as seems appropriate.) The motive for this division of labor is that the two periods raise significantly different issues when regarded in terms of Oakeshott's work on rationalism. In this chapter's survey of the history of the Roman republic prior to the revolution, we will attempt to answer two broad questions:

(1) Did the Roman republic, in fact, exemplify the style of politics that Oakeshott clearly preferred, the one that he, earlier in his career, characterized as 'traditional', but that he later came to characterize as 'practical'?

(2) What (if anything) does Rome's early history (from the republic's founding, roughly around 500 BCE, to the middle of the second century BCE) allow us to conclude about the dispute between Oakeshott and those of his critics who protest that a polity grounded in tradition and guided by practical concerns will not be as capable of coping with changing conditions as one possessed of more abstract principles by which to guide its affairs? Especially, did the Romans fail to preserve their freedom because, as Hayek would suggest, they lacked a 'dogmatic' adherence to certain principles, and instead respond to novel circumstances on a pragmatic basis?

The relevance of the second question relies, of course, on answering the first one in the affirmative, so I am not spoiling any surprise ending by revealing that the general answer to the first question will be 'yes', the Roman republic was, to a great extent, a suitable example for Oakeshott to invoke. And the great flexibility the Romans displayed in responding to changing circumstances allows us, I contend, to declare that, in this case, at least, a polity guided by practical concerns, rather than theory, was well able to adjust to radical alterations in its circumstances, as it evolved from an insignificant city-state in an obscure backwater of the Mediterranean world to the dominant power of that region.

So, to take up the first of the above questions, to what extent was Oakeshott's image of Roman politics accurate? Oakeshott himself made scant effort to justify his employment of Rome as an exemplar. Almost without exception his remarks concerning ancient Rome are broad, sweeping generalizations, disdaining the tedium of undertaking any detailed examination of particular historical episodes. In consequence, it is unclear to what degree Oakeshott himself regarded his own account of Rome as a generally faithful, if very sketchy, portrait, as opposed to an admittedly one-sided caricature of his subject drawn to put a face on an abstract concept. Therefore, it is worth our while to examine Roman history in more depth than did Oakeshott (at least in his written work!), with the goal of determining how appropriate was the example he chose. Of course, in a work of this length, and one not devoted exclusively to Roman history, we will still be leaving out an enormous amount of detail that might prove relevant to answering this question. It is certainly the case that a detailed analysis of how the history taken up in this chapter alone relates to Oakeshott's work on rationalism could easily run to many volumes. Nevertheless, I believe that, by broadly surveying the conclusions of a number of prominent historians who *have* examined this era in great depth, as well as looking to primary sources that seem especially salient to the topic at hand, we can at least gain a greater sense of the plausibility of Oakeshott's view of ancient Rome than we can from his own works.

The Roman 'constitution' was quite unlike the typical modern conception of what characterizes a 'proper' constitution. Explicit declarations as to how the government was to operate and formal limitations on the scope of legitimate political activities were only minor components of the framework supporting the Roman republic. As Lintott put it,

> [Rome's] constitution... consisted of far more than statutes: it was based on traditional institutions defined by precedent and examples. These were above all embodied in stories... Thus *the constitution did not stand above politics like a law-code*: it is what the Romans thought to be right and did, and in more senses than one it was the product of history. (Lintott, 1999: 26, emphasis mine).

Similarly, Scullard asserted, 'The Roman constitution was the remarkable product of a long period of trial and error on the part of a practical and conservative people...' (2006 [1959]: 9). And he noted that the Romans had an instinctive aversion to abstract theorizing, since 'it might even endanger their *mos maiorum*' (2006 [1959]: 11). To add just one more voice from amongst the many supporters of this view it would be possible to cite, Stewart wrote:

> The Romans thought and acted in terms of historical precedents, institutionalizing historical precedent as *mos maiorum* (the custom of the ancestors)... *mos maiorum* in politics produced an essential conservatism in the institutionalized mechanisms of social and political action and interaction, like the administrative procedures for election, formal entry into office, declaring war, and welcoming a triumphant commander. Moreover, the religious context of the political rituals added a second impulse towards conservatism, for strict and rigid adherence to traditional or at least prior behavior was facilitated by the ritual mechanism of *instauratio*, persistent repetition until flawless performance [was achieved], and was enshrined in the principle of *pax*

deorum, peace with the gods, which linked public disaster to faulty ritual disrupting good relations with deity. (Stewart, 1998: 1–2)

(The religious context of political actions in the Roman republic will gain additional significance when we consider Eric Voegelin's analysis of the downfall of the republic as arising from its ceasing to be representative of the Roman people's understanding of their place in the cosmic order.)

Even at a quite late date in the life of the Roman republic, indeed, on the verge of its demise, we find Cicero continuing to assert the superiority of a practical understanding of politics to that found in 'the philosophers', as witnessed by the following quotations:

In fact, although all the writings of [philosophers] contain the richest sources for virtue and knowledge, if they are compared to the actions and accomplishments of [statesmen] I am afraid that they seem to have brought less utility to men's activities than enjoyment to their leisure. (Cicero, 1999: 2)

Even if the intellectual possession of knowledge can be maintained without use, virtue consists entirely in its employment; moreover, its most important employment is the governance of states and the accomplishment in deeds rather than words of the things philosophers talk about in their corners. Philosophers, in fact, say nothing (at least nothing that may be said decently and honorably) that does not derive from the men who established laws for states. (Cicero, 1999: 3)

Our commonwealth, in contrast, was not shaped by one man's talent but by that of many; and not in one person's lifetime, but over many generations... there never was a genius so great that he would miss nothing, nor could all the geniuses in the world brought together in one place at one time foresee all contingencies without the practical experience afforded by the passage of time. (Cicero, 1999: 33)[1]

The person who has had the will and capacity to acquire both — that is, ancestral learning and philosophical learning — is the one who I think has done everything deserving of praise. But if it should be necessary to choose one path of learning or the other... civic life is both more praiseworthy and more glorious... (Cicero, 1999: 61)

Of course, the fact that we find such explicit arguments for the greater virtue of practice compared to theory precisely at a time when the traditional practices and ways of life that had sustained the Roman republic were collapsing raises the issue of whether MacIntyre, as discussed in Chapter 3, was indeed on target in suggesting that 'when

---

[1] An interesting foreshadowing of Hayek's (1973) case for the superiority of common law to legislative decree!

the conservative offers his contemporaries good reasons for returning to an earlier relatively unreflective mode of social life, his very modes of advocacy provide evidence that what he recommends is no longer possible' (1988: 54). Is today's 'Oakeshottian' in a similar position to the late Roman republic's Cicero or Cato (whom we will look at in the next chapter), futilely endorsing an approach to politics that has ceased to be a live option in his contemporary situation? Was Hayek correct in contending that, since conservatism cannot indicate a viable alternative to an undesirable direction in current politics, inevitably the conservative will wind up acting as a mere brake being dragged along a path laid out by his opponents? I believe that this question represents a significant challenge to any program seeking to employ Oakeshott's critique of rationalism as a facile argument for 'getting back to the old ways'. But Oakeshott's point that the way forward still rests in the intimations of a polity's traditions stands, I think.

Roman political practice was constrained primarily by the reverence for *mos maiorum*, a reverence kept vital through the centrality of ancestor worship to Roman religious practice. The chief institutional safeguards of the republican liberty that the Romans understood themselves to enjoy, such as limited tenure in office, collegiality, and deference to the most politically experienced members of the nobility that composed the Senate, derived their fundamental authority to set the boundaries of any acceptable political activity, not from having been written down in some constitutional document that declared them to trump any contrary considerations, but from having been sanctioned by the accumulated wisdom of generations of practice. It is likely to strike a modern, neophyte student of ancient Rome as incredible that the Senate, despite its formal status as a strictly advisory body possessing no legislative authority, nevertheless was the most powerful political force in the republic for several centuries. However, a member of one of Rome's popular assemblies in that period was habitually averse to questioning the preeminence of the Senate. Although there was no written law requiring him to heed the policy advice that the Senate issued to him and his peers, he habitually did so — the wisdom of tradition and experience speaking through the institution of the Senate had served the republic so well in the past that only a fool or madman would ignore its counsel today. As Scullard wrote, 'custom, not law, enabled [the Senate] to govern' (2006 [1959]: 5).

In short, there is strong evidence, both from leading historians of Roman history and from the writings of contemporary witnesses and participants, that Oakeshott was justified in locating the Roman republic well towards the pole marked 'pragmatist' in his abstract pragmatist/rationalist schema for classifying polities. Of course, there were countervailing forces present in the history of the Roman republic, such as the growing influence of Greek philosophical thought in Roman life, as well as the tendency of those opposing that influence to transform the Roman tradition of pragmatism into an ideology of traditionalism. But, as pointed out earlier, Oakeshott never suggested that the abstractions he was presenting had ever been, or even ever could be, pristinely exemplified by any concrete polity. The most we can ask of any of his examples is that employing his ideal types in examining that example renders its concrete history to some extent more intelligible. And, I suggest, we do, indeed, comprehend the Roman republic more fully if we regard it as, among other things, an instance of a pragmatically oriented polity.

Does a pragmatic polity have the resources to respond to changing conditions?

We contended in Chapter 3 of this work that Oakeshott's critics who attacked his support for pragmatic politics as advocacy of social stasis or of a locking-in of the status quo were mischaracterizing his position. He denied their claim that only rationally derived, abstract principles could offer sufficient guidance to political actors confronting novel conditions. (Indeed, he went further, arguing that even those who purport to be guided by such abstractions are deceiving themselves, since they inevitably will wind up falling back on some traditional way of acting in devising their supposedly purely rational response.) As he wrote:

> And anyone who has studied a tradition of customary behaviour (or a tradition of any other sort) knows that both rigidity and instability are foreign to its character. And secondly, this form of the moral life is capable of change as well as of local variation. Indeed, no traditional way of behaviour, no traditional skill, ever remains fixed; its history is one of continuous change... [N]othing is more traditional or customary than our ways of speech, and nothing is more continuously invaded by change. (1991 [1962]: 471)

So let us see what evidence the history of the Roman republic during its first several centuries of existence offers for or against Oakeshott's contention. The Romans, as we have seen, leant heavily upon the lessons of their past to formulate a response to any new situation, and had little sympathy for abstract political theory. Nevertheless, contrary to the view that a reliance on tradition entails an inability to cope with novel circumstances, they were able, for the most part, to adjust their institutions and their behavior to successfully meet the challenges presented to them by the dramatic transformation of their polity from an insignificant city-state located at the fringe of the civilized world to the master of the entire Mediterranean basin.

The flexibility of Roman political practice when faced with changes in 'exogenous' factors was apparent even before the radical alteration of its geopolitical position. During the period immediately after the founding of the Republic, sometimes described as 'the struggle between the orders', the noble class was confronted with repeated challenges to its privileged status by the plebeian majority. As early as 494 BCE, plebeian soldiers 'went on strike' during a conflict with the Aequi and the Volsci, in response to which the aristocracy granted the plebeians the right to elect officials who could guard their interests against autocratic usurpation. A few decades later, plebeian agitation achieved the publication of the laws of the twelve tables, which rendered the proper procedures to be followed in judicial trials a matter of public record accessible to any citizen. Similarly, as Abbott described the evolving role of the tribunes:

> The original function of the tribune was to protect citizens against the magistrate by personal interference in specific cases... the bitterness of the long struggle which the plebeians made for the consulship, led to a continual clashing between the tribunes and the magistrates executing the decrees of the senate... it was felt, therefore, that it would be far better to get the opinion of the tribunes with reference to a bill under consideration in the senate, before action was taken on it. With this purpose in mind they were given seats in the senate, and were allowed to interpose their objections formally at any point in the proceedings. (Abbott, 1901: 38)

This pattern of aristocratic concessions to the demands of the plebeians, accommodations that ensured the continued and necessary (to the military success of Rome) allegiance of the plebeians to the republic as in some sense 'their own', and not merely the imposition of an alien ruling class, was manifested repeatedly throughout early Roman history. As McDonald put it, 'In public affairs the struggle of patrician nobles and the plebs led more often than not to practical compromise' (1966: 45), compromises that allowed the Roman republic to work reasonably well for more than three centuries. Indeed, one historian recently commenting upon this period has contended that the Romans were so flexible in adapting their traditions to the circumstances that they faced that it makes more sense to speak of 'the Roman Republics' than of 'the Roman Republic' (Flower, 2010).

Hannibal's invasion of the Italian peninsula during the Second Punic War (218–201 BCE), and particularly his victories at Trebia and Trasimene and, most traumatic of all, his rout of the Roman army at the Battle of Cannae, during which the Romans lost tens of thousands of soldiers, and which resulted in the defection of several of Rome's Italian allies to the Carthaginian cause, presented the Romans' traditional way of conducting politics with a serious challenge. For one thing, a host of political leaders had lost their lives in those three defeats, particularly at Cannae. And the defeats themselves challenged the Romans' image of themselves as a people of destiny. But, as Scullard contended, the republic was able to respond to this unprecedented threat, and ultimately emerged victorious:

> An immediate task [following the defeat at Cannae] was to revise the list of senators so sadly depleted by war. Many ex-consuls, praetors, and aediles had fought and fallen as military tribunes at Cannae, and senators of all grades had voluntarily served in the ranks... Unusual methods were adopted. Instead of the election of censors a second dictator was appointed... M. Fabius Buteo... was chosen and the Senate summoned Varro to name him. Buteo expressed disapproval of the procedure, removed no one from the senatorial role, appointed all those who had held curule or other office and then those who had distinguished themselves in war, 177 new members in all; his task completed, he promptly laid down his dictatorship. Thus a striking change came about in the composition of the senate... (Scullard, 1973: 56)

Another alteration of circumstances faced by the Romans, as their domain of rule expanded, was an increasingly intimate contact with the older and more sophisticated Greek culture that dominated the eastern Mediterranean as well as southern Italy and Sicily. They were able to adapt to this change as well; Smith wrote:

> This period witnessed the great inrush of Hellenic influence in the form of literature, philosophy, art and by no means least the Greeks themselves. Such influences from without were not new to Rome; Etruria had profoundly influenced Rome in art, architecture and religion since the time of the kings; and though the influence of Etruria was no longer felt at Rome, she had learnt from this experience how to adopt and to adapt. (Smith, 1955: 11)

The Roman republic also displayed the ability of 'practical politics' to respond to changing circumstances in its approach to the Greek colonies it conquered in southern Italy; as McDonald writes, those cities 'had a Greek tradition, which they sustained with pride, e.g. Cumae and Capua... [and] were ready to live with Rome, providing they continued their own life, and the Romans respected their wishes' (1966: 49). Indeed, Rome was remarkably flexible as to the status of its conquered peoples in general; Abbott described this characteristic of Roman policy thus:

> A uniform system of government was by no means adopted for all the people in the limits of a single province. In fact, the way in which the degree of civil liberty enjoyed by the peoples in different cities under one governor varied is one of the unique features of Roman provincial government. The Romans accepted in most cases the political units which they found already in existence, and treated the different communities generously or harshly, according to their previous attitude toward Rome. (Abbott, 2006: 90)

Flower lists a substantial number of major Roman political innovations that occurred in the second century BCE. These include changes in the characteristics of colonization (discussed above), changing the start of the political year from March 1 to January 1, which 'gave counsels who did not need to leave immediately for distant wars much more time in office before the traditional start of the campaigning season for the armies on March 15' (2010: 68), the creation of the first permanent jury court in 149, a significant change in foreign policy, agrarian reform, the introduction of the secret ballot, frequent changes in the design of Roman silver coinage, and changes in army recruitment. The secret ballot was so controversial an innovation that Cicero had Quintus complain about it:

> Who does not realize that the entire authority of the *optimates* was stolen by the ballot law? When the people were free they never wanted it, but they demanded it when they were beaten down by the oppressive power of leading citizens... For that reason the powerful should have been deprived of their excessive desire for balloting in bad causes rather than giving the people a hiding place in which the written ballot could conceal a flawed vote while the respectable citizens were ignorant of each person's sentiments. Therefore no respectable citizen has ever been found to propose or support such a measure. (Cicero, 1999: 170)

As Flower put it, during this period Roman political practice was characterized by 'a willingness to consider patterns of peaceful political reform and successful initiatives that departed in radical ways from inherited political practices...' (2010: 78). A polity oriented around the knowledge gained from earlier practice is not necessarily a polity that rejects reform and change!

As a final example of the ability of the Romans' pragmatic approach to politics to adapt to changes in their 'environment', I offer an emblematic event that occurred in 168 BCE. Antiochus IV, the ruler of the Selucid Empire (centered roughly in modern-day Syria), had marched a large army south to invade Egypt, with which Rome had had a relationship of *amicitia* (friendly alliance) for more than a century. The Roman Senate was anxious to prevent the Selucids from interfering in Egyptian affairs, but rather than attempting to dissuade Antiochus by dispatching a military expedition capable of matching his own, the Senate sent a lone representative, accompanied only by his *lictors* (essentially personal bodyguards and symbols of his authority), to confront his vast army and make its sentiments know. Scullard described the encounter as follows:

> The Senate sent a peremptory order to Antiochus to evacuate Egypt and Cyprus. The Roman envoy, Popillius, handed the Senate's dispatch to the king, who asked for time to consider; but Popillius merely drew a circle round Antiochus and bade him answer before stepping out of it. The king meekly obeyed and withdrew from Egypt. (Scullard, 1980: 288)

The significance of this event, for our purposes, is that Rome was coping successfully in the world of international power politics while continuing to follow its ancient customs: we must picture this unadorned, simply dressed old man, backed only by a handful of personal assistants, confronting a resplendent Hellenistic god-king, at the head of a mighty fighting force, and turning Antiochus back by threatening him with the animosity of the Roman people should he fail to heed Popillius's warning. Rome had not abandoned its traditions by attempting to meet this god-king with an oriental-style potentate of its own, but instead had found in the resources contained in those traditions the means to defeat this foe on its own terms. As Everitt summed up this Roman trait, 'for most of its history Rome's leaders showed a remarkable talent for imaginative improvisation when they met intractable problems' (2003: 12). Or, per Smith:

> Considering that Rome was in origin and organization a city-state, had come suddenly to importance in the Mediterranean world, and had not the political experience of the Greek States, we should be surprised rather that their political instinct was able to adapt its organization to the needs of the time as well as it did; that was in itself no mean achievement and showed that, though conservative, they were not reactionary. (Smith, 1955: 72)

The Roman government as representative

At this point, invoking Eric Voegelin's notion that any successful government must be 'representative', will prove useful both for comprehending why the Roman republic worked as well as it did for as long as it did, and, as will be taken up in the next chapter, for understanding why it finally expired.

Voegelin was a political philosopher admired by Oakeshott.[2] His work is largely compatible with Oakeshott's case against rationalism, while offering insights all its own.[3] Voegelin understood politics not as an autonomous sphere of activity independent of the rest of a culture, but as the public articulation of how some society conceives the proper relationship of its members both to one another and to the rest of the cosmos. Only when a society's political institutions are an organic product of a widely shared and existentially satisfactory conception of mankind's place in the universe will they successfully and stably order social life. Voegelin's conception of a sound political order is reminiscent of Plato's and Leibniz's, but differs from theirs in having a stronger historical component.[4] As a corollary of his understanding of political life, Voegelin was dismissive of the contemporary, rationalist faith in the power of 'well-designed', written constitutions to ensure the continued existence of a healthy polity. He wrote, 'If a government is nothing but representative in the constitutional sense, a representational ruler [meaning a ruler who in some way represents the prevailing worldview of the populace] will sooner or later make an end of it... When a representative does not fulfill his existential task, no constitutional legality of his position will save him' (1987: 49–50). For him, a truly 'representative' government entails, much more crucially than the relatively superficial fact that citizens have some voice in who will serve in their government and what laws it will enact, that the political order must represent the people's understanding of their place in the cosmos.[5]

---

[2] For instance, Oakeshott introduced a talk by Voegelin at LSE by calling his *New Science of Politics* 'a brilliant and alas too little read work' (1962), and he recommended Voegelin to David Boucher as providing 'most enlightening discussions' of the history of political thought (private correspondence, relayed to me by Boucher himself).

[3] Corey (2006: 16) argues that Voegelin's concept of 'gnosticism' and Oakeshott's of 'rationalism' share a 'fundamental equivalence'. While I agree that they are a: least similar, I do not believe they are equivalent.

[4] See Jolley (2005: 176-200) on Leibniz's political thought.

[5] A contemporary philosopher whose work begs for comparison to Voegelin's idea of representation is Charles Taylor; his notion of moral 'frameworks' strikes me as resonant with what 'representation' means to Voegelin, where a representative government in Voegelin's sense is one that, in Taylor's

The Roman republic, throughout the centuries during which it succeeded in rising to meet its domestic challenges and came to dominate the Mediterranean world, was representative, in Voegelin's sense of that term, in that all of its citizens, of whatever class, felt that they were a part of the *mos maiorum* and the *pax deorum* (peace with the gods), and that they were participants in the great destiny history had set aside for the Roman republic; in short, they had a civil religion that gave them all, however exalted or lowly, a place in the cosmic order. As Smith put it:

> Before we discuss the aims and limitations of the domestic and foreign policy, it will be well to glance briefly at the concern shown by the nobles for the protection and defence of the ethos of their society. They felt themselves to be the guardians of that tradition of Romanism, the *mos maiorum*, which gave their society its peculiar and remarkable quality and its citizens their special character; that quality and character which had enabled them to surmount the Hannibalic threats and which, they believed, had come to them from Heaven…

> The *mos maiorum* was the foundation of Rome's society, the sum of all the customs, practices, training and education by which the Roman character had been developed, and to the maintenance of the ethos of Roman society the nobles paid particular attention. For although to only the nobles were the glories of a public career open, yet all classes had their place in society, which was one and indivisible, and undesirable novelties and influences in one section could only have a deleterious effect upon the whole. The society must be kept pure of taint, and only the governors could do that. (Smith, 1955: 10-11)

---

terminology, operates according to a 'framework' that is widely embraced by its citizens—see Taylor (1989). And it is worth noting that there is some acknowledgement of this idea in Oakeshott, for instance, when he defines political philosophy as 'what occurs when this movement of reflection takes a certain direction and achieves a certain level, its characteristic being the relation of political life, and values and purposes pertaining to it, to the entire conception of the world that belongs to a civilization' (1991 [1962]: 224).

Chapter 6

The Roman Revolution: Could the Embrace of Rationalist Principles Have Saved the Republic?

One of the most frequent criticisms of Oakeshott's work on rationalist politics is that he severely undervalues the efficacy of rationalist 'principles' as guides to political activity. For instance, Raphael writes:

> [Oakeshott] agrees that principles have their place as an 'abridgement' of tradition, and that this abridgement can properly be used to explore the 'intimations' of tradition. But how is this exploration to be carried out? The 'intimations' of a tradition do not often point one way only... the rationalist, who thinks in terms of justification, tries to tell us. He will often go wrong but at least he is addressing himself to the right question... he is able to say which tendency should be fostered, and which checked, because he is ready to use principles (ideology, if you like) as a standard. (Raphael, 1964: 212–214)

Oakeshott responded to Raphael as follows:

> I have no horror of principles — only a suspicion of those who use principles as if they were axioms and those who seem to think that practical argument is concerned with proof. A principle is not something which may be given as a reason or a justification for making a decision or performing an action; it is a short-hand identification of a disposition to choose. [The 'principles' so beloved by the rationalist are] in reflecting upon a response to a practical situation... [only part of] a variety of beliefs — approvals and disapprovals, preferences and aversions, pro- and con-feelings (often vague), moral and prudential maxims of varying application and importance, hopes, fears, anxieties, skill in estimating the probable consequence of actions, and some general beliefs about the world. These beliefs, in so far as they are normative, are not self-consistent; they often pull in different directions, they compete with one another and cannot all be satisfied at the same

time, and therefore they cannot properly be thought of as a norm or a self-consistent set of norms or 'principles' capable of delivering to us an unequivocal message about what we should do. (2008: 186)

What does the episode known as the 'Roman revolution', typically conceived as covering the years between the tribunate of Tiberius Gracchus in 133 BCE and the Battle of Actium in 31 BCE, tell us about this dispute? This is a period during which the Roman republic's reliance on what Oakeshott would have praised as a tradition-driven, practical approach to politics might, at first glance, appear to have failed it. So it is worthwhile to examine this history in more detail — to what extent does a closer look at the events of the Roman revolution support Raphael's case for the importance of rationally derived, abstract principles in political life — was 'the constitution [and its lack of rational design]... the Republic's greatest weakness', as Everitt claims (2003: 11)? Or can Oakeshott's thesis withstand this possible counterexample?

What was the 'Roman revolution'?

The term 'revolution' must be understood as used here in an idiosyncratic way. As Garrett Fagan notes:

> We can see right from the start that the Roman Revolution unlike many modern concepts of revolution was somewhat different. It was not a planned event, like the Russian Revolution, enacted for ideological reasons, [nor] was it a restricted, catastrophic, short period of activity as the French Revolution was. It was a long, drawn-out protracted spiral of disorder. This is because, as we have seen, the so-called constitution of the Roman Republic, the *mos maiorum*... was just that, an assemblage of accepted practices and patterns of behavior that allowed the Romans to govern the state in the way that they did. (Fagan, 1999: 111)

As such, many of the 'revolutionary' actions making it up were not even, strictly speaking, illegal — due to the traditional character of the Roman constitution, they consisted, instead, of technically legal but unprecedented acts that flouted that tradition.

The unusual character of the Roman revolution has led some historians to question the very use of that label for the time in question. For instance, Erich Gruen, arguing for rejecting the term, writes:

> In order to explain the republic's fall, it has seemed appropriate to ransack preceding generations for symptoms of decline and signposts for the future. The portrait is shaped to suit the result — a retrojected prophecy. Yet Cicero's contemporaries did not know what was in store.

Nor should their every action be treated as if it conspired to determine the outcome. (Gruen, 1974: 2)

Gruen has a point, in that it is important, in historical analysis, to resist the temptation to 'read history backwards'. Nevertheless, I believe his complaint is overstated: for an historian seeking to explain the downfall of the Roman republic, the only relevant material lies in the course of events that preceded it. From such a perspective, it is beside the point whether or not Cicero and his contemporaries saw what was coming, or if any of them intended the eventual outcome in choosing their actions. The fact is that those choices, whatever the aim of the agent making them, *did* lead to the downfall of the republic and the establishment of the principate. Therefore, even in light of Gruen's critique of the concept, so long as the inherent limits of historical understanding are kept in mind — historical explanations can show only how a particular episode is made more intelligible by its antecedents, and not that it was the 'inevitable' result or that it should have been 'predictable' to those participating in that sequence of events — then the use of the term 'Roman revolution', as well as the search for the causes of the fall of the republic in the events of the preceding century, is unproblematic.

The roots of the Roman revolution, I contend, lie in the changes in social conditions that crucially differentiate the revolutionary period from the time of relative political stability that preceded it, and not in any paucity of rationalist principles with the guidance of which the Romans would have been able to preserve their republican liberty. While the Roman constitution, grounded in tradition, had done its job for several centuries, that reliance on the *mos maiorum* began to lose its effectiveness in the face of the vast power and wealth that Rome's expanding empire offered to anyone willing to ignore accepted practice, as well as the widening gulf separating the fortunes of the Roman elite, of which the Senate was the prime, formal representative, and the great majority of the citizens of the republic. As the historian Carl Richard argues,

the Romans' rapid conquest of the Mediterranean basin helped destroy... the republic. By further increasing the vast inequalities of wealth between the rich and the poor, the new Roman expansion generated class warfare, which, in turn, produced the chaos and violence that paved the way for the emperors. (Richard, 2008: 131)

Populist leaders, whether they were sincerely motivated by the plight of the commoners or merely exploiting the grievances of the masses to enhance their own power, could use the leverage provided by large-scale discontent to break down, piece by piece, the edifice of tradition that had shaped Roman politics throughout most of the republican era. The history of this period illustrates that to flourish, a political order must represent the people's understanding of their role in the cosmos. Once the Roman government was no longer representative in such a sense, it was only a question of when, not if, it would be replaced by a new order that *was* representative.

As an example of this failure of representation, consider Cicero's criticism of the use of the lot in assigning political offices as follows:

> If it does so by haphazard, it will be as easily upset as a vessel if the pilot were chosen by lot from among the passengers. But if a people, being free, chooses those to whom it can trust itself — and, if it desires its own preservation, it will always choose the noblest — then certainly it is in the counsels of the aristocracy that the safety of the State consists, especially as nature has not only appointed that these superior men should excel the inferior sort in high virtue and courage, but has inspired the people also with the desire of obedience towards these, their natural lords. (Cicero, 1877: 384)

But, as Stewart contends, 'I show that ritual definition of the allotment identifies it as an auspice and as one further element of legitimation that identified Jupiter's patronage of the Roman political system, as a random drawing but not simply so' (1998: 13). If Stewart is correct (and she makes a strong case for her contention), then Cicero's disparagement of assigning political offices by allotment, on the part of one supposedly committed to the preservation of the traditional order, illustrates how the rituals of that order had ceased to have the meaning, by Cicero's time, that they had carried for his ancestors. And a similar contempt for the auspices is shown by the story of Caesar's failure to pay heed to the many auspical signs warning him not to appear before the Senate on the *ides* of March.

A crucial factor increasing the power of the *populares*, as the revolutionary politicians were then designated, was the gradual disappearance of the yeoman farmer, the ideal type of the Roman citizen, whose sturdy, agrarian virtues and austere outlook on life had been the foundation of Rome's unprecedented rise from an obscure and insignificant town in a world of great empires to its position of dominance over the entire area of Mediterranean civilization. Given that Rome, during the decades prior to the revolution, was almost constantly at war with one enemy or another, the owners of small farms, who comprised the bulk of the army, were often required to be away from their land for decades at a time. Naturally, the viability of their farms was compromised by these prolonged absences on the part of the proprietor. Meanwhile, the spoils of Rome's conquests, which flowed chiefly to the aristocratic officers given credit for any victory, enabled those aristocrats steadily to enlarge their *latifundia* — vast agricultural estates, which were able to produce foodstuffs at a lower cost than were their yeoman competitors, as the owners of the *latifundia* could exploit the forced labor of the multitudes of the defeated enslaved by Roman armies. The small farmers had little choice but to abandon their holdings and see them absorbed into some aristocrat's estate, and then to seek their sustenance by becoming a *cliens*, a faithful political supporter, of one or another of their former officers. Thus, there arose a growing population of dispossessed, disgruntled, and involuntarily idle citizens, readily available to serve as an angry mob or a band of thugs advancing some demagogue's quest for power.

The social arrangements that, for several centuries, had harmonized the interests of the aristocracy and of the commoners, had been erected upon a sufficiently sound foundation that the erosive effects of the transformations in land ownership and the distribution of wealth were not readily apparent for many decades after the point when, as we might judge in hindsight, they had begun wearing away that base. The durability of those bonds, even in the face of the increasing hardships endured by the average citizen, is demonstrated in a speech that Livy reports as having been delivered in 169 BCE, by a veteran infantry soldier, Spurius Ligustinus. The intent of the speaker was to shame those other veterans who had balked at re-enlisting to fight the Third Macedonian War, because the rank they were offered in this new campaign was lower than that which they had previously held. (Whether or not Livy is presenting a literally true account of an actual speech, or an imaginative reconstruction of one he believes to be representative, is, as with most instances in which an ancient historian offers his readers the text of a speech, an open question. Nevertheless, Livy had access to contemporary sources for the time under consideration, and there is little reason to doubt that he is offering a genuine portrayal of a sentiment that then had significant force amongst the peasant soldiers.)

> After the consul had said what he wanted to say, one of those who were appealing to the tribunes — Sp. Ligustinus — begged the consul and the tribunes to allow him to say a few words to the Assembly. They all gave him permission, and he is recorded to have spoken to the following effect: 'Quirites, I am Spurius Ligustinus, a Sabine by birth, a member of the Crustuminian tribe. My father left me a jugerum [less than an acre] of land and a small cottage in which I was born and bred, and I am living there today. As soon as I came of age my father gave me to wife

his brother's daughter. She brought nothing with her but her personal freedom and her modesty, and together with these a fruitfulness which would have been enough even in a wealthy house. We have six sons and two daughters. Four of our sons wear the *toga virilis*, two the *praetexta*, and both the daughters are married. I became a soldier in the consulship of P. Sulpicius and C. Aurelius. For two years I was a common soldier in the army, fighting against Philip in Macedonia; in the third year T. Quinctius Flamininus gave me in consideration of my courage the command of the tenth company of the hastati. [Spurius Ligustinus goes on to list numerous further military assignments he carried out without complaint, and the many honours he received.] I have served for twenty-two years in the army and I am more than fifty years old. But even if I had not served my full time and my age did not give me exemption, still, P. Licinius, as I was able to give you four soldiers for one, namely, myself, it would have been a right and proper thing that I should be discharged. But I want you to take what I have said simply as a statement of my case. So far as anyone who is raising troops judges me to be an efficient soldier, I am not going to plead excuses. What rank the military tribunes think that I deserve is for them to decide; I will take care that no man shall surpass me in courage; that I always have done so, my commanders and fellow-campaigners bear witness. And as for you, my comrades, though you are only exercising your right of appeal, it is but just and proper that as in your early days you never did anything against the authority of the magistrates and the senate, so now, too, you should place yourselves at the disposal of the senate and the consuls and count any position in which you are to defend your country as an honourable one.'

When he had finished speaking, the consul commended him most warmly and took him from the Assembly to the senate. There, too, he was thanked by the senate, and the military tribunes made him leading centurion in the first legion in recognition of his bravery. The other centurions abandoned their appeal [to have their former ranks restored as a condition for re-enlisting] and answered to the roll-call without demur. (Livius, 1905)

Does the failure of the reforms of the Gracchi brothers exhibit a shortcoming of pragmatic politics?

The period of the Gracchi brothers, running from roughly 133 to 121 BCE, is an episode that some (explicit or implicit) critics, such as, for instance, Raphael or Hayek, might cite as counterevidence to Oakeshott's proposition that abstract political 'principles', the universal validity and applicability of which supposedly are the deductive consequences of sound political theorizing, cannot actually provide the unambiguous guide to political decision-making that rationalists hope they can. The events in question, so the critics' argument might go, illustrate the inability of Rome's 'conservative', traditionalist politics to respond creatively to novel situations; or, as Hayek had it,

> It is that by its very nature [that conservatism] cannot offer an alternative to the direction in which we are moving. It may succeed by its resistance to current tendencies in slowing down undesirable developments, but, since it does not indicate another direction, it cannot prevent their continuance. (Hayek, 1960: 398)

However, I believe that Oakeshott's thesis emerges from the confrontation with these occurrences unscathed: the Romans' pragmatic, untheoretical manner of addressing political dilemmas had proved itself fully able to cope with equally grave situations during the previous several centuries, as we saw earlier in the previous chapter. Therefore, I suggest, it is implausible to attribute the destructive handling of the problems presented by the Gracchi to some lack of theoretical grounding for Roman politics, especially given that the accelerating dissolution of the Roman social order furnishes us with an explanation of this change in affairs pointing to a factor that itself was a change, rather than to one that had remained substantially constant. And, in fact, as we shall see, once the traditionalists became 'dogmatic', as Hayek recommended the defenders of freedom ought to do, they hastened rather than prevented the downfall of the republic.

The stage was set for the drama of the Gracchi brothers by the fact that, although, as noted above, the strength of the tradition-grounded solidarity between the Roman social classes meant that their bonds did not fail easily or rapidly, eventually the frays in those bonds, growing apace with the divergence between the fortunes of the Roman aristocrats and the commoners, became too alarming to be dismissed. One of the first Roman leaders to comprehend the importance of this social transformation and to perceive the threat it posed to the stability of the republic was Tiberius Gracchus. Although Tiberius was himself of the Roman aristocracy, he apparently was genuinely moved by sympathy for the plight of the common farmer when, 'traveling through Etruria on his way to Spain[, he saw] the large estates worked by slaves [and] the absence of free peasants [so that] he realized the need for reform' (Scullard, 2006 [1959]: 24). But he was not alone in his perception of the gravity of that situation, for his demands for reform initially were 'backed by a powerful group in the Senate' (Scullard, 2006 [1959]: 25).

Tiberius was elected tribune in 133 BCE, a position he was determined to use to enact the land reforms he saw as necessary to reverse this ill-boding transformation of Roman society. He proposed legislation that would redistribute all public lands utilized by individuals in excess of the oft-ignored legal limit of roughly 300 acres to citizens without real property. Tiberius had the advantage of his distinguished lineage — his father had been elected consul twice and censor once, and his mother was the daughter of Scipio Africanus, the general legendary for defeating Hannibal — and, as mentioned above, he had many potential allies in the Senate. In light of those resources at his disposal, as well as the strong case that could be made for both the justice and the practical benefits of his proposal, Scullard contends that 'if [Tiberius] had followed the normal procedure of bringing his bill to the Senate before taking it to the People, there is no justification for believing that it would not have received a fair hearing' (2006 [1959]: 26). However, for reasons that are obscure to modern historians, Tiberius flouted custom and went straight to the Tribal Assembly of the Plebs with his bill. Although there was nothing formally illegal in that procedure — there was no Roman body analogous to the U.S. Supreme Court to condemn his action, and no written document that such a body, if it had existed, could have invoked in declaring the maneuver 'unconstitutional' — nevertheless, it represented a blatant disregard for the traditional constitutional principle that the judgment of the Senate, as embodying the seasoned wisdom of the Roman nobility, was the prime voice of authority in the republic's decisions. Deference to its authority, especially on a major and controversial issue such as these proposed land reforms, was made requisite by the centuries of experience demonstrating that the Roman state had prospered and expanded by heeding the wisdom of its senior statesmen.

The Senate, unable to abide Tiberius's challenge to its status, convinced one of his fellow tribunes, Octavius, to veto his bill. At this point, the customary precedence given to the maintenance of *concordia*, or political harmony, over the pursuit of any particular policy goal, however important it might be deemed, called for Tiberius to recognize that his chosen course of action had proved unduly divisive. The proper response then was for him to give ground and seek an acceptable compromise. But instead, no doubt chagrined that a measure he viewed as vital to the well-being of the republic was being blocked, he defied custom by continuing to push for the passage of his legislation. First Tiberius begged Octavius to withdraw his veto, and, when that failed, he took the radical step of having Octavius, through a vote of the people, removed from office for his obstinacy. This was an egregious violation of the constitutional principle of collegiality, which required that an officeholder respect the veto power of his cohorts.

Thus was added a third offense against the Roman constitution to Tiberius's two previous instances of constitutional malfeasance. But even though Tiberius again had displayed a flagrant disregard for tradition, it is worth noting that, just as in the earlier cases described above, his deviance from customary practice was not explicitly prohibited by any legislative act, and so there were no pre-established penalties in place to punish his transgression. In earlier times, it simply had been the case that politicians, however strong were their personal ambitions for power and glory, exercised those ambitions within the confines of the *mos maiorum*. The traditional value system of the republic, far from denigrating such ambitions, saw them as an integral part of the great man's *virtu*. But it was understood that the necessary context for the expression of individual *virtu* was woven from the cloth of reverence for time-tested customs, and consequentially the question of how to handle blatant disregard for the wisdom of the city's ancestors had not arisen.

Tiberius, having gotten Octavius out of the way, saw his land-reform bill passed by the popular assembly. However, the Senate was not prepared to roll over in the face of his radical procedures, and attempted to render that passage meaningless by refusing to provide the funding required to implement the legislation. As Scullard says, '[the Senate] insulted Tiberius by offering him an allowance of about two shillings a day for his expenses' (2006 [1959]: 27). The movement for land reform appeared to have been thwarted when, by a stroke of luck, a way around the obstacle erected by the Senate was opened: while the fate of Tiberius's project hung in the balance, Attalus III, the ruler of the Hellenistic kingdom of Pergamum in Asia Minor, died. Attalus had been without heir, and, fearing a war of succession for the throne, he unexpectedly had decided to bequeath his entire realm to the Roman people. Pergamum was a wealthy kingdom, and Tiberius seized upon this fortuitous event, shepherding legislation through the assembly of the plebs directing that a portion of this newfound revenue be devoted to underwriting his reform effort.

Whatever tolerance the Senate had remaining for the unprecedented course Tiberius was taking probably evaporated at this point. As Scullard declares,

This was going too far: until now the Senate's control of finance and foreign affairs had been unchallenged, but Tiberius was interfering in both spheres. His action must have destroyed any sympathy that still remained for him in the Senate: his reliance on the People will have increased senatorial fears of his aims. (2006 [1959]: 27)

By his unwillingness to forward his reforms using the traditional procedures, a reluctance possibly stemming from a sincere belief that the success of his project was even more important than honoring the *mos maiorum*, but was an example of 'politics as the crow flies', Tiberius had gone from being a respected member of the ruling class to being viewed as an aspiring tyrant.

The Senate, faced with the constitutional crisis Tiberius had created, could come up with no way of handling the emergency less radical than murdering the man responsible, along with several hundred of his supporters. The same 'problem resolution technique' was employed by the Senate a decade later, when Tiberius's brother Gaius emulated him in trying to achieve his policy aims by transgressing traditional restraints on political action. This could be cited as a failure of the Romans' contingency-driven political style—perhaps if they had spent more time devising a rational political system in advance, they could have foreseen this situation and had measures in place to deal with it less drastically? However, as we will see later in this work, the rationalist designers of the American constitution failed to foresee something as fundamental as the rise of political parties, leading to the nearly disastrous election of 1800, a disaster that was only averted by contingency-driven political action!

The careers of the Gracchi brothers set the pattern for much of the political history of the century, beginning with the tribunate of Tiberius. Again and again, following the precedent of the Gracchi, some ambitious politician, finding his agenda blocked along all constitutional routes, flouted tradition and used popular sentiment along with the threat or actual employment of mob violence to achieve his ends. How would Oakeshott have addressed such episodes? I believe his strongest response here to critics would point to a resource of which he did not make use, namely, Eric Voegelin's theory of representation, which was introduced in the previous chapter. The problem, per this line of address, was not a failure of pragmatic politics, but a failure of the Roman social compact. This response might appear ad hoc, but I believe that surveying the failure of more rationalist reform efforts, as we will do in the next sections of this chapter, will at least partially dispel that appearance.

Gaius Marius and Sulla:
planning to halt the revolution proves fruitless

The relevance of the next stage of the Roman revolution we will examine to our broader enquiry is that, during this period, several efforts were made to steer the course of political affairs by means much closer to the counsels of the rationalist than previous Roman political practice had ventured. However, contrary to the hypothesis, embraced, for instance, by the key advocates for the adoption of the new American constitution of 1787, that what ailed the Roman republic was a deficiency of explicitly expounded and theoretically devised-to-be-tamper-resistant mandates dictating the basic structural shape of the body politic, these attempts to perpetuate by decree a republican form of government for Rome came to naught.

We will begin our account of this phase of the revolution in 107 BCE, when one of the consuls for that year, Gaius Marius, in order to raise sufficient troops for his campaign against Jugurtha in Africa, chose to ignore the long-standing minimum property requirements for service in the Roman army, which had arisen from the fact that soldiers were expected to supply their own arms. Marius, in a significant break with centuries of Roman tradition, actively recruited troops from among the *capite censi*, the 'head count', a term that signified the citizens who, at the time of a census, essentially could declare as property only their own heads (and bodies). Per Beard and Crawford:

> Important consequences followed. Soldiers who lacked wealth and property in Italy necessarily rested all their hopes on military service and, in particular, relied on their general to secure them land on retirement. The general, in turn, was encouraged to enter the political arena to provide for his men; and found himself in that arena with an armed force owing him personal loyalty. This was a dangerous interdependence, which quickly proved explosive. (Beard and Crawford, 1999: 7)

Behind the necessity that Marius felt to recruit troops from among the propertyless lay the increasing dispossession of the Italian peasantry. But his decision not only sprang from that circumstance, it also served to intensify its effect on Roman political affairs, by further diminishing the attachment of the landless to the good of the *res publica*. Instead, the new recruits saw their welfare as primarily dependent upon the fortunes of some powerful aristocratic general, who could promise to alleviate their plight, especially by securing them land grants in return for their military service. In return, their general, by directing the focus of their loyalty to his person rather than to the state of which he supposedly was only an agent, gained a potent weapon he could wield in conflicts with his aristocratic rivals.

Marius is also notable in our synopsis of the Roman revolution for glaringly disregarding the constitutional principle of limited tenure of office by serving as consul six times between 107 and 100 BCE. Lest this episode be laid at the feet of the Roman reliance on tradition, it is worth noting that the traditional injunction against repeatedly holding the same office was formalized in law, at least in regards to the consulship, in 151 BCE, by legislation requiring a minimum of 10 years to pass between any individual repeating as consul. However, formalizing this constitutional principle did not stop Marius from flagrantly violating it.

He again enters our story, in 88 BCE, as a key player in yet another blow to the stability of the republic, when the elderly Marius was selected by the populist tribune Sulpicius to take command of the war against Mithridates in the east. That ploy, aimed at increasing Sulpicius's power by bringing the supporters of Marius onto his side, was a slap in the face to senatorial authority over foreign affairs, as the Senate already had assigned that command to Marius's former lieutenant, Sulla. When the resulting conflict descended into violence and threatened Sulla's life, he responded by mustering six loyal legions and marching on Rome, an unprecedented tactic. There was still enough veneration for the republic's traditions that all but one of Sulla's top officers refused to take part in what was essentially a military coup, but Sulla's ploy nevertheless succeeded in driving Marius and his supporters from the city, and resolving the dispute over who should command the campaign against Mithridates in his own favor.

However, executing that command required Sulla to leave Rome far behind, and, despite his efforts to secure his position there before departing, Marius regained control of the city by force in 87 BCE, after which he took vengeance on his perceived enemies, and was declared consul for the seventh time in 86 BCE, sharing that magistracy with his ally Cinna. They exiled Sulla, but Marius did not live to enjoy his latest ascendancy for long, dying only days after taking office, leaving Cinna alone at the top of the Roman political world. Meanwhile Sulla triumphed in the east, in a conflict that included the bizarre situation of two Roman armies, one officially authorized by Cinna and the other, operating without the approval of its own government, commanded by Sulla, simultaneously active in the field but without any measure of cooperation or coordination of their efforts. His victory having re-established Roman dominance over the eastern Mediterranean for at least the near future, in 83 BCE Sulla again marched his troops through Italy, where they routed the forces of his 'Marian' opponents. Once he regained control of Rome, he instituted a reign of terror based on 'proscribing' various citizens whom he claimed to be enemies of the state, a procedure that involved posting the names of the proscribed in the Roman forum, a posting that invited anyone who had the opportunity to murder the proscribed person and claim a substantial reward from the public purse upon delivering the victim's head to the proper authorities.

No longer willing to trust in the ability of the traditional institutions of the republic to adapt successfully, as they had done so often over the centuries, in meeting the challenges presented by novel circumstances, Sulla had himself declared dictator in the winter of 82–81 BCE. He used his unchecked authority to enact a number of reforms intended to restore the Senate's lost status as the ultimate arbiter of Roman political life. To bring that body back up to the numerical strength it had had before its membership had been ravaged by the recent wars and waves of political executions, he appointed many new senators, in the process packing the body with his own supporters. To prevent ambitious demagogues from passing laws without senatorial approval, he made it illegal for the tribunes to propose legislation directly to the popular assemblies. He also put in place new laws concerning treason in order to block officials in command of legions in the provinces from usurping the Senate's control of the forces for themselves, a usurpation that, if successful, would enable a general to turn the military might of his legions against the Roman state, the very institution they had been raised to defend – much as Sulla himself had done!

Sulla, believing he had succeeded in securing the continuation of republican government against future threats from would-be tyrants like himself, voluntarily relinquished the post of dictator and retired to his country villa. But his key measures largely were reversed within a decade after his death, through a counter-counter-revolution in which one of Sulla's chief supporters, Pompey, played a leading role. Clearly, he hoped that erecting explicit, legal barriers to populist assaults on the sanctity of the ancient constitution could succeed in preserving it where the fading reverence for the *mos maiorum* had failed. But his faith in the power of formal legislation to sustain traditional practices that were no longer held dear by the citizens they were supposed to be guiding proved unfounded, and his measures proved to be not lasting bulwarks protecting the republic, but only temporary hindrances to the populist revolution he sought to thwart. In Sulla's defense, I suggest that the failure of his reform program resulted not from any flaw in it he might have been able to avoid through greater attention to its details, but because it was an attempt to halt the progression of an untreatable disorder in the body politic—with the social conditions that for centuries had sustained the vitality of the republic vanishing, no attempt to revive the patient by legislating that it be healthy was likely to work.

It is worth noting that Oakeshott's handling of incidents such as the reign of Sulla display his tendency to view Roman history in a somewhat superficial and sugarcoated fashion. In this case, he may be engaged to an extent in what O'Neill called 'idealization' rather than mere abstraction. That he did so may cast some doubt as to the legitimacy of his citing Rome as a concrete instance of a polity closely approaching the ideal type he opposes to rationalist politics. Nevertheless, despite that Oakeshott's Rome is, indeed, a romanticized portrait that omits the warts and blemishes of the actual subject, I contend that he still was essentially justified in characterizing Roman politics as he did.

To illustrate this problem in Oakeshott's invocations of ancient Rome, let us first contemplate Plutarch's account of the proscriptions of Sulla:

> Sulla now began to make blood flow, and he filled the city with deaths without number or limit; many persons were murdered on grounds of private enmity, who had never had anything to do with Sulla, but he consented to their death to please his adherents. At last a young man, Caius Metellus, had the boldness to ask Sulla in the Senate-house, when there would be an end to these miseries, and how far he would proceed before they could hope to see them stop. 'We are not deprecating,' he said, 'your vengeance against those whom you have determined to put out of the way, but we entreat you to relieve from uncertainty those whom you have determined to spare.' Sulla replied, that he had not yet determined whom he would spare. 'Tell us then,' said Metellus, 'whom you intend to punish.' Sulla said that he would... Sulla immediately proscribed eighty persons without communicating with any magistrate. As this caused a general murmur, he let one day pass, and then proscribed two hundred and twenty more, and again on the third day as many. In an harangue to the people, he said, with reference to these measures, that he had proscribed all he could think of, and as to those who now escaped his memory, he would proscribe them at some future time. It was part of the proscription that every man who received and protected a proscribed person should be put to death for his humanity; and there was no exception for brothers, children, or parents... But what was considered most unjust of all, he affixed infamy on the sons and grandsons of the proscribed and confiscated their property. The proscriptions were not confined to Rome; they extended to every city of

Italy: neither temple nor hospitable hearth nor father's house was free
from murder, but husbands were butchered in the arms of their wives,
and children in the embrace of their mothers. The number of those who
were massacred through revenge and hatred was nothing compared
with those who were murdered for their property... Quintus Aurelius, a
man who never meddled with public affairs, and thought he was no
further concerned about all these calamities except so far as he
sympathised with the sufferings of others, happened to come to the
Forum and there he read the names of the proscribed. Finding his own
name among them, he exclaimed, 'Alas! wretch that I am; 'tis my farm at
Alba that is my persecutor'. He had not gone far before he was
murdered by some one who was in search of him. (Plutarch, 1899: 371–
373)

In light of such horrors, what does Oakeshott make of Sulla's reign?
The only remark of his I have found on that period nonchalantly
mentions that '[f]or a brief period there was some semblance of order
under an appointed dictator named Sulla...' (2006: 198). I have
introduced this issue here because this particular instance of Oakeshott
glossing over some unpleasant aspect of Roman history concerns the
events just discussed; I will return to this topic and address it in more
depth a bit later in the present chapter.

The ascendancy of ideological politics

Oakeshott held a rather dim view of what he understood to be the
ideological style of dealing with politics. As he characterized the
ideologue's obsession with removing all ambiguity from choosing
among political alternatives:

> This multi-voiced creature [of pragmatic political considerations] seems
> to be a most unreliable oracle. How can conduct be assimilated to a
> norm while there remains a variety of often circumstantially conflicting
> norms all demanding to be taken into account? And, in order to get his
> straight answer, [the ideologue] proceeds, by a process of selection,
> abridgement and abstraction, and guided by his own prejudices, to
> construct a permanent, stable, universal, self-consistent 'creed' or set of
> 'principles' out of this somewhat miscellaneous material. This makes
> him feel more comfortable, and it induces the illusion that having
> acquired a self-confident guide he will never be led astray. (2008: 184)

We now will turn our attention to the period in the Roman
revolution that presents us with what is arguably the first significant
appearance of ideological politics on the Roman scene, and ask whether

or not the events under examination support Oakeshott's critique of political ideologies.[1]

As the steady decline of republican institutions became too obvious to ignore, an adamantly conservative faction, called the *Optimates*, appeared in the Senate. Consisting of nostalgic traditionalists and led by Cato the Younger, the *Optimates* were committed to thwarting all proposed departures from customary political practices, seemingly without regard for whether or not they offered the most promising response to the existing political realities. In their hands, what had been a natural disposition to respect traditional ways of doing politics was turned into an inflexible ideology of unwavering adherence to tradition. While the motives driving their refusal to seek workable compromises with their chosen foes very well may have been admirable—a plausible case can be made for either side on that issue, for, on the one hand, the *Optimates* were fighting to preserve a system in which every individual's yearning for political power, including their own, was restrained by respect for principles greater and more lasting than himself, while, on the other hand, they themselves were the most privileged participants in that order—the actual effect of their efforts often was to hasten along the very changes that they desperately sought to prevent. For example, the formation of the so-called 'First Triumvirate', an event frequently cited as a major milestone along the downward course of the fortunes of the republic, largely was motivated, per Scullard, by 'the demands of Pompey, Caesar, and Crassus [in 60 BCE], which were by no means outrageous, and the short-sighted reaction of the die-hard *Optimates* [to those demands]' (2006 [1959]: 112). Pompey, for instance, only asked for land for his victorious veterans returning from an eastern campaign and Senate ratification of the treaties and territorial arrangements he had made during that venture, neither of which requests were unprecedented nor at least on their face a blatant ploy to seize power for himself. But Cato and his cohorts, determined not to suggest that the ultimate authority of the Senate was subject to negotiation or to circumstantial considerations, refused to reach any accommodation with men whom they saw as unsavory demagogues. However, rather than extending the lifespan of the republic, which a reasonable compromise might have accomplished, the intransigence of the *Optimates* almost surely reduced the years remaining to republican government in Rome. By

---

[1] Gruen (1974) makes a strong case for the continuing importance of family ties and patronage networks throughout the period of the 'revolution', but does not deny the growing importance of ideology during this time.

frustrating the achievement of the relatively modest goals their three leading foes initially had pursued, the *Optimates'* chosen course prompted the trio to join forces and create an alliance with enough power that they no longer needed to confer with the Senate at all, and could, as they did in 60 BCE, meet in private and effectively divide up control of the entire Roman Empire amongst themselves. While the *Optimates* were not delusional in suspecting that Pompey, Caesar, and Crassus each individually posed a potential threat to the traditional dispersal of power among the whole noble class—subsequent events demonstrate that at least Caesar was quite willing to seize dictatorial power for himself, given the opportunity to do so—those dangers clearly were dwarfed by the threat to republican institutions created through the alliance of all three. As Scullard notes, 'The policy of the Senate was unrealistic, and even a [more practical conservative such as] Cicero complained that Cato talked as if he were in the Republic of Plato, and not in the sink of Romulus' (2006 [1959]: 113)—Cato's devotion to ideological purity kept him from seeing the situation in which he actually acted. The union of the already significant clientele, noble support, and *auctoritas* each triumver had had on his own allowed the triumvirate to exercise nearly complete command over the most important matters in Roman politics, which was certainly not the situation the *Optimates* had hoped to bring about. Similarly, a decade later, the senatorial conservatives forced Caesar's back up against a wall, rather than trying to address his well-founded concerns about the fate of his career and his very life, should he be forced to disarm while Pompey, who by then was no longer Caesar's ally but instead his rival, was allowed to retain command of his own legions. By placing Caesar in such an untenable situation, the purported defenders of the republic prompted him, if only from an interest in self-preservation, to bring his troops across the Rubicon and into Italy proper, thereby declaring war on his own country and once again hastening the republic's demise. Ideological politics again proved less capable of dealing with reality than its pragmatic alternative.

Another example of the inability of reforms deliberately aimed at halting the Republic's degeneration occurred in the 60s BCE, when, amidst growing concern over electoral abuses, a number of legislative efforts were made to curb their prevalence. For instance, law was passed banning the use of *nomenclatores*, campaign workers who assisted a candidate in recalling (or pretending to recall) the names of individual voters. Gruen writes that 'Young M. Cato, carefully cultivating a reputation for rectitude, embarrassed his rivals when he stood for the military tribunate: he alone scrupulously obeyed [the]

recent law that forbade candidates to employ *nomenclatores*' (1974: 216).
But despite the legislation and Cato's example, the use of such
assistants went on; according to Gruen, 'That convenient institution,
which enabled candidates to greet voters by name, was too useful to be
dropped. Legislation violating accepted standards proves generally
unenforceable. Even Cato recognized its futility and resumed
employment of *nomenclatores*' (1974: 217). What's even more telling is
that these repeated legislative attempts to clean up the electoral process
were rendered pointless by the increasing employment of gangs of
thugs and mob violence to control the results of elections during the
60s and 50s. Indeed, as Shotter notes of Cicero, the *Optimates* were most
effective only when they abandoned their ideological purity:
'Ultimately, Cicero was too constrained by the system, as is
demonstrated by the fact that his great moments of effectiveness (63
and 44–43 BC) coincided with behaviour on his part that was in legal
terms outrageous' (1994: 97).

The actions of the *Optimates* in this period and the gulf between the
intended and the actual effects of those actions exhibit the defects that
Oakeshott argued were inherently present in all instances of ideological
politics. As McIntyre sums up Oakeshott's critique of ideology:

> Technical knowledge in its political forms as ideology is a confusion
> of practical recommendation and philosophical elucidation. The
> abstraction from concrete tradition renders ideology irrelevant in the
> practical world of politics and morality, while the retention of practical
> presuppositions undermines its claims to be philosophical knowledge.
> (2004: 58)

The ideologue has pledged his full allegiance to an abstract conception
of the ideal polity, and as a consequence regards any acceptance of
deviations from that ideal, other than as a stepping-stone along the
shortest path to his utopia, as an unprincipled compromise between
virtue and vice. Thus, the ideologue is contemptuous of attempts by
more practical and modest political actors to comprehend the actual
political circumstances of their particular place and time so as to pursue
those improvements to present conditions that are realistically
achievable. Although the ideological purist flaunts his unwillingness to
compromise his principles as evidence of his moral superiority over the
political pragmatist, in fact it is evidence that he has failed to grasp the
ethical truth that an action, however laudable the intentions behind it,
is lacking in virtue to whatever extent the agent undertaking it has
neglected to give prudent consideration to its probable outcome in the

real world, rather than merely his own fanciful wishes for what his action will bring about.

In the meantime, returning to our historical narrative, we note that the result of Caesar's decision to enter Italy under arms was a civil war between his supporters and those backing Pompey, a war that spanned the entire breadth of the Mediterranean basin, from Spain to Asia. Caesar, as we all know, emerged from that conflict victorious, now the sole master of the Roman world. Following the example Sulla had provided more than three decades earlier, Caesar had himself appointed dictator. However, unlike his model, he had no intention of ever surrendering that power, and was, in yet another egregious violation of constitutional principles, declared dictator for life in 44 BCE. When, soon thereafter, in what was almost certainly a staged piece of political theater, Caesar was thrice offered a royal crown, which on each occasion he declined, a group of senatorial republicans interpreted the play's purpose to be softening the resistance to Caesar's imminent elevation to kingship, by trying to demonstrate that he really didn't seek or even desire the role of monarch, but at length had had it forced upon him by the demands of the Roman people. It had been more than four centuries since the Romans had been ruled by a king, and during that entire time avoiding the danger of losing their cherished liberty through the ascendancy of a new monarch had been a guiding principle of their political affairs. Now, with the prospect of that relapse into tyranny looming before them all too closely, those senators believed it to be their patriotic duty to pursue the only course of action they saw as definitively safeguarding Rome's freedom from being extinguished: Caesar must be eliminated for the good of their country. On the ides of March in 44 BCE the conspirators assassinated Caesar, confident that their act, though extreme, had been necessary to save the republic. But again, much as we saw earlier, the actual consequences of an idealistic attempt to preserve Roman liberty were very different from those desired by the idealists. Caesar's rule, while it undeniably had been autocratic, had not been vicious: he not only had refused to seek vengeance against those who had opposed him in the civil war with Pompey, he even had granted some of the most prominent of his erstwhile opponents posts in his own government. His successors would not rule with such charity: the Second Triumvirate of Antony, Octavian, and Lepidus, who headed the Caesarean forces in the new civil war following Caesar's death, pursued a far more brutal course. As Scullard writes:

> The triumvirs needed political security and money; they therefore forgot
> the example of Caesar and remembered Marius and Sulla. They carried
> out a ruthless proscription, in which they signed the death warrant of
> some 300 senators and 2000 knights. Since they had forty-five legions
> behind them and their victims included so many knights, whose share
> in politics will often have been negligible, their dominant motive will
> have been the need to confiscate estates with which to pay their
> troops... The most famous victim, on whose death Antony insisted, was
> Cicero... Antony had his head and hands hung up on the Rostra in the
> Forum at Rome: such was the barbaric revenge that he took on the man
> who had dared to challenge him in the name of the Republic...
> (Scullard, 2006 [1959]: 158–159)

What's more, in an outcome essentially a direct reversal of that
sought by the 'liberators' who had killed Caesar, the Caesarean party
eventually crushed the republican forces, with the consequence that
almost every republican voice that had been of recent prominence in
Roman politics was now dead, often killed by their own hand.
Although it succeeded in winning its civil war, in the wake of victory
the Second Triumvirate, as might have been predicted given that it was
composed of aspirants to fill the position vacated by Caesar's death,
proved as unstable as had its predecessor, and, in yet another civil war,
Octavian rose to sole command of the entire Roman world.

This history provides evidence countering critics of Oakeshott such
as Eccleshall and Freeden (see Chapter 3). First of all, it contradicts their
claim that all politics is ideological politics. Of course we may simply
define politics so that their proposition is true, and it is also true, as
Winch (1990) notes, that we can always extract *some* rule from all
purposeful behavior, and, therefore, we could amass a 'book' of such
rules from any historical period and call it 'an ideology'. Nevertheless,
there is a clear distinction between the pragmatic respect for the past
exhibited throughout the early centuries of the Roman republic and the
dogmatic adherence to tradition displayed by the *Optimates* (although
there are hints of the latter already in, for instance, the career of Cato
the Elder). And it seems quite sensible to categorize the difference as
that between pragmatic and ideological politics. Second, far from it
being the case, as Freeden would have it, that 'if a constructed
ideological harmony with the capacity for cultural survival emerges, it
becomes an asset for any society, enhancing its communicative
capacity, adumbrating boundaries among alternative ideological
patterns' (2001: 10), quite to the contrary, the emergence of ideological
politics proved a disaster for the Roman republic and set the stage for
empire-wide civil war and bloodshed.

In more than 50 years, from 88 to 31 BCE, Rome had endured seven violent overthrows of its established government, at least four other episodes that represented serious threats of a coup, and three empire-wide civil wars. At length, the Roman people were willing to embrace almost any political arrangement that promised to bring an end to the decades of chaos and violence, and so they placidly accepted the one-man rule of Octavian, which, although a dictatorship in all but name, veiled its authoritarian character behind a flimsy fabric of faux republicanism. Even though all but the hollow shell of the Roman republic had been abandoned, it is worth noting that the substance with which the Romans filled that shell still was not a product of a rationalist design; they may have lost their republican ideals, but the Romans had not lost their pragmatic and experientially oriented character. Scullard writes, '[Octavian] did not sit down and draft an ideal solution on paper and then try to implement it. Rather, he proceeded by a slow process of trial and error, feeling his way forward with patient care...' (2006 [1959]: 208). That is the germ of truth contained within Oakeshott's overly rosy depiction of the principate, a topic that we will explore in more detail in the next section.

Oakeshott's understanding of the Roman revolution

As mentioned previously, given the importance of Rome for Oakeshott, as an exemplar of the style of politics he admired, it is appropriate to ask how accurate was his portrayal of Roman political life. And, as I indicated earlier, I believe that, while his handling of the revolutionary period is unsatisfactory in several respects, the broad sweep of Roman history largely supports the use to which Oakeshott puts it. However, lest we too blithely excuse his shortcomings in this regard, it is appropriate that we first review them. To begin with, and quite surprisingly, at one point he gets the plain chronology wrong: 'And in the later part of this period [before the destruction of Carthage]... Roman armies, in a major military effort, invade and conquered Greece, Asia Minor, Egypt, and Spain' (2006: 194). Carthage was destroyed in 146 BCE, and it is true that, by that time, Rome had two provinces in Spain and ruled Greece. But the first Roman province in Asia Minor was gained, not by conquest, but, as mentioned above, because the last monarch of Pergamum willed his kingdom to the Roman people, and that was not until 133 BCE. And Egypt was not annexed until after the Battle of Actium, in 31 BCE, more than a century after the annihilation of Carthage.

More significant for our purposes, Oakeshott attributes the onset of the crisis of the republic to the coming of peace, which, he argues, disturbed the long-established pre-eminence of the Senate over the popular assemblies, inspiring the latter bodies to challenge the authority of the former. He writes, 'But wars come to an end; and it is almost a maxim of Roman political experience that peace and the cessation of danger is the signal for a renewal of the internal tensions of Roman politics' (2006: 197). However, it is not at all evident that the years of the revolution encompassed any time of peace long enough to differ in kind from the many respites from war that had occurred in earlier centuries. The revolutionary period witnessed the Social War, the war against Jugurtha in North Africa, war with the Cimbri (a Germanic tribe), two wars against Mithradites in Asia Minor, Caesar's famed Gallic Wars, and two wars with Parthia, one led by Crassus and the other by Antony. As I argued above, the increasing woes of the republic owed much less to any novel onset of peace than they did to the lure of the easy affluence available through unflinchingly exploiting the lands and inhabitants of the ever-expanding empire.

Finally, Oakeshott adopts a quite sanguine view of the transition from republic to principate. The germ of truth in his depiction of that process, as noted previously, is that the principate genuinely was the product of the Roman predilection for proceeding according to the shifting demands of the concrete situations encountered along one's way, rather than trying to follow some rationalist blueprint drawn up in advance of one's embarkation. He is accurate in contending that the principate:

> was generated with remarkable political economy, out of materials which lay ready to hand. The Romans never indulged in political invention, if they could find among their institutions something suitable to meet the situation. The new order of government (as it came to be called) which gradually emerged was an immensely subtle rearrangement in which sheer invention played a negligible part. Each phase of the change was unobtrusive because it differed minimally from what had gone before. (2006: 200)

However, missing from Oakeshott's admiring account of the principate's formation is any recognition of the dark side of the transition: while it is true that it was not a transformation tortured into conformance with some rationalist vision, it nevertheless entailed tremendous brutality and the ever-present threat of violent retribution awaiting anyone who opposed, in any significant fashion, the consolidation of all real political authority in the person of the emperor. As Voegelin noted, of the document in which Augustus 'enumerates the laudable deeds of his reign... the emperor could omit, probably in all sincerity, the minor fact that every cent... spent [in achieving those deeds] was robbed, confiscated, extorted from persons killed, blackmailed, left destitute, and driven to suicide' (1997a: 141).

The transition from republic to principate proceeded in such a way that the average Roman citizen could pretend that nothing of basic importance about his government had changed, and that he was still a free participant in a republican polity, so that Oakeshott is justified in his claim, quoted above, that 'each phase of the change was unobtrusive because it differed minimally from what had gone before'. But his account neglects the important fact that any nascent urge to call attention to what might have been objectionable in those changes was aborted not only because they were gradual, but also because essentially all of the leading republican advocates had been killed or had been reduced to killing themselves, and because of the unspoken but tacitly understood threat that anyone who might consider taking up their lost cause would meet a similar fate.

Our examination of Roman history, while being itself very much a quick sketch omitting a plethora of details, still represents a closer look at its subject than that offered by Oakeshott. Even this modest increase in image resolution reveals that, while Oakeshott's depiction of Rome's political life is not grossly distorted, it is more a caricature of the subject, one that exaggerates a few chosen features while ignoring others, than it is a realistic portrait. In elaborating upon his general critique of rationalism, Oakeshott singled out Rome as a notable, historical instance of a polity largely conforming to the ideal type of a social order guided by the wisdom embodied in its time-tested traditions and intimately familiar customs, the type that he opposed to the rationalistic approach to governance. Oakeshott's case is bolstered by the fact that the reliance of Roman citizens on their traditions for guidance in their political life worked well for several centuries. Furthermore, when the customs that sustained their republic began to decay, attempts to rationally legislate adherence to those mores had little success. Nevertheless, I believe that Oakeshott's sanitized version of Roman history unnecessarily raises scepticism about his case for readers who are familiar with the particulars of that time.

In the introduction to this work, we addressed the issue of the discrepancy between Oakeshott's contention, in his work on the philosophy of history, that the 'ideal type' method of doing historical work, while not without merit, was inherently inferior to a more concrete exploration of historical matters, and his own nearly exclusive reliance on just such ideal typification whenever he addressed historical material himself. But that still leaves open the question of why Oakeshott, in painting his flattering portrait of Roman political experience, largely chose to gloss over the many prominent and unsightly features that made his subject significantly less attractive in reality than it appeared in his depiction of it. Here, I think, the best explanation lies in Oakeshott's conviction that the human condition, while susceptible to moderate and gradual melioration, is fundamentally impervious to all attempts at radically transforming it to reflect some utopian vision of what mankind ought to be. As a result, it is an idle fantasy to demand of any actual polity that it must eliminate all corruption, cupidity, cruelty, and other characteristic human vices before it could be worthy of appreciation. I suspect that, for Oakeshott, the darker episodes in Roman history were only to be expected in the lives of flawed human beings, and that he saw them as being of trivial significance for his tale of what was singular and admirable in the political experience of the Roman nation.

The importance of the Roman revolution for the American republic

As mentioned previously, the downfall of the Roman republic takes on added significance for our study given the importance the American founders placed on that historical episode and the influence their conception of it had on their design for the newly born United States. As Richard put it:

> The period of ancient history that most enthralled the Founding Fathers was the era that witnessed the decline and fall of the Roman republic... The founders' intense scrutiny of the late Roman republic resembled an autopsy. The purpose of this autopsy was to save the life of the American body politic by uncovering the cancerous growths that had caused the demise of its greatest ideological ancestor. (Richard, 2008: 129)

The lesson the founders learned from Plutarch, Sallust, and Cicero, Richard continues, was 'that if republics wished to survive, they must exercise eternal vigilance against cunning, ambitious individuals who would seek to advance their own power at the expense of the republic. Conversely, republics must also encourage the patriotic spirit of self-sacrifice' (2008: 150–151). As Richard documents, it was great praise for a founder to be compared to Cato the Younger, Cicero, Brutus, or Cassius, and the highest calumny for one to be called a new Caesar.

Indeed, both ends of the ideological spectrum likened the leaders of their opposition to Caesar: Hamilton believed that Jefferson and Burr resembled Caesar in employing populist rhetoric and flattery of the masses to hide their tyrannical ambitions, while Jefferson thought that Hamilton's advocacy of a strong central government was meant to pave the way for dictatorship (Richard, 2008: 156–157).

Despite their intense interest in the story of the Roman republic's fall, the American founders had a very one-sided understanding of the causes of its collapse. The founders divided the cast of Roman historical characters as unambiguously belonging either to a party of good or a party of evil. Richard contends, 'Most of the founders attributed the downfall of the Roman republic to ambitious individuals like Caesar. Only rarely did anyone attribute it to social institutions...' (2008: 158). Their focus on conspiracies blinded them to the dependence of a polity for its health upon an underlying conception of just social order, an order seen as an expression of humanity's properly understood place in the cosmic scheme of existence.

The fact that Rome and America, arguably the two most influential republics in world history, can be opposed to each other as exemplifying Oakeshott's ideal types of the pragmatic and the rationalist polity without too severely contorting their histories to fit the desired molds, alone suggests them to be interesting candidates for testing his theory against historical evidence. That the American founders had the aim of avoiding the fate of the Roman republic at the forefront of their thoughts when designing the U.S. Constitution makes the case for the comparison even stronger. Given that aim, we are justified in asking to what extent it was achieved: could the principles of Enlightenment rationalism succeed in sustaining a republican government where the Roman reliance on tradition, custom, and veneration of one's glorious ancestors ultimately had failed?

Would the employment of rationalist designing have been an effective treatment for the ills of the Roman republic?

In deciding whether the history of the Roman republic, on net, supports or argues against Oakeshott's critique of rationalism in politics, it is likely that we immediately will be struck by the curious situation that the story of that republic suggests a natural division of the whole into two chapters, one of which, at least on first impression, seems likely to back Oakeshott, while the other initially would appear to undermine his case. Which of the two, then, is more deserving of our attention: Should we point to the several centuries during which the Roman republic flourished as confirming the general soundness of Oakeshott's thesis, or should we, instead, cite the tumultuous period of the republic's collapse as offering a telling counterexample to its general relevance? Neither emphasis appears indefensible on its face, and the American founders, as we have seen, largely read Rome's history as a cautionary tale, understanding the revolution to illustrate the danger in forgoing the rational design of political institutions, a danger that they sought to avoid in their own enterprise. However, I contend that the lesson they read in the downfall of the Roman republic has less historical support than does its alternative: Oakeshott was more perceptive here than the founders, since, as I will try to show, the absence of rationalist politics had little to do with the death of the Roman republic.

Historical counterfactuals are never, of course, susceptible to indisputable demonstration. However, the above-cited incidents strongly suggest that a written, rationally designed constitution, in the end, no more would have been able to save Roman republicanism than was the faith in the *mos maiorum*. The Romans' 'failure', as some would see it, to formalize the constitutional principles guiding their republic by setting down those precepts in a written and purportedly inviolable document was not a major factor in the death of their republic.

In making my case, I acknowledge that, as Oakeshott pointed out in his work dealing with the philosophy of history (see especially Oakeshott, 1999), a fully satisfactory historical explanation of any occurrence will incorporate the entire myriad of prior circumstances and actions that the historian understands as having contributed to the appearance on the scene of the event under consideration. However, such an analysis of the Roman revolution is far beyond the scope of the present work. Fortunately, the theoretical possibility of such an ideally exhaustive explanation in no way precludes a less complete examination from offering its own, admittedly more partial, comprehension of the episode in question. From among the plethora of significant antecedents that might be invoked in explaining any particular historical event, the theorist can select a much smaller set of factors that she posits as being especially relevant and important for understanding the import of the event in answering the specific question guiding her current effort. In that spirit, I will propose several crucial contributors to the downfall of the Roman republic that, taken together, I believe are sufficient to defend the thesis that Rome's lack of a written constitution was not a decisive factor in the republic's passing.

First of all, as we have seen, the failure of the informal Roman constitution to constrain political actors came only in the wake of the breakdown of the social arrangements of which it was an expression. History does not suggest that a social order, once it has collapsed, is a likely candidate for resuscitation, but failing the improbable revival of the Rome built upon the foundation of independent, peasant farmers, the constitution was bound to expire once cut off from the source of its vitality. Even Polybius, despite his famous praise of the balanced Roman constitution, acknowledged it to be a dependent rather than a self-sufficient source of the republic's vitality. As Voegelin writes:

> [Polybius] predicts that the possession of the perfect constitution will not prevent the decay of Rome, again because the constitution is not the important factor, but because victory and new wealth will ruin morale and precipitate the development toward mob rule and leadership... If men's private lives are righteous and well-ordered, the state will be good; if men are covetous and unjust, the state will be bad. Rome is not better than other states [at the time of Polybius, circa 150 BCE] merely because it possesses a balanced constitution, but rather because an aristocracy with certain standards of conduct guides the affairs of the state. The end of Rome [or at least of the republic] will come when the masses 'will no longer consent to obey or even to be the equals of the ruling caste' (Voegelin, 1997a: 127).

Intimately connected to that transformation in social conditions, but still worth noting as a conceptually distinguishable factor, is that, in vastly expanding their empire during the centuries preceding the revolution, the Romans had repeatedly snuffed out the liberty of those they conquered, enslaving many of the defeated to work their *latifundia* and tutor their children, for the sake of increasing their own glory, power, ease, and wealth. Garrett Fagan notes that a 'tipping point' in this regard may be detected in 146 BCE, a year in which the Romans, seemingly in the absence of any compelling strategic motives, razed to the ground two ancient centers of Mediterranean civilization, Carthage and Corinth. It is interesting to note that those events only preceded the rise of Tiberius Gracchus by a little more than a decade. Having valued their own desire for personal aggrandizement over the liberty of others, the Roman aristocrats inevitably lost the passion for liberty necessary to defend their own political freedom against the depredations of the most ambitious of their fellows. When the aristocracy ceased to display 'certain standards of conduct', it lost its source of authority vis-à-vis the masses, and the Roman social compact fell apart. While the republic could not survive that collapse, Voegelin contends that 'historical factors had tipped the scale for the survival of Rome just long enough to carry the state over into the imperial expansion and then keep it going by the organized plunder of the *orbis terrarum*...' (1997a: 133).

Augustine emphasized this moral failing in refuting the contention that abandoning the traditional pagan gods and embracing Christianity was the cause of the Empire's decline:

> Now, if these were the days in which the Roman republic shows fairest and best, what are we to say or think of the succeeding age, when, to use the words of the same historian [Sallust], 'changing little by little from the fair and virtuous city it was, it became utterly wicked and dissolute?' This was, as he mentions, after the destruction of Carthage. Sallust's brief sum and sketch of this period may be read in his own history, in which he shows how the profligate manners which were propagated by prosperity resulted at last even in civil wars. He says: 'And from this time the primitive manners, instead of undergoing an insensible alteration as hitherto they had done, were swept away as by a torrent: the young men were so depraved by luxury and avarice, that it may justly be said that no father had a son who could either preserve his own patrimony, or keep his hands off other men's.' Sallust adds a number of particulars about the vices of Sylla, and the debased condition of the republic in general; and other writers make similar observations, though in much less striking language.
>
> Here, then, is this Roman republic, 'which has changed little by little from the fair and virtuous city it was, and has become utterly wicked and dissolute'. It is not I who am the first to say this, but their own authors, from whom we learned it for a fee, and who wrote it long before the coming of Christ. You see how, before the coming of Christ, and after the destruction of Carthage, 'the primitive manners, instead of undergoing insensible alteration, as hitherto they had done, were swept away as by a torrent; and how depraved by luxury and avarice the youth were'. Let them now, on their part, read to us any laws given by their gods to the Roman people, and directed against luxury and avarice. And would that they had only been silent on the subjects of chastity and modesty, and had not demanded from the people indecent and shameful practices, to which they lent a pernicious patronage by their so-called divinity. (Augustine, 1950: 57–58)

The final influence sapping the strength of the republic that we will note, one again intimately intertwined with the failure of the social compact, and one which also was not amenable to treatment by a written constitution, was the gradual fading away of Roman paganism's ability to provide a viable understanding for its adherents of their relationship with the cosmos. Voegelin points out that the pagan religion of Rome, with its civic focus, was the foundation upon which Roman political life rested. However, as the Romans exported their armies and their rule to more and more of the known world, they, willingly or not, imported the ideas of the people they had conquered back to Rome. In particular, the Roman's encounters with Greek philosophy and the novel religions they met in their eastern provinces, most notably that of the Hebrews, gradually eroded their confidence in the superiority of their indigenous mythology. A perceptive Roman leader such as Augustus clearly understood the debilitating effects of this loss of religious conviction on Rome's civic health, and sought to revive traditional beliefs through measures aimed to turn back 'widespread scepticism and rationalism' (Scullard, 2006 [1959]: 233), but such policies proved to offer not cures but temporary palliatives. It was not until the ascendancy of Christianity, several centuries later, that the Roman world finally rediscovered a cosmological basis upon which a coherent civil order could be erected. How could the hypothetical existence of a written constitution have succeeded in animating a political body whose soul was fading from the world? As R. E. Smith would have it, 'Thus concludes our study of the Republic's failure, a failure of the spirit, not of government...' (1955, 163) Or, as he wrote in another passage:

> The history of the last century of the Republic is the history of a disintegrating State and society, in which men became selfish and self-seeking, while social and political problems became the tools of contending factions fighting for their personal power, and those spiritual and religious qualities which are both cause and effect of an integrated State were atrophied and died, leaving to replace them their material counterparts, greed and the lust for power and personal advantage. (Smith, 1955: 75)

In short, there is scant reason to believe that any significant blame for the demise of the Roman republic should fall upon an absence of rationalist design of its institutions, or that the undertaking of such design could have extended its life but briefly. The Roman republic had ceased to be representative, in Voegelin's sense of the word, and efforts to preserve it by writing the traditional practices that had previously sustained it into law proved fruitless. And the form of government that actually extended the life of the Roman state for several more centuries was the principate, a form that was arrived at by a process of trial and error, and that was not something anyone foresaw as a possibility during the revolution.

Conclusion

Our examination of Rome has largely supported Oakeshott's use of it as an exemplar of the style of 'pragmatic politics'. While, as we have seen, Oakeshott did tend to take a superficial view of Roman history, and to sugarcoat certain unsavory episodes, those who have devoted their careers to this topic concur that Roman politics differed markedly from common modern practice in the Romans' abjuring of theory in favor of practical concerns, and in their reliance on precedent rather than on formal constitutional measures to regulate political activity. The result was not, as some critics of Oakeshott contended would be the case, a polity lacking flexibility or foundering for direction when confronted with novel situations: instead, the Roman republic worked remarkably well for several centuries, and Roman political practice was able to adapt successfully to tremendous change in the situations faced by the state. It is true that the republic finally fell, but, aside from Switzerland, history offers us no examples of a republic enduring longer than did the Roman. And, as we have seen, there is little cause for laying the blame for the Roman republic's demise on a lack of rationalist design or the absence of a guiding ideology.

Chapter 7

Rationalism in the American Founding

We now turn to an examination of selected episodes from the history of the American republic, to see what evidence they provide weighing for or against Oakeshott's thesis on rationalism. As mentioned earlier, Oakeshott held up the American founding as an exemplar of the rationalist style of politics. He wrote:

> The early history of the United States of America is an instructive chapter in the history of the politics of Rationalism. The situation of society called upon without much notice to exercise political initiative on its own account is similar to that of an individual or a social class rising not fully prepared to the exercise of political power; in general, its needs are the same as theirs. And the similarity is even closer when the independence of the society concerned begins with an admitted illegality... [T]he intellectual gifts of Europe to America (both in philosophy and religion) had, from the beginning, been predominantly rationalistic... [Colonial Americans] were disposed to believe, and they believed more fully than was possible for an inhabitant of the Old World, that the proper organization of a society and the conduct of its affairs were based upon abstract principles, and not upon a tradition which, as Hamilton said, had 'to be rummaged for among old parchments and musty records'... The Declaration of Independence is a characteristic product of the *saeculum rationalisticum*. It represents the politics of the felt need interpreted with the aid of an ideology. (1991 [1962]: 31–32)

In his essay 'Rational Conduct', Oakesott sets out a number of characteristics of the rationalist understanding of the 'rational' mode of conduct.[1] We will review these characteristics here so that we may use them as guides through the material in this chapter.

---

[1] As Oakeshott pointed out, the rationalist may very well acknowledge 'that human beings do not often achieve this mode of conduct...' (1991 [1962]: 104) but that, nevertheless, it is both *a* possible and *the* most desirable mode of conduct.

First of all, the rationalist assumes that people have a power of reasoning about things, and that

> this is a power independent of any other powers a man may have, and something from which his activity can *begin*. And activity is said to be 'rational' (or 'intelligent') on account of being preceded by the exercise of this power... (1991 [1962]: 105)

Second, this power of abstract reason implies that a person's 'mind can be separated from its contents and activities', that one can have a 'trained mind' that is trained in nothing in particular, and that the mental acuity this training produces is 'a *consequence* of learning and activity, and is not a *conclusion* from it' (1991 [1962]: 106).

Finally, the rationalist believes:

> the mind will be most successful in dealing with experience when it is least prejudiced with already acquired dispositions or knowledge: the open, empty or free mind, the mind without disposition, is an instrument which attracts truth, repels superstition and is alone the spring of 'rational' judgment and 'rational' conduct' (1991 [1962]: 106)

With these guides in our mind, let us turn once more to some historical material.

From Rome to America through Florence and England

We will begin this chapter's case study by examining the transformations of republican thought that occurred during the centuries separating republican Rome and the American revolution. Roughly eighteen hundred years passed between the end of the Roman republic to the launch of the American attempt to create a free polity made sustainable by achieving a stable balance between the claims of the one, the few, and the many to be the most legitimate possessors of the authority to govern. The Western political mind was not idle during that time, and, while the American founders looked largely to Rome as the exemplar of the political order they wished to create, they, whether aware of it or not, inevitably understood Rome through the filter of political thinkers from the intervening eras. The significance of that filter to the present work is that it gradually came to block out any light emitted by the Roman experience that was out of phase with the increasingly rationalist polarization of European thought.

Our selection of a few persons and episodes from the vast amount of material we might include is guided, again, by theoretical ideas arising in Oakeshott's work. As Franco wrote:

Oakeshott traces the appeal of rationalistic ideologies to the incursion of the politically inexperienced into politics. He gives three examples: the new ruler, the new ruling class, and the new political society. In the case of the new ruler, it was Machiavelli who supplied the need for a technique of politics, a 'crib' to make up for the ruler's lack of political education and traditional knowledge... As examples of cribs for new and politically inexperienced classes, Oakeshott cites Locke's *Second Treatise* and the work of Marx and Engels... Finally, Oakeshott shows how the circumstances of a new political society such as the United States at its founding favored the emergence of a rationalistic politics based on self-conscious reflection and abstract principles. (Franco, 2004: 86)

Therefore, let us choose Machiavelli and Florence and Locke and seventeenth-century England as subjects for our elliptical passage from Rome to America.

Machiavelli and Florence

Pocock presents an extended case that Florentine political thinkers of the Renaissance, especially Machiavelli and Guicciardini, are the key figures transmitting ancient political ideas to the 'Atlantic' realm of England and America: 'It can... be shown how the thought of the Machiavellian epic served to convey the Aristotelian-Polybian tradition to future generations and to lands beyond Italy' (1975: 86). He further contends that 'the classical republicanism to which John Adams still adhered was basically a renaissance rephrasing of the political science set forth in Aristotle's politics...' (1975: 317). It is chiefly the character of that 'rephrasing' that concerns us here.

The Florentine political thinkers made a great effort to come to terms with the tension existing between the reverence for tradition characterizing Rome, which, much like the American founders, they viewed as an exemplar, and the fact that, in proposing new institutional arrangements devised to address the political crisis they saw unfolding in Italy, they were necessarily innovators. Florentine political writers had little doubt that it was Rome that they themselves ought to look to for their models. As Pocock wrote, 'Salutati's and Bruni's Florence learned direct from republican Rome and envisaged itself as Rome's revival' (1975: 62). But, without an extensive history of republican government behind them, and faced with novel circumstances (such as the threats to Italian independence presented by the nascent nation-states of Europe, such as Spain and France), the republicans of the Italian Renaissance could not rely on a native tradition of republicanism as the Romans had done—thus, they sought answers to their difficulties in more abstract political theories.

As a result, there was a notable struggle between two strains in Renaissance Italian political theorizing. On the one hand, Florentine thinkers were wary of too much political novelty. Pocock wrote, 'Machiavelli's emphasis is on usage; nothing else seems capable of providing legitimacy, and the innovator's problem is always that his subjects are not used to him and are used to something of which he has deprived them' (1975: 164).

On the other hand, as they were dealing with a novel situation, they necessarily had a 'lack of political education and traditional knowledge' concerning these circumstances. This lead, as Oakeshott pointed out, to an increasingly rationalist bent of Florentine political thought, as displayed in the following passage from Machiavelli:

> Now in a well-ordered republic it should never be necessary to resort to extra-constitutional measures; for although they may for the time be beneficial, yet the precedent is pernicious, for if the practice is once established of disregarding the laws for good objects, they will in a little while be disregarded under that pretext for evil purposes. Thus no republic will ever be perfect if she has not by law provided for everything, having a remedy for every emergency, and fixed rules for applying it. (Machiavelli, 1882: ch. XXXIV)

There is a clear pre-shadowing here of the attempt by the American founders to create a document that would act as a prophylactic against any forces that might subvert republican virtue. As described by Oakeshott, this is the rationalist error of conceiving that an activity can be 'reduced to knowledge in the form of propositions (and possibly to ends, rule and principles),' but, in fact, 'these propositions are neither the spring of activity nor are they in any direct sense regulative of the activity' (1991 [1962]: 110).

Another idea, arising in this period, which also strongly influenced the American founders, was that this ideal balance of estates could be the result of rationally designed 'political machinery'. Pocock wrote:

> A fully Polybian theory would assert that monarchy, aristocracy, and democracy had each its peculiar merit, or *virtú*, but that each tended to self-corruption in isolation; a true mixed government would employ each *virtú* to check the degeneration of the others, and… it was usually added that the Venetians had achieved this by mechanical and self-perpetuating devices. (Pocock, 1975: 262)

The basic idea of mixed government is not itself rationalist, but was a practical guideline drawn from Aristotle's survey of numerous constitutions and Polybius's analysis of the historical factors explaining Rome's success. (Although, in the latter case, as we cited in the previous chapter, Voegelin argued that the theory of the mixed constitution actually does little real work in Polybius's explanation of the rise of Rome.) But as interpreted by later theorists confronting the precarious circumstances faced by nascent republics, it was turned into an abstract formula whose invocation could inoculate polities against the threat of corruption.

The English transit and Locke

The Puritan movement provided much of the impetus behind the English revolution of the 1640s, and the influence of which continued to be felt strongly across the Atlantic up to and even beyond the American revolution. An early detection of what Voegelin would call the Puritan's 'Gnostic spirit', which is a phenomenon closely related to rationalism, was made by 'the judicious Hooker', who, in the late sixteenth century, remarked upon the Anabaptists as follows:

> In such kinds of error the mind once imagining itself to seek the execution of God's will, laboureth forthwith to remove both things and persons which any way hinder it from taking place; and in such cases if any strange or new thing seem requisite to be done, a strange and new opinion concerning the lawfulness thereof, is withal received and broached under countenance of divine authority... Where [the Anabaptists] found men in diet, attire, furniture of house, or any other way observers of civility and decent order, such they reproved as being carnally and earthly minded... They so much affected to cross the ordinary custom in everything, that when other men's use was to put on better attire, they would be sure to show themselves openly abroad in worse; the ordinary names of the days in the week they thought a kind of profaneness to use, and therefore accustomed themselves to make no other distinction than by numbers... When they and their Bibles were alone, what strange fantastical opinion soever at any time entered into their heads, their use was to think the Spirit taught it them. (Hooker, 1989: 40–43)

I think it is interesting to compare the attitude of these saints towards custom with that of Keynes and his Bloomsbury friends, as cited in Chapter 1 of this work; both groups might be rather surprised to discover their close kinship, if it were possible to revive them and make them aware of it. The relationship between the religious and secular rationalism may appear obscure, since, so often, the secular rationalists declare themselves to be the enemies of religion. But they

are closely related phenomena differentiated primarily by the source
one looks to as grounding one's entry into the elect: the religious
rationalists assert that the individual can cast aside all traditional
wisdom, such as the teachings of any established church, and proceed
to work out his salvation based on Scripture alone, while his secular
counterpart rejects tradition in favor of the revelation offered by
Reason. As Oakeshott wrote:

> This belief, in the authority of 'virtue' and 'wisdom' is, of course, the
> stepbrother of the belief that the 'elect of God' have a right to rule; the
> difference is only that, here, 'enlightenment' is regarded as a 'natural'
> quality and not an endowment of God's grace. (2006: 444)

The Puritans, of course, were a driving force in the English Civil
Wars of 1641–1651. The dispute, initially intellectual and later violent,
between various views of the proper constitution of the English
government, saw monarchial (represented, of course, by Charles I and
Charles II), aristocratic (represented by, for example, the Presbyterians
and City of London alliance), and democratic (represented by the
Independents and the Levellers) views all in play, has great relevance
to the American chapters of our story. As Voegelin wrote:

> The further course of events brought about was to be expected under
> the circumstances: the increased of the relative positions and the
> ensuing friction made it necessary to find formulas for the delimitation
> of jurisdiction. The jurisdictional rules themselves as well as the political
> axioms justifying them are the body of principles of so-called
> constitutional government... Most of the material that assumes an
> important function later in the American constitutional movement is
> already assembled. (Voegelin, 1997b: 78)

The importance for subsequent constitutionalism of these events
hardly can be overstated; as Voegelin wrote:

> The endeavors of the army to secure the gains of the Revolution against
> a Presbyterian-dominated parliament and the City of London resulted
> in the *Agreement of the People*, October 28 1647... a proposal of the army
> that fixed in principle the form and theory of modern constitutions...
> The origin of oppression and misery is seen in 'the obscurity and
> doubtfulness' of earlier legal forms resulting in differences of opinion
> with regard to their interpretation and ultimately in friction and armed
> clashes. (Voegelin, 1997b: 81)

In other words, while subsequent constitutional rationalists saw
themselves as creating an 'empire of reason' based on timeless truths,
in fact, they were drawing upon an historical solution to a set of
contingent circumstances.

The culmination of the struggle between the Parliamentarian forces (representing both the aristocratic and democratic factions in the conflict) and the Royalist party was the execution of King Charles I on January 30, 1649. That event again sets an important precedent for the American founding; to cite Voegelin again, 'The Charge and Sentence were furthermore historically important because they set the pattern for the second bloodless decapitation of an English king, through the American Declaration of Independence...' (1997b: 84).

As a result of the political upheavals of seventeenth-century England, new classes entered the nation's political life, and, as Oakeshott had it, needed a crib sheet. John Locke was able to provide one. Oakeshott said of Locke:

> Some of these writings are genuine works of political vulgarization; they do not altogether deny the existence or worth of a political tradition... but they are abridgements of a tradition, rationalizations purporting to elicit the 'truth' of a tradition and to exhibit it in a set of abstract principles, but from which, nevertheless, the full significance of the tradition inevitably escapes. This is pre-eminently so of Locke's *Second Treatise of Civil Government*... (1991 [1962]: 30).

Although Locke attempted to present his case as the conclusion of rational considerations, to a great extent he was, as Oakeshott pointed out, simply executing a rationalist gloss on the prevailing view of liberty characteristic of the bourgeoisie English landowner of his time. Voegelin was perhaps even more dismissive of the philosophical value of Locke's 'abridgement of a tradition' than was Oakeshott. For instance, in order to offer a rational justification for the traditional rights of Englishmen, Locke resorted to a construction of extremely dubious merit, his theory of 'self-ownership', of which Voegelin wrote:

> Whether God is a proprietor [of man] or not, what really matters is that man is the proprietor of himself. No pretext of derivation is made for this second step... The appearance of man as the proprietor of his person would have fascinated Hobbes had he lived to witness it. He might have classified it as a variety of madness similar to that of the man who believes himself God. The history of political thought does not offer an attack on the dignity of man comparable to this classification of the human person as a capital good, to the undisturbed economic use of which one has a natural right. (1997b: 147–148)

As Oakeshott wrote, Locke, recognizing 'no firm distinction be explanation and prescription... moves, often inadvertently, between these two disparate worlds of discourse, giving a spurious air of principle to his recommendations and a false air of practical applicability to his explanations...' (1998: 163). And this construct did not die with him; the concept of 'self-ownership' plays a key role in the thought of later American libertarians, such as Rothbard, whom we discussed in Chapter 4.

After the shockwaves of the Puritan revolution had subsided and the 'Glorious Revolution' of 1688 had taken place, the next debate in English politics of significance to this work was that between the competing visions of what constituted a healthy polity forwarded by the factions that came to be known as the 'Court' party and the 'Country' party. Here, as with previous episodes we have taken up, the importance of this topic for us rests upon the fact that it continued to reverberate forward in time and across the Atlantic, so that its echoes can be clearly heard in, for instance, the conflict between the Hamiltonian and Jeffersonian ideals for the character of the American republic.

The Country party consisted of those who saw English republican virtue as based upon agrarian life and ties to the land. They perceived a grave danger in the emergence of powerful, wealthy political actors whose status arose not from landholding but from financial speculation. A representative expression of this view was voiced by the Scottish political writer Andrew Fletcher, who described the change in life circumstances facing Britons at the dawn of the 'modern era', and its relationship to politics:

> These things brought a total *alteration* in the way of living, upon which all government depends. It is true, knowledge being mightily increased, and a great curiosity and nicety in everything introduced, men imagined themselves to be gainers in all points, by changing from their frugal and military way of living, which I must confess had some mixture of rudeness and ignorance in it, though not inseparable from it. But at the same time they did not consider the unspeakable evils that are altogether inseparable from an expensive way of living. (Fletcher, 1698: par. 25)

Once more, as during the Roman revolution, we can detect the emergence of ideological traditionalists. The Tory party here plays the role of the *optimates*. As discussed in Chapter 3, an important question here for Oakeshott's theory is whether, once tradition itself becomes another ideology in competition with rival ideologies, is it possible to have anything *but* rationalist politics? Oakeshott himself was not optimistic on this matter. As Gray expressed the dilemma faced by the critic of modern rationalism:

> [Oakeshott] has also shown us that the origins of modern disorder and rationalist illusion go back a long way — to the very beginnings of our

cultural tradition. But, if this is so, then we can hardly hope for any easy or swift release from our condition. Indeed, given that the deformation of thought by rationalist error has now produced a comprehensive loss of confidence in many areas of practical life, it is hard to see how a return to practice can help us, since practice itself is sick. (Gray, 1989: 213)

So, we see that the American founders received the ancient republican political tradition as it was transmitted to them along an increasingly rationalist route passing through Florence and England. Therefore, it should not come as a surprise if they, as Oakeshott contended, had a touch or more of the rationalist flu themselves. But how deeply had the bug entered their systems?

Did the American founders exhibit Oakeshottian rationalism?

Now, let us turn to the question, 'To what extent is Oakeshott correct about the rationalist character of the American founding?' As with Rome, we do not expect a simple yes/no answer either indicating that the above portrait was entirely accurate or completely mistaken, since Oakeshott recognized that he was abstracting what he saw as a broad tendency in American thought, rather than trying to paint a complete portrait of all of its complexity and depth.

To the degree that we find Oakeshott's caricature accurately depicts some of the distinctive features of America at its founding, the next logical question to ask is whether the outcome of this attempt rationally to design a polity generally supports Oakeshott's contention that rationalist schemes never really proceed as the rationalist intends, but, instead, wind up falling back on some tradition of behavior that the rationalist has supposedly eschewed? In other words, how much of the post-founding history of the American republic unfolded according to the founders' plans, and how much of it was the result of 'human action but not of human design'? We will take up the first of the above questions in this chapter, conducting our analysis guided by the themes from 'Rational Conduct' we outlined above, and devote the subsequent chapter to considering the second.

In fact, there have been political theorists, and even political theorists largely sympathetic to Oakeshott's ideas, who have argued that he was mistaken in his understanding of the American founding. For instance, Haddock, disputing Oakeshott's view, wrote, 'To assume that a text like *The Federalist Papers* discounts the significance of experience surely misses the point... [It], surely, is the "pursuit of intimations" at its very best' (2005: 14). So what should we make of this difference of interpretation?

It is worth noting here that, according to Oakeshott, Haddock must be, in one sense, correct: since rationalist politics is, in Oakeshott's understanding, an inaccurate understanding of politics, which cannot actually be put into practice, it follows that the politics of the American founders was necessarily the 'pursuit of intimations' if regarded in terms of how they actually proceeded. The question at hand is not whether the founders, in fact, wound up ordering the new republic's political life by drawing on traditions with which they were familiar — as Oakeshott saw it, they could not have done otherwise, and, as Voegelin pointed out in noting the role of the *Agreement of the People* in subsequent constitutional thinking, they did not do otherwise — but whether they understood themselves as primarily grounding their politics in previous practice or in a rationalist vision of how politics ought to proceed. In other words, was the work of the American founders the pursuit of intimations 'at its very best', as Haddock contends, or was it such a pursuit hamstrung by the embrace of rationalist precepts as to how political conduct should be directed? In this section, we will present evidence from original source material and from historians specializing in revolutionary-era America that suggests Oakeshott, contra Haddock, was more on target in his depiction of the U.S. founding, although, of course, Haddock's point is not without merit.

American political thought and the founding

One of the foremost historians of the American founding, Bernard Bailyn, presents an extensive case for the proposition that the founders were very much children of the Enlightenment, and to a great extent interpreted their revolutionary project in the terms of the concepts bequeathed to them by Enlightenment rationalists. As he describes their intellectual world,

> directly influential in shaping the thought of the Revolutionary generation were the ideas and attitudes associated with the writings of Enlightenment rationalism... The ideas and writings of the leading secular thinkers of the European Enlightenment — reformers and social critics like Voltaire, Russo, and Beccaria as well as conservative analysts like Montesquieu — were quoted everywhere in the colonies by everyone who claimed a broad awareness. (Bailyn, 1992 [1967]: 26–27)

Recognizing the leading role played by the rationalism of the Enlightenment in the drama of the intellectual movement that eventually led the American colonies to embrace rebellion against and independence from their mother country does not lead Bailyn to deny any significant parts to other currents of thought. As Oakeshott claimed the rationalist must, the colonists drew heavily upon various traditions; they were captivated, for instance, by the sagas of republics that had braved the stormy seas of self-governance before them; most of all, as noted earlier in this work, they held the Roman republic before them as an exemplar of republican virtue, and thus perceived a grim and overriding warning in the tragedy of its eventual demise. Another important source of guidance on their journey towards understanding the situation they faced was the political traditions that they had inherited from their mother country, England, in particular, the idea of a polity in which power is distributed among several distinct offices. Bailyn contended, 'The categories within which the colonists thought about the social foundations of politics were inheritances from classical antiquity, reshaped by 17th-century English thought' (1992 [1967]: 272). Nevertheless, as he demonstrates convincingly, Americans of the years immediately preceding and the years comprising the revolution and the devising of the constitution typically reshaped those categories so that they could be incorporated coherently within the conceptual framework erected by the thinkers of the Enlightenment, and, as we noted earlier, the English tradition itself had grown increasingly rationalist, even in its conservative strains.

Seconding Bailyn's view of the importance of Enlightenment rationalism to the American founding, legal scholar Steven D. Smith wrote of the revolutionary era:

> It was a confident, even a cocky age; and the founders did not feel themselves seriously constricted by the claims of modesty as they introduced their newly concocted Constitution to the world. Thomas Jefferson declared it to be 'unquestionably the wisest ever yet presented to men'...

> [Such] sanguine claims were corollary to another — that the Constitution the founders devised was a manifestation of 'reason'. Past governments had always resulted either from violence or from blind accumulations of tradition, ambition, fortune, and fortuity. This Constitution, by contrast, was the product of conscious, mindful design — of deliberation guided by the newly improved science of politics. (Smith, 1998: 3)

And this confidence was not over their ability to handle something they saw as a small matter; rather, they saw themselves as facing 'the most important question that was ever proposed [to] any people under heaven' (Brutus, 1787: 164). What is more, as Smith goes on to note, the great advantages to be conferred by having a written constitution versus the shortcomings of the traditional constitution that the founders saw as having failed Rome was a crucial element in their confidence:

> As noted, the framers believed they had made a great discovery in political science in recognizing the advantages of a written constitution. The exercise of governing reason itself had been made possible by a sort of special dispensation from the usual irrational forces of history and human nature; but... fixing the conclusions of reason was possible only because of, and through the use of, a written legal text. (Smith, 1998: 58)

John Marshall, in fact, declared 'the greatest improvement on political institutions' to be 'a written constitution' (1967: 89). Smith has noted the founders emphasis on technical details, especially the enumerated powers strategy (1998: 45–46), showing clear evidence of the roots of their approach in Bacon and Descartes.

This emphasis on technical matters is noted by another contemporary scholar of this period, Ackerman, who wrote,

> Begin with the Founding, and its Enlightenment pretensions. The Constitutional Convention had its share of compromises, but it was also betting on ideas. Men like James Madison and James Wilson were trying to base their constitution on the best political science of their time. (Ackerman, 2005: 16).

And the Cartesian influence on the founders appears distinctly in the diary of the young John Adams, which 'shows a young man enjoying his liberation from the psychological imperatives and intellectual blinders associated with an inherited culture' (Thompson, 1998: 261). He was, as we quoted Oakeshott characterizing the rationalist earlier in this chapter, aspiring to 'the open, empty or free mind, the mind without disposition'.

In fact, even as the American revolution was unfolding, various contemporary observers realized that there was something novel about its being driven more by abstract principles than any unendurable oppressions, which is not to deny that the colonists also were motivated to rebel by various actual British measures, such as the Stamp Act. Historian Gordon S. Wood quotes Edmund Randolph marvelling that the American rebellion was 'without an immediate oppression, without a cause depending so much on hasty feeling as *theoretic reasoning*' (emphasis mine, quoted in 1998 [1969]: 4). And Wood's own analysis of the character of the rebellion echoes

Oakeshott's view: 'From the outset the colonists attempted to turn their decade-long controversy with England into a vast exercise in the deciphering and applying of the philosophy of their age' (1998 [1969] : 5). Wood further notes that the colonists' writings, peppered as they were with quotes from Enlightenment thinkers and common law judges, displayed 'a more obviously rational, rather than an experiential, understanding of the nature of politics' (1998 [1969]: 7). A paradigmatic example of this rationalist understanding can be found in Hamilton, from *The Federalist* No. 9:

> The science of politics, however, like most other sciences, has received great improvement. The efficacy of various principles is now well understood, which were either not known at all, or imperfectly known to the ancients. The regular distribution of power into distinct departments; the introduction of legislative balances and checks; the institution of courts composed of judges holding their offices during good behavior; the representation of the people in the legislature by deputies of their own election: these are wholly new discoveries, or have made their principal progress towards perfection in modern times. They are means, and powerful means, by which the excellences of republican government may be retained and its imperfections lessened or avoided. (Hamilton, 1787: 340)

Thomas Paine, whose work *Common Sense*, enjoyed an unprecedented popularity in revolutionary-era America, is a particularly salient representation of the rationalist strain of thought at work in the revolution. Paine quite explicitly declares himself a rationalist epigone of Descartes:

> I do not believe in the creed professed by the Jewish church, by the Roman church, by the Greek church, by the Turkish church, by the Protestant church, nor by any church that I know of. My own mind is my own church.

> All national institutions of churches, whether Jewish, Christian or Turkish, appear to me no other than human inventions, set up to terrify and enslave mankind, and monopolize power and profit. (Paine, 1995b: 666)

The state, for Paine, has a rationally discernible purpose that can be specified in advance: 'Here too is the design and end of government, viz. freedom and security' (1995a: 4). To the contrary, as Oakeshott noted, 'there is no way of determining an end for activity in advance of the activity itself' (1991 [1962]: 111). Traditional polities, even if they had the evidence of centuries of lived experience on their side, deserve no presumptive respect: '[T]he constitution of England is so exceedingly complex, that the nation may suffer for years together without being able to discover in which part the fault lies' (1995a: 5). Paine can only see 'tyranny' in the office of the monarch and the institution of the aristocracy; he has no affinity for the Aristotilean-Polybian ideal of a mixed constitution. It is interesting to contrast this paradigmatic rationalist with de Tocqueville, who, despite carrying no banner for the nobility, had the benefit of intimate familiarity with aristocratic governance, and wrote: 'Aristocracies are infinitely more expert in the science of legislation than democracies ever can be. They are possessed of a self-control which protects them from the errors of temporary excitement' (2001: 101).

Slaves and women

Two salient cases of how the American founders were not doing what they thought they were doing are the status of slaves and the status of women at the time of the founding. The founders were purportedly setting up a system of government following the 'self-evident' principle that 'all men are created equal', a form of government that was universally, and not contingently, valid.[2] Therefore, it might seem that the status of African slaves, who were treated much more like farm animals than like human beings, and women, who were denied many of the basic rights of free men, should have troubled them much more than it did.

Now, it would be overstating the case to claim that no one in the founding generation was troubled at all by the status of slaves. As we will see in the next chapter, Jefferson risked his political career to write against slaveholding. During the debates over the adoption of the constitution, Luther Martin declared '*slavery* is *inconsistent* with the *genius* of *republicanism*, and has a tendency to *destroy* those *principles* on which it is *supported*, as it *lessens the sense* of the *equal rights* of mankind, and habituates us to *tyranny* and *oppression*' (1788: 646). Similarly, during the same debates, Simeon Baldwin wrote, 'Humanity will mourn that an odious slavery, cruel in itself, degrading to the dignity of man, and shocking to human nature, is tolerated, and in many instances practised with barbarian cruelty' (1788: 525). And Zachariah

---

[2] Franklin nicely summed up this universalism in the following: 'God grant that not only the love of liberty but a thorough knowledge of the rights of man may pervade all the nations of the earth, so that a philosopher may set his foot anywhere on its surface and say, "This is my country."' (Quoted in Bowen, 1966: 17.)

Johnston called slavery 'the foundation of that impiety and dissipation which have been so much disseminated among our countrymen. If it is totally abolished, it would do much good' (1788: 755). (It is interesting to see that Johnston seems more concerned with the effects on the slave owners than on the slaves.)

But if the recognition that slavery is incompatible with the supposedly universal principles that the founders embraced was only slowly spreading, the notion that the same was true of the status of women was not even on the horizon. I have not discovered a single writer or public speaker addressing this matter at the time of the founding. As Amar contended, 'the question of woman suffrage [was] a nonissue in the late 1780s...' (2006: 393).

It's not rationalism all the way down

As we have stressed, the 'rationalist political actor' is an ideal type, which never appears in history in its pure form, and thus the rationalist component in American founding thought was not unmingled with more traditional elements. Furthermore, the American revolution was not nearly as rationalist as its French counterpart; Sandoz correctly pointed out that:

> In short, then, neither in spirit nor substance was American Whig liberty at all the same as French Jacobin liberty. The American founding generation's resistance to tyranny and claim to liberty as free men echoed themes as old as the civilization itself and constantly recurred to that tradition. Coming during the Golden Age of the classics, the American appeal was grounded in philosophy as expressed in Aristotle, Cicero, Aquinas, Harrington, Locke, and Thomas Reid; in Protestant Christianity in the form of a political theology that mingled religious revival, keeping the faith and fighting the good fight, providential purpose, and a palpable sense of special favor or choseness; and in a constitutionalism that recapitulated all of the arguments seventeenth-century Englishmen had thought valid in resisting the tyranny of Stuart kings by invoking common law liberty back to Magna Carta and the ancient constitution... (Sandoz, 1994: 606)

Of course, Sandoz includes here a number of rationalist elements amidst these 'themes as old as the civilization itself', such as the philosophy of Locke, and the peculiar American form of Protestantism,[3] but his point is still well taken: the American founders, while strongly exhibiting rationalist influence, were not insensitive to

---

[3] And the Stuart kings were hardly tyrants!

the value of tradition—as noted at the beginning of this section, while I believe that Oakeshott's view of the American founding was largely accurate, Haddock's counter-argument that the revolutionaries were pursuing the intimations of their tradition is not baseless.

McDonald sounds another somewhat dissenting note, seeing the founders as *more* rationalist than they knew:

> Now, the Framers of 1787 have been justly acclaimed as a hard-headed, practical band of men who disdained chimerical theory, but they could not entirely disregard these various bodies of theory. The theories had already produced consequences that amounted to prior commitments... Moreover, as was suggested earlier, the theories permeated the thinking of the Framers far more deeply than they cared to admit – and perhaps more deeply than they knew. (McDonald, 1985: 59–60)

McDonald's contention lends support to Haddock's argument that the American founders were 'pursuing intimations', an argument that, as mentioned above, is not really at odds with Oakeshott's view of them as rationalists, since rationalists, even when they most vehemently deny it, are pursuing the intimations of their traditions willy-nilly; moreover, McDonald's suggestion that the founders were not aware of their theoretical commitments largely is contradicted by the quotes and the conclusions of historians specializing in this era cited above.

Noah Webster provides an interesting example of this mixture of rationalist and more pragmatic political thought in the pro-constitution essay he penned during the debates over ratification taking place in 1787. He displayed his more utopian, rationalist side on several occasions, writing, for instance, 'In the formation of our constitution the wisdom of all ages is collected... In short, it is an *empire of reason*' (1787: 129). Or consider his evaluation of representation: 'the moderns have invented the doctrine of *representation*, which seems to be the perfection of human government' (1787: 130). He assures his readers that the method designed for electing the president 'almost precludes the possibility of corruption' (1993a: 135)—it instantiates politics as the crow flies. And he defended the lowering of the age necessary to qualify for the top American political office compared to the Roman case (thirty-five for president versus forty-three for consul) by citing 'the improvements in [political] science' (1993a: 136). The rationalist cheat sheet can make up for a lack of experience! But then he leavens his rationalist dough with statements in which he sounds much more like an ancient Roman than an Enlightenment rationalist: 'Experience is the best instructor—it is better than a thousand theories' (1993a: 132).

It was all planned

Another unprecedented aspect of the American revolution and the roiling cauldron of still forming political ideas that led up to it is how central conspiracy theorizing was in the thought of the colonists. Wood argued:

> The notion of conspiracy was new in Western history. From Sallust's description of Catiline through Machiavelli's lengthy discussion men were familiar with the use of conspiracy in politics. Yet the tendency to see events as the result of a calculated plot, especially events in time of public tumult, appears particularly strong in the eighteenth century, a product, it seems, not only of the political realities and assumptions of the age, but of its very enlightenment... What ever happened in history was intended by men to have happened. (1998 [1969]: 40–41)

The importance of conspiracy theories in the revolution provides another piece of evidence attesting to the rationalist flavor of the rebellion—not only ought the coming, improved social order be deliberately designed around rationally discovered universal principles, but the already existent society was also the intended result of conscious planning. The difference between the old and the new orders was that those who had devised the old one had been corrupt power-seekers, while the emerging, ideal polity would be based on the blueprints of altruists drawn up to maximize the common good. (The ideas of the Scottish Enlightenment, announcing that actual, historical institutions could be, as Adam Ferguson put it, 'the result of *human action*, but not the execution of any *human* design' (1782: par. 381), had apparently not yet made a significant impression on the American mind.)

Does Burke's understanding of the 'American situation' contradict Oakeshott's?

So far, we have presented what I believe to be a strong case that the American founding plausibly can be seen as an example, although of course not an unambiguous example, of rationalism in politics. However, it behooves us to consider a thinker who might seem to contradict that view, namely, Edmund Burke. Burke and Oakeshott are often paired as similar political theorists, both stressing the value of tradition for political practice. But Burke, at least at first glance, seemed to hold a more favorable opinion of the American rebellion than did Oakeshott.

Oakeshott admired the writings of Edmund Burke, and Burke is often seen as a precursor of Oakeshott's thought.[4] Therefore, if Burke's view of the American Revolution is fundamentally at odds with Oakeshott's, as some have contended, then it would present a puzzle that a defender of Oakeshott's view might want to solve.

However, I believe that the appearance of a conflict between Burke and Oakeshott is illusory. What Burke defends in his speech to parliament, 'On Moving his Resolutions for Conciliation with the Colonies,' is not the American Enlightenment project of creating a '*novus ordo seclorum*', but rather the colonists' defense of their traditional rights as Englishmen. His goal was to promote conciliation between Britain and its American colonies within the existing order, and not to support the founding of a new nation based on rationalist precepts.

Burke made his scepticism of 'rationally' designing a polity clear when he wrote, 'I have in general no very exalted opinion of the virtue of Paper Government [i.e., the attempt to devise a form of government through a written constitution], nor of any Politicks, in which the plan is to be wholly separated from the execution' (1993: 209).

Indeed, far from advocating American independence, Burke urged acknowledging the justice of American grievances as a way of keeping America British:

> America, Gentlemen say, is a noble object. It is an object worth fighting for. Certainly it is, if fighting a people be the best way of gaining them... But, I confess... my opinion is much more in favour of prudent management, than of force; considering force not as an odious, but a feeble instrument, for preserving a people so numerous, so active, so growing, so spirited as this, in a profitable and subordinate connexion with us. (Burke, 1993: 220)

It was proper respect for English tradition, and the colonists' birthright as inheritors of that tradition, that Burke offered as a less 'feeble' means for maintaining America's ties to Britain:

> My hold of the Colonies is in the close affection which grows from common names, from kindred blood, from similar privileges, and equal protection. These are ties, which, though light as air, are as strong as links of iron. Let the Colonies always keep their idea of their civil rights associated with your Government;--they will cling and grapple to you, and no force under heaven will be of power to tear them from their allegiance. (Burke, 1993: 265)

---

[4] See, for instance, Roberts and Sutch, 2004: 241–266.

Thus, Burke's sympathy for the American rebellion was grounded in his admiration and respect for English political and cultural traditions, and his view that England's overseas progeny were no less the heirs of that tradition than were their kin who had remained in the mother country, and ought not to be identified with the colonists' project of forming a 'Paper Government' of rationalist origin. While Oakeshott may have lacked, and certainly never expressed, Burke's degree of appreciation for the justice of many of the colonists' complaints, there is no fundamental conflict between his characterization of the American founding as a rationalist enterprise and Burke's defense of the colonial cause.

Conclusion

In summary, while it is certainly the case, as Haddock argued, that the American founders were pursuing the intimations of their traditions, the evidence assembled here suggests that they did so, as Oakeshott argued, under the influence of a strongly rationalist understanding of how 'pursuing' those intimations ought to be done.

We have seen that the increasing rationalism characterizing the Enlightenment played a significant, although not exclusive, role in the ideas leading to the American founding.[5] Given that conclusion, the next logical question for us is whether or not the subsequent history of the American republic supports Oakeshott's thesis that rationalists can never really execute their designs as they intend. We turn to that topic in the next chapter.

---

[5] Although it appeared as this book was being prepared for print, and thus too late to use extensively, it should be noted that Wood (2011) strongly supports the conclusions of this chapter, especially in chapters 4 and 9.

Chapter 8

Were the American Founders Able to Realize Their Design?

In this chapter we will examine two notable episodes from the American founding, the career of Thomas Jefferson and the election of 1800, as well as looking at the overall development of the American political system towards what Arthur Schlesinger (1973) termed 'the imperial presidency', investigating to what extent these stories support Oakeshott's thesis that the rationalist cannot succeed in directing actual conduct according to his rationally derived blueprint. As Oakeshott put it:

> What we are considering is not, in fact, a way of behaving, but a theory of behaviour. And since, as I hope to show, it is an erroneous theory, a misconception of human behaviour, it is impossible to produce any clear and genuine example of behaviour which fits it. If this is 'rational' behaviour, then it is not merely undesirable, it is impossible. Men do not behave in this way, because they cannot. No doubt those who have held this theory have thought that they were describing a possible form of behaviour; and by calling it 'rational', they recommended it as desirable: but they were under an illusion. (1991 [1962]: 108)

So, what light can our case studies shed on the 'illusion' Oakeshott ascribes to the rationalist? We will first turn to the example of a paradigmatically rationalist political theorist, Thomas Jefferson, to begin answering that question.

The case of Jefferson

The tension exhibited in the public career of Thomas Jefferson between the theoretical ideals he espoused and his concrete performances as a political actor is such that the two aspects of his character at times seemed so disconnected that various observers found it hard to imagine them coexisting in one person, presenting a mysterious figure, a riddle so vexing that he has been called the 'American sphinx' (Ellis, 1998). How was it that 'the strict constructionist of constitutional powers purchased Louisiana and adopted the embargo' against Britain and France (Levy, 1963: 16)? In the interest of enforcing his unconstitutional embargo, Jefferson suspended *habeas corpus*, a power reserved for Congress (Levy, 1963: 89), and showed little interest in 'the violations of the Fourth Amendment that resulted from his policies' (Levy, 1963: 105). As a result of his almost fanatical devotion to the embargo, 'the privilege against self-incrimination was rendered meaningless; the right to trial by jury made a farce [and] the protection against property being taken without due process of law ignored' (Levy, 1963: 138), leading Levy to conclude that for Jefferson, in the conduct of his actual, political activity, 'constitutional proprieties were not permitted to interfere with vigorous leadership' (1963: 113); all of this was from a man who once wrote, 'To take a single step beyond the boundaries thus specially drawn around the powers of Congress, is to take possession of a boundless field of power, no longer susceptible of any definition' (Jefferson, 1975: 262).

As mentioned above, in Oakeshott's view it essentially was a foregone conclusion that Jefferson the political practitioner could not live up to the idealized standard of political behavior posited by Jefferson the rational theorist. To support this understanding of Jefferson, we will first attempt to demonstrate that he was, indeed, as paradigmatic an example of the Oakeshottian rationalist as the real world might present, and then illustrate how his actual behavior in power departed significantly from his ideals.

The rationalist Jefferson

We have explored how the writings of leading American-revolution-era thinkers and the conclusions of historians specializing in this era can help us to understand better Oakeshott's critique of rationalism in politics. Now let us look for similar illumination from the particular case of Jefferson.

For instance, after he was admitted to the bar, Jefferson wrote, concerning the then prevailing practice of having neophyte lawyers undergo a period of apprenticeship with a seasoned mentor, that 'the placing of a youth to study with an attorney was rather a prejudice than a help... The only help a youth wants is to be directed what books to read, and in what order to read them' (quoted in Cunningham, 1987: 8). If Jefferson had intended to provide an illustration of the rationalist disdain for practical, tacit learning and his belief in the superiority of explicitly stated technique, which Oakeshott saw as one of the most damaging features of rationalism, he hardly could have done a better job.

Kirk listed, as one of the key components of 'radicalism at the end of the eighteenth century', the tenet, 'Mankind, capable of infinite improvement, is struggling upward toward Elysium, and should fix its gaze always upon the future' (1987: 27). Ellis finds this trait strongly displayed in Jefferson the Declaration writer: 'His several arguments for American independence were all shaped around a central motif, in which the imperfect and inadequate present was contrasted with a perfect and pure future, achievable once the sources of corruption were eliminated' (1998: 69).

When the constitutional debates were in progress, Jefferson's concern was not with whatever reforms to the Articles of Confederation might be appropriate given the specific circumstances of the United States, but rather 'the very ground on which any and all political structures must be constructed' (Ellis, 1998: 119). Jefferson proclaimed that, if the first shot at writing a constitution should go wrong, 'we can assemble with all the coolness of philosophers and set it right' (quoted in Ellis, 1998: 121).

As Ellis documented, Jefferson's rationalist faith led him to seriously misread the events unfolding around him in France in the late 1780s. Even when, in 1789, 'Paris exploded in a series of riots and mob actions', Jefferson 'never questioned his belief in the essential rightness of the cause or the ultimate triumph of its progressive principles' (1998: 130). With the Terror yet ahead, Jefferson serenely wrote, 'Quiet is so well established here that I think there is nothing further to be apprehended' (quoted in Ellis, 1998: 131). The impracticality of Jefferson's idea, formulated in France, that every 'generation' should start with a legislative blank slate led Madison to observe that he was 'engaged in magic more than political philosophy... But whatever practical problems the idea posed, whatever its inadequacies as a realistic rationale for legal reform, [Jefferson] clung to it tenaciously, introducing it in conversations and letters for the rest of his life' (Ellis, 1998: 132).

Jefferson also was confident in the power of abstract thought to enumerate a small set of fundamental and morally inviolable human rights. Furthermore, the state's observance of the limits to its legitimate scope of action implied by the existence of those rights could be enforced by explicitly forbidding it from violating them in its constitution. For example, in a letter to Madison, he wrote, 'A bill of rights is what the people are entitled to against every government on earth, general or particular, & what no just government should refuse, or rest on inferences' (quoted in Dunn, 2006: 281).

The practical Jefferson

In this section we will examine how Jefferson's concrete actions, both as an office-holder and in his personal affairs, were often strikingly at odds with his more theoretical pronouncements. We will limit our attention to a handful of especially notable episodes from his life, in particular: his inconsistency on the matter of slavery, the lack of regard for the freedom of the press he displayed in his presidential actions, his decision to purchase the Louisiana territory from France despite recognizing that he lacked the constitutional authority to do so, his violation of several of the basic principles of Anglo-American law in seeking to punish the leaders of the alleged 'Burr Conspiracy', and the increasingly repressive measures he adopted in pursuing his obsessive quest to make the embargo of 1808–1809 work as he had intended it to. No doubt, other illustrative examples of this divergence between Jeffersonian theory and practice could be located.

Slavery

Jefferson was among the earliest of prominent American statesmen to publically support abolishing the institution of slavery in the New World. In the late 1770s, as a member of the Virginia House of Delegates, he introduced 'a bill to emancipate all slaves born after the passage of [that] act' (Cunningham, 1987: 61), but he failed to persuade a sufficient number of legislators of its wisdom and the measure was stillborn. Throughout the early 1780s, Jefferson forwarded proposals for 'an end to the slave trade, the prohibition of slavery in all Western territories and the establishment of a fixed date, he suggested 1800, after which all newly born children of slaves would be emancipated' (Ellis, 1998: 172). In his *Notes on the State of Virginia,* a work published in 1785, which, in fact, would turn out to be the only book of Jefferson's released for public consumption during his life, he wrote:

There must doubtless be an unhappy influence on the manners of our people produced by the existence of slavery among us. The whole commerce between master and slave is a perpetual exercise of the most boisterous passions, the most unremitting despotism on the one part, and degrading submission on the other.... [Along] with the morals of the people, their industry also is destroyed. For in a warm climate, no man will labor for himself who can make another labor for him... And can the liberties of a nation be thought secure when we have removed their only firm basis, a conviction in the minds of the people that these liberties are of the gift of God? That they are not to be violated but with His wrath? Indeed I tremble for my country when I reflect that God is just... (quoted in Dunn, 2006: 275–276)

Not only did Jefferson present an eloquent and stirring condemnation of slavery, but he published those uncompromising words despite his serious fears, which he voiced in a letter to Madison, that their expression would 'be displeasing to the country [and] perhaps to the [Virginia] assembly or to some who lead it. I do not wish to be exposed to their censure...' (quoted in Ellis, 1998: 101).

However, the same man whose theoretical case against slavery justifies his being honored as a visionary thinker at the leading edge of the advance of human rights in his day, confoundingly continued, throughout his adult life, to own roughly 200 slaves, whom he employed as laborers on his farms and as his personal servants (Ellis, 1998: 171). Furthermore, it now appears nearly certain that he sired several children by one of his slaves, engaging in a sexual relationship that, given the vastly greater possibilities for autonomously directing the course of the affair available to the master compared to the highly restricted set of options facing his slave, could hardly be deemed consensual. How can we comprehend the existence of this yawning, seemingly unbridgeable, chasm isolating the country inhabited by Jefferson the theorist from the land on the other side of the divide, home to Jefferson the practical actor? I propose that Oakeshott's abstraction of the rationalist ideal type out of the welter of all 'goings-on' can be employed to dispel, at least partially, some of the fog obscuring the figure of our subject.

In pursuing the implications of his foundational political principles, Jefferson realized that the existence of fellow humans living in bondage was incompatible with his vision of the ideal society, one composed of individuals free to direct their own lives and to choose for themselves how they would interact with others.

Exhibiting laudable intellectual honesty and courage, Jefferson accepted and publically endorsed that conclusion, even while recognizing that his position would anger many of those upon whom his future political success would depend. This puzzling gap between Jefferson's theory and practice becomes more explicable in light of Oakeshott's thesis that the rationalist can never put his program into practice. It might be argued, against that suggestion, that it is simpler to view him as a mere hypocrite, spouting noble-sounding ideas but too self-interested to put them into practice. That Jefferson risked his career in publically condemning slavery is strong evidence, I believe, that this simple hypothesis won't do. Surely no simple hypocrite would go out on a limb as Jefferson did in this instance?

But, in spite of this admirable courage in his theorizing, Jefferson never was able to bring his concrete actions into line with his abstract principles. Whatever inclinations he might have felt to resolve that conflict were stifled by his failure to conceive of how he could achieve the domestic utopia he sought without the labor of his own slaves, or how the emancipation called for by his theories could be made tenable in practice. His rationalist ideals simply were too disconnected from his practical situation for him to be able to integrate the two.

Freedom of the press

Jefferson the theorist assigned a prominent role to a free press in protecting republican liberty from its would-be usurpers, but Jefferson the practitioner was far less sanguine concerning the effects of allowing unrestricted criticism of government agents. When faced with harsh critiques of his own actions or proposals as president, he responded by attempting to use the coercive powers of the state to silence his most vociferous and nettlesome opponents.

As Levy pointed out, in Jefferson's theoretical understanding of governance, 'The concept of sedition could exist only in a relationship based on inferiority, when people were subjects rather than sovereigns and their criticism implied contempt of their master' (1963: 54). He also noted, '[Jefferson's] draft constitution for Virginia in 1783 proposed that the press "shall be subject to no other restraint than liableness to legal prosecution for false facts printed and published"' (1963: 46). And Jefferson was a leading opponent of the Adam government's Sedition Act.

Nevertheless, when faced with the practical difficulties involved in actually governing, he was unable to realize his rationalist ideals. For example, he allowed cases brought by Judge Pierpont Edwards against various Federalists for seditious libel of the president (Jefferson) to proceed for some time; Levy wrote: 'he learned of [the cases] in

December of 1806, nearly four months before they were scheduled for trial, and he did not disapprove of them until expediency forced him to do so some months later' (1963: 62).

As Levy noted:

> [Jefferson] cared deeply for the intellectual liberty of religious, scientific, or philosophical heretics, but not for the freedom of opinion of political heretics — unless political heresies of his own adherence were involved... His consistent recognition of the concept of verbal political crimes throughout the Revolution continued in the period of peace that followed. (1963: 45–46)

The quite plausible idea that Jefferson was merely a hypocrite on this topic again is not supported by the historical evidence; as Bailyn put it, 'He truly wished for free speech and a free press; but the complexity of these liberal goals, their inner ambiguities in application, came to him only gradually' (2003: 53). These were not 'principles' susceptible to deductive application, but the 'admitted goods' of America's political life, the attainment of any one of which must be balanced against the attainment of other such goods. Levy pointed out, 'Jefferson's diagnosis of the ills of the press lacked a realistic understanding of partisan politics' (1963: 67); once again, we see the difficulty rationalism causes its adherents in their attempts to deal with practical reality. In brief, as a rationalist theorist, Jefferson was quite sincere about the freedom of the press, but when it came time to put his ideals into practice, he was unable to do so.

The Louisiana purchase

The opportunity to purchase most of France's then remaining North American colonial territory, which arose in 1803, as Napoleon sought to raise funds to support his armies in Europe, presented Jefferson with a conundrum. The U.S. Constitution clearly did not contain any provision authorizing the president to expand the territory of the nation; on the other hand, removing a European power's ability to interfere in American affairs from an established position along the country's borders, as well as the opening of a vast new territory to American settlement, offered obvious practical benefits to the new republic.

The status of the Louisiana territory, and particularly of the key port city of New Orleans, became urgent when the Jefferson learned through channels that Spain was on the verge of returning the territory to France. Spanish possession of Louisiana, especially given the Spanish-American treaty granting American merchants the right to deposit their goods at New Orleans while they were transferred from river-going to ocean-going vessels, and Spain's relatively indifferent attitude towards the territory, was relatively unproblematic. But the possible transfer of the territory to France, a militarily expansive nation recently at war with Great Britain, was very troublesome. Jefferson wrote his Minister to France, Robert R. Livingston, that it would be 'impossible that France and the U.S. can continue long friends when they meet in so irritable a position... From [the moment France took control of New Orleans] we must marry ourselves to the British fleet and nation' (quoted in Cunningham, 1987: 260). In response to this threat, Jefferson dispatched his friend James Monroe to France, with the secret mission of trying to purchase New Orleans and perhaps West Florida from that nation. To Monroe's surprise, Napoleon, having abandoned his plan for a new French empire in the Americas and facing a depleted treasury on the eve of renewed conflict with Britain, offered to sell the United States the entire Louisiana territory, which would more than double the size of America. Monroe swiftly signed on to the deal.

Jefferson acknowledged one small problem in seeking Senate approval for the treaty: 'The general government has no powers but such as the constitution has given it; and it has not given it a power of holding foreign territory, and still less of incorporating it into the Union' (quoted in Cunningham, 1987: 265–266). While at first he conceived of a constitutional amendment being passed to permit the purchase, he finally became convinced that 'the extraordinary circumstances of the moment required that Congress act without waiting for an amendment' (Cunningham, 1987: 266) — successful practical reasoning requires flexibility in dealing with just such contingencies. The friendly Republican majorities in both houses of Congress did not question their president's decision or belabor the constitutional niceties of the matter; the Senate approved the treaty in an almost straight party-line vote and the House allocated the funds necessary for the purchase.

As Bailyn wrote of this episode:

> He was a fervent constitutionalist, indeed a strict and narrow constructionist, especially in fighting the Alien and Sedition Acts in 1798; but five years later, in arranging for the purchase of Louisiana, he deliberately exceeded the bounds of the Constitution. 'The less we say about the constitutional difficulties respecting Louisiana', he told Madison, his secretary of state, 'the better'. (Bailyn, 2003: 41)

It was perhaps fortunate for the fledgling nation that the constitutional theorist lost out to the pragmatic politician in this case; whether or not that is so, once again Jefferson found his practical sense at odds with his rationalist principles, and acted according to sense.

The Burr conspiracy

Rationalists, Oakeshott contended, may think they are following precepts derived, starting from a *tabula rasa*, by 'pure' reasoning, but, in fact, they are always responding to contingencies by employing elements of learned traditions of activity. Consider, in light of that, the history of Jefferson and Aaron Burr. Jefferson regarded Burr, who had served as his vice president during his first term, as an unscrupulous schemer who presented a danger to the fledgling American republic. He had denied Burr a second term as vice president in 1804, and then had worked behind the scenes to see his bid for the governorship of New York defeated. But, however sincere were his misgivings in regards to Burr's character, when Jefferson saw a chance to bring his opponent down, after an alleged plot by Burr to separate the Western territories of the United States from the rest of the nation, from there invade Mexico, and form his own empire as a result, in pursuit of his quarry Jefferson egregiously violated the legal principles he theoretically embraced. For Jefferson, Wheelan wrote, 'it mattered little that Burr's expedition, when captured on the Mississippi River above New Orleans... had turned out to be pathetically small – just sixty men, women, and children' (2005: 2), and it mattered little that the chief evidence against Burr came from supposed co-conspirators, such as General James Wilkinson, whose reputation was not above reproach.

Historians still dispute what the true goal of Burr's expedition was – Burr himself claimed he only intended to take possession of land in Texas that had been granted to him by the Spanish government. However, the problem with Jefferson's conduct during this case is not a matter of whether Burr was truly guilty of treason, or whether Jefferson truly thought him so; it is that, as Levy wrote:

> Having convicted Burr before the bar of public opinion prior to his apprehension, the first Magistrate proceeded relentlessly to mobilize executive resources to prove the preconceived guilt... The object was not to secure Burr's guilt – or innocence – fairly determined, but to secure a conviction, no matter how, on the charge of high treason. (Levy, 1963: 71)

Jefferson publically declared, prior to Burr's trial, that the defendant's 'guilt is placed beyond question' (quoted in Wheelan, 2005: 8). Levy commented upon such statements, writing: 'Jefferson... was satisfied with mere probable suspicion as to the accused's guilt, whereas the law required proof of probable guilt before commitment and a prima fascia case of guilt before trial' (1963: 77).

In pursuing Burr, the Jefferson administration

> would spend nearly $100,000, without congressional authorization, the rough equivalent of $2 million today. Besides throwing open the executive purse, the president had sent [U.S. Attorney] Hay a sheaf of blank pardons. Use them, he instructed Hay, 'at your discretion, if you should find a defect of evidence, and believe that this would supply it...' (Wheelan, 2005: 100)

Wilkinson, whom Jefferson had appointed governor of the Territory of Louisiana, despite Wilkinson's having been suspected of earlier plotting to separate Kentucky and Tennessee from the union, went after Burr's purported co-conspirators via distinctly unconstitutional means, subjecting them to military imprisonment and bypassing normal channels of judicial review. But, Levy wrote, 'Jefferson's reaction to his general's conduct... was to applaud a job well done... Jefferson measured Wilkinson's arrests by neither legal nor moral standards, but only by the extent by which public opinion would support them' (1963: 83–84).

Jefferson, aware of the questionable legal standards involved in those arrests, sent a message to Congress hinting, as Levy put it, that 'the prisoners would surely be freed on writs of habeas corpus as soon as military jurisdiction over them ended' (1963: 86). In response, Levy wrote:

> On receiving this message, the Senate, the following day, acted with unbelievable haste to please the President... a bill was quickly passed, without debate, suspending the writ of habeas corpus for three months in all cases of persons charged with treason or other high crimes against the United States and arrested or imprisoned on authority of the President or anyone acting under his direction... (Levy, 1963: 85–86)

The jury in Burr's trial, following the opinion of Chief Justice John Marshall that to be guilty of treason required an overt act and not mere intention, in the end acquitted Burr, much to Jefferson's chagrin. As Wheelan summed up this episode:

> From habits of thinking acquired during the systematic eradication of Burr's political hopes, Jefferson was able to contrive treason out of a slipshod filibuster, and, without a shred of solid evidence, fix it thus in

the public mind... Had a more pliable judge than... Marshall presided over Burr's treason trial, the Judiciary might have evolved into an instrument of repression, as it is in other nations. (Wheelan, 2005: 285)

The embargo

Although, as Oakeshott noted, the rationalist cannot put his principles into practice, the attempt to do so is not without consequences. During Jefferson's second term, the United States found itself caught in the middle of the ongoing conflict between France and Great Britain. As Levy put it, both of 'the two mightiest powers in the world had been guilty of acts warranting a declaration of war by the United States' (1963: 93). But Jefferson, no doubt motivated by his theoretical conviction of the danger that embracing militarism posed to a people's liberties, desperately sought to avoid taking that route. His alternative response to those provocations relied on attacking the aggressors' pocketbooks by denying them the benefits of trade with Americans. Levy argued:

> The success of the embargo depended ultimately on the willingness of a free people to suffer acute economic privation for a great national goal... [However,] widespread coercion of Americans to enforce a policy of passive resistance [by the U.S. to Britain and France] resulted in failure of the policy. Jefferson needed more than a substitute for war; he also needed a substitute for the patriotic behavior stimulated by war. (Levy, 1963: 93)

Convinced that the rational justification for the course he had chosen was self-evident, Jefferson failed to present the American people with a case for the embargo that could gain their emotional willingness to endure the hardships it entailed. Increasingly frustrated by their lack of cooperation with what he saw as the only reasonable method of addressing the nation's dilemma, he turned to ever more authoritarian means of forcing his solution on an 'irrationally' recalcitrant populace, employing measures wildly ignoring the boundaries his theories had set for the domain within which the state may legitimately exercise its coercive powers. Jefferson biographer Dumas Malone contended that Jefferson was 'so obsessed with the immediate problem of making the embargo work as to be unmindful of republican theory' (quoted in Cunnningham,1987: 315).

Jefferson went even further in seeking to avoid the theoretical evil of war. Levy characterized the Fifth Embargo Act of 1809 as being 'to this day... the most repressive and unconstitutional legislation ever enacted by Congress in time of peace' (1963: 139). He argues that 'military preparedness against France and England was actually a policy of realism' (1963: 140), in contrast to the 'noble dream to attempt to use pacific sanctions against them' (1963: 93). But Jefferson, in typical rationalist fashion, mistook his theoretical case against militarism and standing armies, which was not without its merits, for an unambiguous guide to action rather than one consideration to be weighed against others, and thus was driven to adopt policies far more directly and immediately destructive of republican liberty than were the dangers they sought to preclude. And those policies did not even counterbalance the loss of freedom they imposed on American citizens with some geopolitical benefit; as Levy concluded, 'As a means of peaceably coercing European powers to rescind their harmful decrees against American commerce, the embargo policy was a total failure' (1963: 140). It 'was the plan of an idealist, trapped and bewildered by the foreign situation, who gambled the nation's welfare on the outcome of an unrealistic scheme' (1963: 95). Once again, Jefferson the practical politician could not actualize the ideas of Jefferson the rationalist theorist, the difference in this case being that he tried to cling to his ideology despite its disastrous practical consequences.

Is hypocrisy a reasonable explanation for the Jeffersonian paradox?

While this question was raised above, I think it is salutary to revisit it a final time. For some of those who fought for American independence, Jefferson's behavior in office was interpreted as just one more manifestation of an ongoing betrayal, on the part of its self-appointed leaders, of the revolution's ideals, a betrayal that had commenced even before the military conflict with Britain had been decided. As Alfred Young wrote:

> Many [ex-Revolutionary soldiers] would have shared the sense of the Revolution as not fulfilling its promises, as expressed by Herman Husband, leader of two backcountry rebellions in North Carolina in the 1770s and in western Pennsylvania in the 1790s that were both put down with force: 'In Every Revolution, the people at large are called upon to assist true Liberty', but when 'the foreign oppressor is thrown off, learned and designing men' assume power to the detriment of the 'laboring people'. (Young, 2006: 3)

However, I believe that the historical evidence suggests that the gulf separating the ideals espoused by Jefferson the theorist and the actual behavior of Jefferson the politician and practical actor represent not so much a betrayal as an unavoidable consequence of the rationalist's inability to realize the abstract designs he has sketched, while working in a realm of pure thought standing apart from all circumstantial contingencies and inherited practices, of the real world. From this perspective, Jefferson appears, not as a schemer cynically offering the people whatever platitudes they find appealing whilst blithely disregarding his own words in practice, but as an unfortunate victim of the rationalist fantasy that had so enraptured his age, and which still casts its spell over our own time. As Bailyn contended:

> If he had been less responsive to the principles of freedom as they had emerged in the initial struggle with Britain, less committed to the vision of a golden age, and more cautious in seeking it, he might, when in positions of power, have been less likely to have had to modify or complicate or contradict his principles in attempting, in his efficient way, to effect them, and so in the end might have seemed more consistent and less likely to be thought hypocritical...

> [Jefferson had] caught a vision, as a precocious leader of the American Revolution, of a comprehensive Enlightenment ideal, a glimpse of what a wholly enlightened world might be, and strove to make it real, discovering as he did so the intractable dilemmas. Repeatedly he saw a pure vision, conceptualized and verbalized it brilliantly, and then struggled to relate it to reality, shifting, twisting, maneuvering backward and forward as he did so. (Bailyn, 2003: 46–47)

Jefferson was an ideological rationalist, who hoped that a constitution, incorporating a bill of rights, could be binding on the future actions of the new government he had helped to create. However, when faced with the practical tasks of governing an actual polity, he energetically violated the very same rights that Jefferson the theorist had viewed as sacred. As we have pointed out above, we have here a paradigmatic case of Oakeshott's dictum that the rationalist cannot really follow his rational scheme; rather, his concrete practice will always draw far more on available tradition than he intends: in the case of Jefferson, that tradition was one of a single, sovereign ruler doing whatever he saw as being in the best interests of his realm.

The crisis of the election of 1800

The election of 1800 presents a notable instance of the inability of rationalist planners to devise a scheme that could foresee the multitudinous contingencies thrown up by actual political practice, again offering an illustration of Oakeshott's contention that the rationalist program is incapable of being implemented as the rationalist planner intends it to be. The fledging American republic survived the crisis due to the practical political wisdom marshalled by a handful of key players, who were impeded in their efforts by the written constitution. As Bruce Ackerman contended, in his study of this episode, which we will draw upon heavily in this section,

> If the nation survived the crisis, it wasn't because the Constitution provided clear rules for the political game. The Framers of 1787 made an alarming number of technical mistakes that invited partisans to inflame an already explosive situation. (Ackerman, 2005: 4)

The American founders had failed to foresee the rise of party politics — indeed, they had viewed parties as damaging 'factions', to be studiously avoided. Ackerman wrote,

> The 1787 text reveals the Founders at their Enlightenment best — and worst. If politics had evolved as they had expected, the Founders' design of the electoral college would have proved to be very clever. But unfortunately their scheme was not very robust and quickly collapsed under the weight of the rising party system. (Ackerman, 2005: 27)

The system they devised for selecting the president and vice president envisioned an open election in which the cream of the nation's political crop competed for those positions in the absence of party allegiance. Therefore, when, by 1800, the American political landscape was dominated by two rival parties, the Federalists and the Republicans, the founders' mechanisms proved ill-suited to the new reality. Per Ackerman, 'When they looked at the presidency, the Convention feared a demagogue, and it designed the electoral college to reduce the chances that a political opportunist could ascend to power. But the onset of party politics undermined its basic premises' (2005: 5).

The genesis of the crisis was the founders' scheme to avoid the election of a demagogue by having citizens vote, not directly for the president, but for electors who would make up an 'electoral college'. These prominent and experienced electors were thought to be less susceptible to the seduction of demagoguery than was the common man in the street. Each voter in the electoral college would cast two votes, one of which had to be for a candidate not from the elector's home state, that requirement being meant to restrict the influence of regional partisanship. The highest vote getter would be awarded the presidency, and the runner-up the vice presidency. As Ackerman describes it, 'The aim of this *Enlightenment machine* was to create the artificial impression that the president was a man of truly national character even if the pickings were pretty slim' (2005: 28, emphasis mine). The electors, each voting for those who were, based on their individual judgments, the best candidates to lead the American republic, would naturally divide up their votes amongst a variety of candidates, making a tie highly unlikely.

However, the rise of party politics changed those odds dramatically. With the electors running as party partisans, by 1800 being representatives of parties that had put forward their own choices for those two offices, they would tend to vote as a block for the two candidates nominated by their party. And that is exactly what happened in the election of 1800, so that the victorious Republican electors all voted for both Jefferson and Burr, resulting in an Electoral College tie for the presidency. While the possibility of such an outcome had not totally eluded the writers of the constitution, it turned out that they had not dealt with it adequately. As Ackerman wrote, 'In designing the presidency, the Framers made blunder after blunder...' (2005: 14). For one thing, the office given the task of supervising the count of presidential ballots was that of the president of the Senate — in other words, the vice president, who, in the specific case we are examining, turned out to be Jefferson himself. Per Ackerman:

> The vice president may be a fine ceremonial leader of the Senate, but he is a natural candidate in the next presidential contest. It is a bad mistake to designate him as the presiding officer of the counting of electoral votes... this mistake was exacerbated by another blunder. The Constitution doesn't clearly say what should happen once a vote-counting problem arises. (Ackerman, 2005: 58)

And a vote-counting problem did arise! The ballot of the electors from the state of Georgia failed to meet the technical requirements for a valid ballot laid out in the constitution, as they lacked the signatures of the electors in question. And without the four electoral votes of Georgia's delegation supporting the Republican candidates, the constitution required that a House run-off, the technique that had been devised to deal with the Electoral College failing to choose a clear victor in an election, would have had to include the Federalist candidates for president — who were, of course, preferred by the lame-duck, Federalist-controlled House — in addition to Jefferson and Burr. As Ackerman notes,

> the Framers mistakenly allowed the retiring president and Congress to control affairs for an extended lame-duck period after they lost an election. This gave the Federalists a chance to use their last days in

power to push for a statute that would have authorized their new chief justice to displace Jefferson as president of the United States. (Ackerman, 2005: 14)

The crucial question raised by Georgia's nonconformant ballots was whether or not an entire state should be disqualified from having a voice in choosing the next president simply because of a procedural error, even though there was little doubt as to the residents' true choice in the matter. Jefferson, due to the Framers' errors, was placed in the awkward position of having to act as judge over a legal question in which he was personally far from neutral. It was, in fact, not even clear as to whether he had the constitutional authority to make such a decision; Ackerman argued that 'the truth is that the Framers had utterly failed to resolve the issue, leaving it wrapped in the mystery of the passive voice: "and the Votes shall then be counted"' (2005: 59). But authorized or not, Jefferson decided to admit Georgia's votes despite their technical invalidity, a decision that Ackerman commended in light of the possibility that, had Jefferson not done so, the Federalists might have been able to elect a member of their party to the office, in clear contravention of the choice of the American people.

However, admitting Georgia's votes, while eliminating the Federalist candidates from contention, did nothing to break the tie between Jefferson and Burr. Attempts to resolve the crisis continued into the middle of February 1801. While the constitution had tasked the (lame-duck) House of Representatives with the role of breaking the deadlock, it mandated that the House's choice be made, not by a simple majority of representatives, but by a majority of states, with the votes of a state's representatives aggregated. Because of that requirement, the Federalists were able to prevent either candidate from emerging victorious for the first 35 ballots. The conflict grew so heated that both some Federalist-leaning and some Republican-leaning states threatened to send their militias marching on Washington should the ultimate outcome displease them. There were even calls for a new Constitutional Convention, which would have meant the new republic would have operated under three different constitutions in just twenty years. As the end of the sitting president's term drew near, Ackerman points out that quite another design flaw in the constitution became apparent:

If neither Jefferson nor Burr won nine [out of 16 states'] votes by March 4, who would become president at the end of Adams's term in office? In its rush to the finish line, the Convention missed this issue entirely. In a breathtaking show of incompetent draftsmanship, the delegates failed to provide an explicit answer to this obvious question. (Ackerman, 2005: 37)

Rushing to fill this void, an essay, published under the pseudonym 'Horatius', appeared in Washington papers arguing that the outgoing Federalist congress ought to appoint an interim president pending the resolution of the disputed election. The most obvious choice to fill this position was the sitting secretary of state and newly appointed chief justice of the Supreme Court, John Marshall. And Ackerman makes a plausible case that 'Horatio' was none other than Marshall himself, so that, 'as the Founding system spun out of control, Marshall loomed as acting secretary of state, permanent chief justice of the Supreme Court, and potential interim president of the United States!' (2005: 45)

As it turned out, the crisis was resolved, without civil war or constitutional chaos, by means of the practical political sense possessed by some of the key actors in the fray. Aaron Burr, for instance, might well have gained the presidency had he chosen to travel down from Albany to Washington to lobby Federalist congressmen to choose him as the lesser evil in comparison to Jefferson, who was clearly the more radically Republican of the two. But Burr, following an 'old-fashioned set of conventions', chose to remain in Albany, since 'under the classical republican view, it was utterly wrong for a would-be [George] Washington to launch an aggressive campaign for office' (Ackerman, 2005: 103). And the congressman who ultimately broke the deadlock, James Bayard, followed 'classical Republican norms' in negotiating a resolution with Jefferson (Ackerman, 2005: 106). Thus, it was pragmatic political traditions, rather than formal, constitutional dictums, that enabled the fledgling republic to survive this crisis.

Ackerman makes a strong case that the crisis in question transformed the written American constitution in fundamental ways. One is that the Republicans' frequent invocations of having a popular mandate for their actions gave rise to the continuing notion that presidential elections are an expression of 'the will of the people', and justify modifying the prevailing interpretation of the constitution. As he put it, 'Although America pulled back from the brink in 1801, the rise of the plebiscitarian presidency triggered institutional confrontations that transformed basic constitutional arrangements by the end of the decade, and in ways that remain relevant today' (2005: 5). This transformation meant that the actual, working constitution guiding American politics was the result of pragmatic compromises, differing significantly from the rationalist design of the founders. This idea of a popular mandate was especially important during the presidencies of Lincoln, in denying the South a right to secession; in that of Franklin Roosevelt, in pushing through the reforms of the New Deal over objections from the Supreme Court; and in the recent one of

George W. Bush, in justifying the unprecedented measures his administration employed in pursuing the 'War on terror'. We will touch upon these episodes in the next section of this chapter.

Jefferson continued to push the idea that 'the people' had rejected the Federalist vision of how the United States ought to be governed, and sought to purge the courts, the last bastion of Federalist power, of the entrenched incumbents who stood in the way of the Republican program. The first assault was the impeachment of District Judge John Pickering, who, although senile and alcoholic, apparently had not committed any 'high crimes and misdemeanors', which transgressions were the Constitution's explicit standard for justifying impeachment. The Senate, as Ackerman notes, 'refused to delay [Pickering's trial], despite the absence of Pickering or his lawyer' (2005: 200), and removed the judge in a mostly party-line vote.

Ackerman continues, 'John Randolph, a manager of Pickering's impeachment... within an hour of his success in persuading the Senate to "remove" Pickering... gained the support of the overwhelming Republican majority in the House to impeach Samuel Chase of the Supreme Court' (2005: 201). Chase was targeted because he had harshly criticized the Republican administration's decision to strip 16 federal circuit judges, whom the Federalists had appointed on the eve of turning over power, of their offices. In a blatant attempt by the Jeffersonians to stifle political speech, based on the charge that Chase's remarks were 'seditious', he was impeached on a party-line vote, despite the fact that the list of charges against him (a list that was subsequently to be revised) was not drawn up until three weeks after that vote. While the attempt to remove a Supreme Court justice from office on political grounds was in progress, the Republicans succeeded in using their legislative majorities to push through the Twelfth Amendment to the U.S. Constitution, which changed the voting procedure of the Electoral College so that each elector cast, not two votes for president, but one for president and one for vice president. That amendment locked in place the system of party politics that the authors of the constitution had sought so vigorously to resist.

Jefferson attempted to influence the vote in the Senate by rewarding friends of the lame-duck vice president, Aaron Burr, who was presiding over the impeachment trial, with political appointments, and by seeking to have the murder charges that followed Burr's killing of Alexander Hamilton in a duel dropped (see Ackerman, 2005: 213), despite the enmity that existed between the two men, an enmity that later, as described above, would lead Jefferson to seek Burr's execution for treason on very shaky grounds. Nevertheless, the Senate ultimately failed to convict Chase on any of the three charges brought against him. This defeat did not prompt Jefferson to abandon his efforts to cleanse the system of Federalist heretics; as Ackerman wrote:

> Despite the failure of impeachment, Jefferson continued to plot further assaults on the Court. But his capacity for presidential leadership diminished over time, and a new institutional equilibrium was emerging: president and party would count for a great deal in the constitutional order that the Founders had never imagined; but judicial independence would survive... (Ackerman, 2005: 10)

One of the chief reasons for the acquittal of Chase, according to Ackerman, was the rise of divisions between the Republican congressional majority and the Republican administration. As he pointed out:

> The Founders did not "intend" this outcome: since they had no inkling of a national party system, they did not consider how such a system would interact with the separation of powers. Nonetheless, the conjunction of the congressionalist legacy of 1787 with the new presidentialism of 1801 provides an introduction to a distinctive dynamic that would recur throughout the next two centuries of American history. (Ackerman, 2005: 217)

Once again, we see that the actual, functioning constitution of the United States was not the one designed by the founders, but was the result of political actors' attempts to cope with the unforeseen contingencies of practical politics.

For our purposes, the question of whether the 'new' constitution arrived at through these pragmatic political maneuverings was some sort of 'betrayal' of the founders' principles, or a sensible modification of their vision in light of new circumstances, is irrelevant. What is important to us is that the founders, just as Oakeshott contended was true of all rationalists, were not able to implement their design as they had planned, despite their best efforts to render their framework inviolable. As noted earlier in the present chapter, rationalism, per Oakeshott, is not an inferior way of conducting political life, but an impossible one, since it is based on a mistaken theory of how human conduct proceeds. The general accuracy of his thesis is lent support by the fact that the actual course of the American polity turned out to be steered by a complex blend of ideas incorporated in the original, written constitution and the quite significant modifications of those ideas achieved in the nitty-gritty fray of practical political affairs, rather than being constrained by the explicit, rationalist principles laid out in the founding document.

The continuing failure of the constitution to realize its authors' designs

The failure of the U.S. Constitution to 'perform' as the founders expected it to hardly ceased with these early episodes. Indeed, an ongoing theme in American politics has been how greatly constitutional interpretation has differed from 'original intention'. A few quotes from the founders suffice to show how different the modern vision of the proper scope of the federal government is from what theirs was. For instance, juxtapose the modern welfare states and the numerous American international relief efforts with this quote from Madison, contemplating federal relief for the St. Domingo refugees: 'Charity is no part of the legislative duty of the government. It would puzzle any gentleman to lay his finger on any part of the Constitution which would authorize the government to interpose in the relief of the St. Domingo sufferers' (Madison, 1794: par. 1).

Or consider what Jefferson held to be the proper scope of government:

[A] wise and frugal Government, which shall restrain men from injuring one another, shall leave them otherwise free to regulate their own pursuits of industry and improvement, and shall not take from the mouth of labor the bread it has earned. This is the sum of good government, and this is necessary to close the circle of our felicities. (Jefferson, 1989: par. 3)

Restraining men from injuring one another — that's it! And while it is no doubt true that a founder such as Hamilton took a somewhat more expansive view of the role of the new federal government, it is hard to imagine that even he would recognize the contemporary, enormous range of federal activities as his legitimate offspring.

Of course, conservatives bemoan the change from that founding vision as a betrayal and liberals generally welcome it as a sign that Americans have a 'living constitution'. However, according to Oakeshott, there was never any chance that 'original intention' — assuming such a united intention existed, at least on some topics — could have been followed, since rationalists can never implement their designs as intended. To conclude this section, let us examine just a few more examples of how this point has been illustrated in U.S. history.

In *The Cult of the Presidency*, Gene Healy has an interesting discussion of the early debate over the role of the U.S. president. John Adams sought a role for the president as a sort of elected monarch, and contended that foreign leaders would not respect anyone with such a plebian title as 'president': 'Even "fire companies and a cricket club" could have a "president"... Adams complained' (2008: 15). He suggested adding honorifics like 'His Highness' to the office. Meanwhile, staunch republicans like Senator William Maclay ridiculed such suggestions as verging on treason to republican ideals. Maclay's side won the day, and Healy sums up the result as follows: 'The titles debate was significant because it reaffirmed the constitutional settlement: the new president would not be an elected king' (2008: 18). But, of course, although the republicans were victorious in terms of *formal legislation*, over the 200-plus years since then, the office of the U.S. president has probably accrued more monarchial splendor than Adams would have dreamed possible: what mattered in the long run was that the American people *wanted* an elected king, not whether or not the written constitution called for one.

As Smith argued, regarding the attitude of the founding generation:

> Both the Federalists and the Antifederalists agreed — or at least they purported to agree — that a consolidation of general governmental power on the national level would be a very bad thing. So both sides employed their full repertoire of argument and rhetoric to persuade the citizenry either that the Constitution would not permit such a consolidation of power (the Federalist argument) or that it would (the Antifederalist argument). This debate culminated in the ratification of the Constitution, and so we might infer that the citizens who participated in the decision — or at least the dominant part of them — ultimately found the Federalist argument more persuasive.

> In retrospect, though, we can also see that they were wrong: The accumulation of national power that the Antifederalists predicted has in fact occurred — many times over... (Smith, 1998: 48–49)

It is worth noting here that no claim is being made as to whether or not this expansion of federal power was a good or a bad thing. Persons of various ideological leanings are likely to differ widely in their answer to that question, with libertarians, in particular, typically seeing the expansion as a tragedy, while modern liberals are liable to view it as a necessary adaptation to changing times. The contention being made here is neutral in regards to the desirability of that expansion; it is, rather, that desirable or not, that expansion is not what the founders intended, that they saw the U.S. Constitution as a formidable barrier to such an expansion, and that their hopes proved unfounded. It is quite beside the point of this work to come down on either side of that debate. Rather, our aim here is to show that this transformation did, indeed, happen, and that the hope of those who want to enforce the founders' 'original intent' is not just a pipe dream today, but always was such. The rationalist cannot do what he purports to be doing, in politics or otherwise.

A critic of this thesis might point to how, say, the First Amendment continues to function as a bulwark for the right to the freedom of speech. But I suggest that is because the sentiment supporting freedom of speech is still strong. When the sentiment lying behind the 'original intent' of some portion of the constitution (to the dubious extent that there ever was such a univocal intent) fades and is replaced by some alternative popular understanding of the issue in question, then that provision is no longer interpreted as it once was. Consider the Second Amendment — can you imagine, if you thought the founders meant it as an individual right, what contemporary advocates of free speech would say if they were told they had the right to speak their mind, just so long as they first underwent a 30-day waiting period, then registered their mind with the state government, and then applied for a special permit to speak freely that required that they demonstrate a serious need for them to speak their minds in public? Or, if you believe, as for instance, Spitzer (2000) argues, that the Second Amendment was originally meant to apply only to militias, then imagine the framers' shock at it being frequently taken to apply to individuals for two centuries. Once again, my point is not to comment on the desirability of this evolved understanding of the U.S. Constitution—restrictions on the right to bear arms may, in fact, be an entirely reasonable response to the changing social and technological circumstances in which that right is to be exercised (or not!)—but only to note that, in light of such changed circumstances and the concomitant changes in popular opinion regarding the right in question, it simply is the case that a written constitution will be read in a way that conforms to the prevailing understanding of how government ought to operate and what powers it ought to possess. Indeed, the very principle of a right to self-governance that the American founders invoked to justify their rebellion against their king's authority over them equally negates their own authority to determine how subsequent generations will be permitted to interpret the document by which they sought to constrain the government they were creating.

As Smith put this point:

> More specifically, the framers' constitutional project of fixing the
> conclusions of reason in a written document presupposed that the
> future interpreters of the constitutional text would be readers who
> would attempt to read and understand the meaning the framers
> intended to convey, not readers who would seek to creatively misread
> that text. The authors of the constitutional text had no power (as authors
> never have power) to compel readers to approach the text in a particular
> spirit or with a particular purpose… (Smith, 1998: 63)

Smith noted an irony in the framers' attempt:

> The framers, as we have seen, tried to implement reason in careful
> legalistic fashion; and so it may seem ironic that the most obvious defect
> in their plan can plausibly be viewed as a technical flaw, or a failure in
> practical legal judgment. Central to their constitutional strategy was a
> misplaced trust in the enumerated powers doctrine — the idea that
> government powers could in practice be confined by listing such powers
> in a written document and specifying that the national government
> would have only those powers actually conferred on it. (Smith, 1998: 49–
> 50)

One of the chief targets of Healy, who was cited on page 182, is John
Yoo, whose is famous (or perhaps infamous) for being the chief legal
theorist behind the George W. Bush administration's expansion of
presidential power. Yoo defended his generous interpretation of the
powers that the constitution granted to the president by claiming, 'The
questions raised by [recent debates on presidential power] are not new
ones but in fact have been unresolved since the birth of the Republic…
President, Senate, and Congress similarly have never settled on the
nature of treaties within our domestic constitutional system' (2005: 3).
He continued, 'Our constitutional system has yet to settle the question
of the allocation of power over the interpretation of treaties, now more
than two hundred years old' (2005: 5). And he further claimed, '[The]
Constitution generally does not establish a fixed process for foreign
relations decisionmaking' (2005: 7–8).

Yoo makes the case that it is primarily the actual practice of
government in foreign affairs, and not the written text of the
constitution or judicial precedent, that has the greatest role in
determining what is 'constitutional' in those regards. Of course, this
kind of 'constitutionalism' negates the binding effect that theorists like
Jefferson, Madison, Buchanan, Wagner, and Elster hold out as the *raison
d' être* of having a written consitution in the first place, but it is, in fact,
just what, from an Oakeshottian perspective, we would expect to be the
case. Yoo further argues that the founders were deeply influenced by
the British constitutional tradition, which made taking the country to

war an executive prerogative. Again, in Oakeshott's view, that is what we should expect—rationalists always draw on some tradition, even if unwittingly.

Healy argues that, to the contrary, the framers certainly did not mean to create the American executive branch on the model of the British monarchy. He quotes a number of writers of the time to make his case; for instance, he cites Alexander Hamilton, perhaps especially relevant as he advocated a stronger executive than did republicans such as Jefferson and Madison:

> Hamilton wrote the *Federalist*'s principal essays on presidential powers, and in them, he took great pains to refute those Anti-Federalists who compared the chief magistrate with an elected king. He no more resembles a king, Hamilton wrote indignantly in *Federalist* No. 69, than he resembles 'the man of the seven mountains'. (Healy, 2008: 24)

From a viewpoint that takes Oakeshott's insights here seriously, the dispute between Yoo and Healy can be resolved by saying that, to some extent, both sides are right. Healy is correct in contending that the imperial presidency we have in the U.S. today was not what the authors of the constitution had in mind when they were designing the office. But Yoo is correct in that the framers were influenced by their tradition in ways of which they were not fully aware.[1] Furthermore, he is correct in that, given that America decided to pursue empire, the kind of presidency we've got was just the kind that was up to the task, and that it is practice that must have the upper hand on such an issue. Historical counterfactuals are, of course, impossible to demonstrate; they can only be presented as plausible. So perhaps it is the case that if the United States had not chosen to purchase Louisiana, to acquire Florida, to attempt to conquer Canada, to annex Texas, to go to war with Mexico and grab a third of that country by conquest, to subvert the kingdom of Hawaii, to take the Philippines and Puerto Rico by force from Spain, to entangle itself in land wars in Europe, and so on, then perhaps the presidency might bear a greater resemblance to the one the founders had envisioned. But the United States did not take that route, and as a result required a president up to the task of running an empire.[2]

---

[1] Interestingly, the same sort of Oakehsottian resolution can be offered for the dispute between the Federalists and Anti-Federalists: The Anti-Federalists were wrong to accuse the Federalists of *intending* to set up an elective monarchy, but right in sensing that that was what was being created.

[2] To be fair to Healy, he showed some recognition of this fact, when he wrote, 'America needs to become a normal country, not one that fancies itself chosen

As Smith put it:

> The framers tried in a cautious way to consolidate the conclusions of reason in a legal document they called the Constitution. But it would take a forgetting — or a repudiation — of the framers' grim awareness of human nature, and indeed of their notions about Nature itself, before 'reason' could expand to claim its full dignity, or to manifest its full pretensions. (Smith, 1998: 69)

We will add that we can go farther than Smith: reason itself is never the free-floating, universal reason dreamed of by Enlightenment thinkers, but is always reason embedded within a tradition, and only when it recognizes itself as such does it ever claim 'its full dignity'.

The modern obsession with constitutional design and instrumental republicanism

I will briefly touch upon several cases that support the general conclusions of this work, and suggest fruitful avenues for further research. Our first case is that of the former Soviet Union, which is of great interest for our present work for two reasons. First of all, in 1936 it adopted a quite liberal, written constitution, the gist of which had almost nothing to do with the actual conduct of the government over the activities of which it supposedly acted as the ultimate authority. As such, the Soviet Union illustrates the impotence of a written constitution in the face of an ideological climate that does not embrace the principles the constitution is purported to safeguard.

Second, the steadfastly avowed aim of the Soviet state, as well as the public story about how the nation actually operated, was to realize full communism. This was attempted in an as-the-crow-flies approach immediately after the 1917 revolution, in a period often called 'War Communism', but the disastrous results that ensued led leaders to back off and opt for a more gradual approach to the communist ideal.[3] That ideal, of course, is one of the most notable and most extreme real-world instances of an attempt to pursue rational politics. The social order to be achieved was entirely theoretical in its conception, as no society had ever come close to functioning in the way the ideal communist nation would — in fact, it was a key tenet of those who imagined its shape that

---

by God to pay any price, bear any burden, to expand the American way of life by force of arms' (2008: 296).

[3] See Boettke, 2001: 133–135.

they were prophesying the imminent birth of a wholly unprecedented condition of human existence, one which represented the culmination of everything that had preceded it.

In light of Oakeshott's contention that the rationalist never can proceed as he proposes to do, and of the radical rationalism driving the Soviet program, it will behoove us to examine how closely actual practice in the Soviet Union approached the ideal it was supposed to embody. If Oakeshott was on target concerning the impossibility of conduct strictly directed according to rationalist principles, then we should find that the real Soviet Union bore little resemblance to its rationalist blueprint.

While the Soviet Union stood, it was widely acknowledged, even by its own leaders, that the country had not yet achieved full socialism. But the market features of its economy that were plainly visible were held to be, by the advocates of the communist dream, merely vestigial remnants of the prior, vanishing stage of the organization of the productive forces, while the bulk of the Soviet economy was seen as already operating on socialist principles. However, after the collapse of the Soviet regime in 1991, vast new amounts of data as to how the country really had functioned became available to scholars for the first time. As a result of investigating this previously classified information, some researchers have concluded that the USSR never represented an instance of a mostly socialist economy at all, but was better characterized as a mercantilist society, operating on the model of a European nation-state of the eighteenth century.

The Soviet economy, according to economist Peter Boettke, chiefly was characterized not by central planning but by cronyism, intervention, and corruption. Soviet industrial concerns, far from being run according to the plans emerging from Moscow that theoretically directed all production, instead operated as though they were the private property of their local directors, who, lacking legal title to the assets they temporarily controlled, exploited the resource for whatever immediate or short-term benefits they could extract from it.[4] Oakeshott had surmized that the Soviet Union was not what it purported to be many years before the documents upon which Boettke's based his work were available in the West; he wrote: 'The Russian Revolution (what actually happened in Russia) was not the implementation of an abstract design worked out by Lenin and others in Switzerland: it was a modification of *Russian* circumstances' (1991 [1962]: 59).

---

[4] See Boettke, 2001: 140-153.

In another example of our general thesis, Wheare confronts an intrinsic difficulty faced by attempts to fully specify the limits of state action in a written constitution using the example of the Republic of Ireland:

> No realistic attempt to define the rights of the citizen, indeed, can fail to include qualifications. Yet when we see the result it is difficult to resist asking the question: What of substance is left after the qualifications have been given full effect? The Constitution of Ireland provides an interesting example of this position... Consider this statement first: 'No citizen shall be deprived of his personal liberty save in accordance with the law.' A little later there follows: 'The dwelling of every citizen is inviolable and shall not be forcibly entered save in accordance with the law.' What does this guarantee amount to? The answer must be: 'It all depends on what the law is...'

> The experience of Ireland in the years immediately following the adoption of the Constitution in 1937 illustrates the dilemma very nicely. In 1940 the Irish parliament passed the Offences Against the State (Amendment) Act', certain provisions of which, in the eyes of some observers, appeared to shred the constitutional rights mentioned above. But when the Supreme Court of Ireland was asked to evaluate the validity of those provisions, it ruled in parliament's favour, deciding that it was the business of the legislature to harmonize the rights of particular citizens with concerns over public peace and safety. (Wheare, 1966: 40–41)

Northern Ireland, upon its creation as a special province of the United Kingdom in 1921, had a written constitution that explicitly forbid the establishment of or favoring of any religious sect. Yet, almost immediately, the Protestant majority began discriminating against the Catholic minority. One tool of this discrimination was the Special Powers Act, passed in 1922 as a temporary, emergency measure. The act declared, 'The civil authority shall have power, in respect of persons, matters and things within the jurisdiction of the Government of Northern Ireland, to take all such steps and issue all such orders as may be necessary for preserving the peace and maintaining order...' The only restraint on the powers granted was that they should interfere with 'the ordinary course of law and avocations of life and the enjoyment of property... as little as may be permitted by the exigencies of the steps required to be taken under this Act' (Civil Authorities (Special Powers) Act, 1922) But, as Finn wrote:

> Desperate measures have a way of enduring beyond the life of the situations that give life to them. As originally drafted, the Special Powers Act was a temporary measure, its duration limited to one year. Stormont annually renewed the act through 1928, when its duration was

extended to five years. In 1933 Stormont simply made the act permanent, thus institutionalizing measures adopted during an emergency that had long since expired. (Finn, 1991: 54)

The nation of Somalia has been the subject of no little attention from the international community of late, because, since the civil war of the early 1990s, the country essentially has been without an effective central government, which has led many to view it as a 'failed state', in need of 'nation building'. (Nation building will be further discussed later in this conclusion.) Ethiopia, Eritrea, the United States, and other nations have sought to intervene in the nation to remedy this perceived problem. But is the plight of Somalia without a central authority as dire as depicted—in particular, is it so dire as to justify these foreign military interventions? Some analysts of the situation have argued that the people of Somalia, operating under the auspices of traditional tribal laws, have actually done better without a central government than they had with one.

Powell, Ford, and Nowrasteh, in their study of Somali, describe the operation of customary law in Somalia as follows:

> Somali law is based on custom, and decentralized clan networks interpret and enforce it. The Somali customary law (Xeer) has existed since pre-colonial times, and it continued to operate under colonial rule. The Somali nation state tried to replace the Xeer with government legislation and enforcement. However, in rural areas and border regions where the Somali government lacked firm control, people continued to apply the common law. When the Somali state collapsed, much of the population returned to their traditional legal system...

> Clan elders chosen on the basis of their knowledge of the law judge cases. The elders cannot create the law; they only interpret the community customs. Elders who make decisions that deviate from community norms are not consulted in future cases...

> After a verdict is reached, the criminal must compensate his victim the appropriate amount. If he is unable or unwilling, his extended family must pay the compensation. Every Somali is born into an insurance group based on their lineage to a common great-grandfather. Out of their own self-interest these insurance groups help enforce the judgment on wrongdoers. When an individual becomes particularly troublesome, a family can publicly declare that the person is no longer a member of their group, effectively making the person an outlaw. Outlaws must find another insurance group willing to sponsor them or be expelled from the larger clan. In cases in which more formal enforcement of the law is necessary, clan elders can call for all clansmen to form a posse to enforce the verdict; clansmen are obligated to answer the call. (Powell *et al.*, 2008: 666–667)

The authors conclude, 'However, we find that rather than [creating] chaos, statelessness seems to have generally improved living conditions in Somalia' (2008: 699), in other words, the reversion to traditional, tribal law has actually improved the circumstances of most Somalians compared to what they had experienced living in a 'modern' nation-state, a condition that rationalist political theory holds out as universally desirable.

'Nation building' is another modern, rationalist exercise, closely related to the faith in written constitutions as a near panacea, since an almost mandatory aspect of nation building efforts is to establish a written constitution for the nation being 'built'. But surveying the outcome of a broad sample of attempts to build nations does not offer much succor to proponents of rationalist politics. For instance, Payne's empirical study shows that less than a third of attempts to establish democracies by force succeed, and it's not clear in many of the cases of success whether a democracy would not have emerged without foreign intervention anyway. He concludes his paper:

> Trying to establish democracy through military occupation is not a coherent, defensible policy... The record shows that it usually fails and even when it appears to succeed, the positive result owes more to historical evolution and local political culture than to anything the nation builders would have done. (Payne, 2006: 607–608)

Our final example concerns the recent 'coup' (I put the term in quotes because one of the chief bones of contention here is whether what transpired actually *was* a coup) that took place in Honduras in 2009. President Zelaya was proposing a referendum on reforming the constitution, a maneuver objected to by most of the National Congress and Supreme Court. The Court wound up ordering the military to remove Zelaya from office and the country. Immediately, some voices called the act an illegal military coup, while others praised it as a defense of the Honduran Constitution. It is no easy matter to adjudicate this dispute; the difficulty arises from the combination of articles 239 and 374 of the Honduran Constitution:

> **ARTICULO 239.-** El ciudadano que haya desempeñado la titularidad del Poder Ejecutivo no podrá ser Presidente o Vicepresidente de la República.

> El que quebrante esta disposición o proponga su reforma, así como aquellos que lo apoyen directa o indirectamente, cesarán de inmediato en el desempeño de sus respectivos cargos y quedarán inhabilitados por diez (10) años para el ejercicio de toda función pública.

ARTICULO 374.- No podrán reformarse, en ningún caso, el artículo anterior, el presente artículo, los artículos constitucionales que se refieren a la forma de gobierno, al territorio nacional, al período presidencial, a la prohibición para ser nuevamente Presidente de la República, el ciudadano que lo haya desempeñado bajo cualquier título y el referente a quienes no pueden ser Presidentes de la República por el período subsiguiente.[5]

Article 374 declares certain constitutional clauses to be immune from amendment. (They can be amended 'en ningún caso', 'in no case'.) These specifically include the subject of Article 239, which itself forbids even proposing changes in itself, and which also declares violators will be removed from office 'immediately' ('inmediato') and will be banned from politics for 10 years thereafter.

While the above seems clear enough, the difficulty in sorting out whether the events took place were a constitutional blockage of an executive power grab or a military coup arises from the fact that the Honduran Constitution utterly fails to set out any procedure for who should determine or how it should be determined that the president has violated Article 239, or what the procedure for 'immediately' removing a convicted (or is the mere accusation sufficient for removal?) offender should be. In other words, we have a rationalist declaration of certain constitutional principles held to be inviolable, but no practical solution to resolving disputes about such a purported violation. Furthermore, the articles cited above simply beg the question of why the constitutional generation *ought* to be able to bind irrevocably all future generations to any of its decisions. And thus we have our current mess, where both sides in the dispute can claim, with some plausibility, that the other is acting unconstitutionally.[6]

Conclusion

We have looked extensively at the fate of the U.S. Constitution, especially in the years immediately after its adoption, and more briefly at the constitutions of the Soviet Union, the Republic of Ireland, Northern Ireland, and Honduras. The pattern indicated is that the fate

---

[5] Georgetown University Political Database of the Americas, 2005.

[6] See, for example, Thoresen (2009) and O'Grady (2009) for examples of the two sides' positions.

of any constitution depends much more on the climate of opinion in the polity that it is thought to 'found' than on the explicit clauses contained in the written work. The case of Somalia suggests that people can manage to establish a semblance of social order even in the absence of any such document. This is all as Oakeshott would lead us to expect.

Conclusion

Is a 'rationally designed' republic superior to one put together on an ad hoc basis, in response to practical contingencies? Can a written, well-designed constitution act to preserve the stability of a republic? Can construction along rational principles help prevent a republic from decaying into a concealed oligarchy, a de facto dictatorship, or a majoritarian tyranny? The American founders certainly hoped that it could do so, and their hopes are echoed by a number of modern, republican theorists, such as Pettit and Viroli, as well as in the actions of contemporary political actors, such as the American occupiers of Iraq noted in the introduction to this work.

Others, however, are not so optimistic about the efficacy of such rationalist design. This work has centered on Oakeshott's critique of attempts to reform a concrete, human practice so as to bring its performances into conformity with a 'rational' design or set of rules. Oakeshott argued that rationalists could not, in fact, reach their goal of directing conduct by a set of abstract principles worked out only after setting aside the prejudicial influence of tradition. He contended that, however strenuous were the efforts of rationalists to start afresh, the results they achieved would always bear the strong imprint of the traditional practices and customary mores in which the designers were embedded. But what they may be able to do, in seeking to implement their schemes, is weaken the ability of a society's traditions to maintain a working, civil order. The typical response of the social engineers, when faced with the 'social decay' that results from their most recent tinkerings, is to cite those problems as urgent reasons to undertake even more vigorous engineering. As stressed repeatedly in this work, the Oakeshottian rationalist is an ideal type, and we do not expect to find a pure instance of him in historical reality. Nevertheless, as argued earlier, republican-era Romans largely conducted their political life in line with the ideal type of a 'practical polity' as described by Oakeshott, and the Enlightenment's faith in the power of rational thought, when it has succeeded in casting off the blinders of received wisdom, was an important influence on the creators of the American constitution. If those contentions are true, then the histories of the Roman and the American republics sensibly can be employed to explore the veracity of Oakeshott's theoretical framework.

The episodes that we have examined in this work support the scepticism about rationalist politics expressed by Oakeshott. As we have seen, the Romans succeeded in maintaining a republican form of polity for roughly four centuries, without a written constitution or much in the way of deliberate attempts to design their institutions according to some theory of political perfection. Instead, the Romans looked to *mos maiorum*, the 'way of the ancestors', to preserve their liberty, and turned to their traditions for guidance in responding to novel situations. Eventually, their republic collapsed, as the lure of controlling and plundering their expanding empire overcame the reluctance of political leaders to violate the customary practices that limited their power. Nevertheless, the longevity of the Roman republic suggests that the Romans' faith in their traditions was not unfounded, and there is no reason to believe that any other form of institutional arrangements would have preserved their republic forever against the vicissitudes of *fortuna*.

As we have seen, the American revolution was largely founded in rationalist principles, including a foremost statement of rationalist politics, the Declaration of Independence. After gaining independence, Americans were faced with the question of what sort of political arrangements should take the place of the colonial governments and the monarch that they just had cast off. The debate as to the best answer was decided, after several years of heated discussion, in favor of those who advocated a strong, central government, the primary features of which would be set out in a written constitution, rationally designed to safeguard the republic against the danger that the state might grow in power and usurp the citizens' liberties.

The subsequent history of the United States offers little support for the American founders' faith in the power of their rationally designed framework of governance to direct the future course of their country's political life. Only 10 years after the ratification of the U.S. Constitution, the Alien and Sedition Acts were made law, seemingly in direct violation of the spirit of the First Amendment of the Bill of Rights. The election of 1800 precipitated a crisis that the rationally designed American constitution was incapable of handling, and which was addressed only by falling back on practical experience of republican politics. Less than two decades had passed after the adoption of the U.S. Constitution before one of the foremost champions of limited government among the founders, Thomas Jefferson, was using his presidential power to purchase the vast Louisiana territory from France, launching the nation on its journey towards the world-dominating empire it has become today, despite his recognition that the constitution did not authorize the office of president to undertake such an action. Meanwhile, he was pursuing political opponents through clearly extra-constitutional means.

Over the two centuries since that time, the U.S. Constitution has repeatedly been interpreted in a manner that would make any proposed direction for the federal government to proceed permissible, if that direction had strong support. For example, since World War II, the fact that the constitution rests the sole authority for declaring war with the legislative branch has routinely been ignored, as presidents simply have declared that military actions they were initiating were not wars at all, but 'police actions' or 'international peacekeeping'. (This issue is currently live in the debate over President Obama's military intervention in Libya.) The U.S. government headed by President George W. Bush habitually ignored the constitutional requirement that the executive branch be bound by the laws passed in Congress, attaching 'signing statements' to bills, which audaciously declared that his administration had no intention of obeying particular parts of the legislation. Along with a number of similar extensions of executive power under Bush, such as the assertion that the executive branch arbitrarily can deny the right of habeas corpus, can undertake wiretaps without judicial review, and that its members can refuse any requests from the legislature to testify before it by invoking 'national security', a pessimist might have cause to declare that the American republic already has met its demise, having survived only about half as long as the Roman republic, which lacked the supposed armor of a written constitution.

Summing up

Our findings would not surprise Oakeshott. As Oakeshott would have it, a rational rulebook for some field of action is only an abstraction from the concrete reality of the practice of that activity, and can never fully capture or convey the tacit knowledge relied upon by a skilled performer. While the American founders were able to draw on the tradition of English liberty, in which they had been educated and within which they had lived, to devise a plausible design for a republic that could embody that tradition, that design could only be realized in so far as the nation's citizens cherished republican liberty and displayed republican virtues. As Boucher wrote, the survival of republican institutions requires:

> not only formal subscription, but also the will and political culture to animate it with the spirit and not merely the principle of law. As both Burke and Hegel told us long ago, and Oakeshott and Wittengstein did more recently, these are the traditional elements of a way of life that become established and grow over a long period of time, and not the product of abstract reason and manufactured institutional design. (Boucher, 2005b: 105)

If the populace of a republic comes to regard other guiding principles for its political life more highly than it does those that support a republican polity, then no written safeguards, however cleverly designed and ostensibly binding, can prevent the demise of the republic they once embodied. When the Roman people became more concerned with acquiring a share of the booty flowing from military conquests and being fed and entertained with bread and circuses than they were with preserving their freedom and civic virtues, the Roman republic was doomed. The victory of the republican party of Brutus, Cassius, Cicero, and Cato over the Caesarian forces in some alternative history at best would have kept the republic on life support for a few more years.

The American founders, for whom the saga of the Roman's loss of their republican liberty loomed as a giant spectre from the past bearing a haunting message of warning, sought to secure their new republic from such dangers by creating a system of institutions with carefully delineated and circumscribed powers, in which each major component of the state would act as a barrier to any attempt by one of the other branches to exceed its constitutional authority. Despite their admirable intentions, the later generations that inherited their legacy read that document as suited their own political ambitions and predilections. As the character of the American people changed, their form of government was transformed as well, so greatly that it is difficult to imagine that the nation's founders, if resurrected today, would believe that the document through which they sought to direct and constrain the activities of the federal government they were creating is still in effect. And that is just what Oakeshott was telling us: rational guidelines purporting to direct our activities are derivative of, and not prior to, our concrete practices, and if those practices should alter significantly, then the rulebooks neither will serve to save the former ways of proceeding from becoming of no more than historical significance, nor can they dictate to the new ways just what course their development must follow.

Bibliography

Abbott, Frank Frost (1901) *A History and Description of Roman Political Institutions*, Boston and London: Ginn & Company.

Ackerman, Bruce (2005) *The Failure of the Founding Fathers: Jefferson, Marshall, and the Rise of Presidential Democracy*, Cambridge, Mass. and London: The Belknap Press of Harvard University Press.

Adams, John (1776) 'Letter to James Sullivan', in Dunn (2006): 204–206.

Adcock, F. E. (1964) *Roman Political Ideas and Practices*, Ann Arbor: University of Michigan Press.

Alexander, Christopher (1979) *The Timeless Way of Building*, New York: Oxford University Press.

Amar, Akhil Reed (2006) *America's Constitution: A Biography*, New York: Random House.

Archer, J. R. (1979) 'Oakeshott on Politics', *The Journal of Politics*, Vol. 41, No. 1: 150–168.

Aristotle (1995) *Politics*, trans. Ernest Barker, rev. R. F. Stalley, Oxford: Oxford University Press.

Aristotle (1999) *Nicomachean Ethics*, 2nd edition, trans. and ed. by Terence Irwin, Indianapolis and Cambridge: Hackett Publishing Company, Inc.

Augustine, Saint (1950) *The City of God*, trans. Marcus Dods, D. D., New York: Modern Library, available at *Questia*, www.questia.com/PM.qst?a=o&d=61633558 (accessed Jan. 24, 2009)

Bacon, Francis (1937) *Essays, Advancement of Learning, New Atlantis, and Other Pieces*, ed. Richard Foster Jones, New York: The Odyssey Press Inc.

Bailyn, Bernard (1967) *The Origins of American Politics*, New York: Vintage Books.

Bailyn, Bernard (1992 [1967]) *The Ideological Origins of the American Revolution*, Cambridge, Mass. and London: The Belknap Press of Harvard University Press.

Bailyn, Bernard, ed. (1993a) *The Debates on the Constitution: Federalist and Antifederalist Speeches, Articles, and Letters During the Struggle over Ratification, Part One*, New York: The Library of America.

Bailyn, Bernard, ed. (1993b) *The Debates on the Constitution: Federalist and Antifederalist Speeches, Articles, and Letters During the Struggle over Ratification, Part Two*, New York: The Library of America.

Bailyn, Bernard (2003) *To Begin the World Anew: The Genius and Ambiguities of the American Founders*, New York: Vintage Books.

Baldwin, Simeon (1788) 'Simeon Baldwin's Oration at New Haven', in Bailyn (1993b): 514–525.

Barber, Benjamin R. (1976) 'Conserving Politics: Michael Oakeshott and Political Theory', *Government and Opposition*, Vol. 11, Issue 4: pp. 446–463.

Barnett, Randy (2004) *Restoring The Lost Constitution: The Presumption Of Liberty*, Princeton: Princeton University Press.

BBC News (2005) 'Iraqi Constitution — Writer Killed', July 19, available at www.news.bbc.co.uk/2/hi/middle_east/4696869.stm (accessed Mar. 3, 2009).

Beard, Mary, and Michael Crawford (1999) *Rome in the Late Republic*, 2nd edition, London: Duckworth.

Bentley, Jon (1986) *Programming Pearls*, Murray Hill, New Jersey: Addison-Wesley Publishing Company.

Boettke, Peter J. (2001) *Calculation and Coordination: Essays on Socialism and Transitional Political Economy*, London and New York: Routledge.

Bosanquet, Bernard (1927) *Principle of Individuality and Value*, London: Macmillan and Co. Limited.

Boucher, David (2005a) 'Oakeshott and the Republican Tradition', *British Journal of Politics and International Relations*, Vol. 7: 81–96.

Boucher, David (2005b) 'The Rule of Law in the Modern European State: Oakeshott and the Enlargement of Europe', *European Journal of Political Theory*, Vol. 4, No. 1: 89–107.

Bowen, Catherine Drinker (1966) *Miracle at Philadelphia: The Story of the Constitutional Convention*, Boston: Little, Brown and Company.

Bowers, C. A. (2005) '"Liberal" and "Conservative" Misunderstood', *The Register-Guard*, No. 6: B1.

Brutus (1787) 'Brutus I', in Bailyn (1993a): 164–175.

Buchanan, James M. (1975) *The Limits of Liberty: Between Anarchy and Leviathan*, Chicago and London: The University of Chicago Press.

Buchanan, James M. And Gordon Tullock (1965 [1962]) *The Calculus of Consent: Logical Foundations of Constitutional Democracy*, Ann Arbor : University of Michigan Press.

Burke, Edmund (1993) *Burke: Pre-Revolutionary Writings*, ed. Ian Harris, Cambridge, England: Cambridge University Press.

Callahan, Gene (2001) 'Historical Explanation and Moral Justification', available at *LewRockwell.com*, www.lewrockwell.com/callahan/callahan60.html (accessed Mar. 3, 2009).

Callahan, Gene (2005) 'Mises and Oakeshott on Understanding Human Action', *Independent Review*, Fall issue: 231–248.

Cartwright, Nancy (1983) *How the Laws of Physics Lie*, Oxford: Oxford University Press.

Cicero (1999) *On the Commonwealth* and *On the Laws*, ed. James E. G. Zetzel, Cambridge, England: Cambridge University Press.

Cicero (1877) *Tusculan Disputations* and *The Nature of the Gods* and *On the Commonwealth*, trans. C. D. Yonge, New York: Harper Brothers, available at www.gutenberg.org/files/14988/14988-h/14988-h.htm (accessed Aug. 28, 2009).

Civil Authorities (Special Powers) Act (Northern Ireland) (1922), available at www.cain.ulst.ac.uk/hmso/spa1922.htm (accessed Mar. 15, 2009).

Cohen, G. A. (2008) *Rescuing Justice and Equality*, London: Harvard University Press.

Collingwood, R. G. (1924) *Speculum Mentis or Map of Knowledge*, London: Oxford University Press.

Collingwood, R. G. (1994) *Religion and Philosophy*, Bristol, England: Thoemmes Press.

Congleton, Roger D. (2011) *Perfecting Parliament: Constitutional Reform, Liberalism, and the Rise of Western Democracy*, Cambridge, England: Cambridge University Press.

Corey, Elizabeth Campbell (2006) *Michael Oakeshott on Religion, Aesthetics, and Politics*, Columbia, Missouri: University of Missouri Press.

Crick, Bernard (1992) *In Defense of Politics*, 4th American edition, Chicago: The University of Chicago Press.

Cunningham, Noble E. Jr. (1987) *In Pursuit of Reason: The Life of Thomas Jefferson*, New York: Ballantine Books.

de Jasay, Anthony (1997) *Against Politics*, London: Routledge.

de Jasay, Anthony (2002) *Justice and Its Surroundings*, Indianapolis: Liberty Fund.

Descartes, Rene (1960) *Descartes' Discourse on Method, and Other Writings*, trans. Arthur Wollaston, Baltimore: Penguin Books.

de Tocqueville, Alexis (2001) *Democracy in America*, ed. Richard D. Heffner, New York: New American Library.

Devereux, Daniel T. (1986) 'Particular and Universal in Aristotle's Conception of Practical Knowledge', *Review of Metaphysics*, Vol. 39: 483–504.

Dunn, Susan, ed. (2006) *Something That Will Surprise the World: The Essential Writings of the Founding Fathers*, New York: Basic Books.

Eccleshall, Robert (2001) 'The Doing of Conservatism', in Freeden (2001): 67–79.

Ellis, Joseph J. (1998) *American Sphinx: The Character of Thomas Jefferson*, New York: Random House.

Elster, Jon (2000) *Ulysses Unbound*, Cambridge, England: Cambridge University Press.

Everitt, Anthony (2003) *Cicero: The Life and Times of Rome's Greatest Politician*, New York: Random House.

Fagan, Garrett G. (1999) *The History of Ancient Rome: Part Two*, Chantilly, Virginia: The Teaching Company.

Ferguson, Adam (1782) 'An Essay on the History of Civil Society', 5th edition, London: T. Cadell, Chapter: 'SECT. II: The History of political Establishments', available at www.oll.libertyfund.org/title/1428/19736/1566171 (accessed Jan. 13, 2010).

Finer, Jonathan (2006) 'U.S. Troop Fatalities Hit A Low; Iraqi Deaths Soar', *The Washington Post*, April 1, available at www.washingtonpost.com/wp-dyn/content/article/2006/03/31/AR2006033101745.html (accessed July 9, 2010).

Finn, John E. (1991) *Constitutions in Crisis: Political Violence and the Rule of Law*, New York: Oxford University Press.

Fletcher, Andrew (1698) *A Discourse of Government with Relation to Militias*, Edinburgh, available at www.oll.libertyfund.org/title/1222/83362/1960666 (accessed Nov. 17, 2009).

Flower, Harriet I. (2010) *Roman Republics*, Princeton, New Jersey: Princeton University Press.

Franco, Paul (2004) *Michael Oakeshott: An Introduction*, New Haven and London: Yale University Press.

Freeden, Michael, ed. (2001) *Reassessing Political Ideologies: The Durability of Dissent*, New York: Routledge, available at *Questia*, www.questia.com/PM.qst?a=o&d=107543984 (accessed Dec. 29, 2008).

Freedom House (2008) 'Freedom in the World', available at www.freedomhouse.org/template.cfm?page=363&year=2008 (accessed July 1, 2009).

Friedman, David D. (1989) *The Machinery of Freedom: Guide to Radical Capitalism*, 2nd edition, La Salle, Illinois: Open Court.

Gray, John (1989) *Liberalisms: Essays in Political Philosophy*, London: Routledge.

Geertz, Clifford (1973) *The Interpretation of Cultures*, New York: Basic Books.

Gerencser, Steven Anthony (2000) *The Skeptic's Oakeshott*, New York: St. Martin's Press.

Grandin, Temple (2005) *Animals in Translation: Using the Mysteries of Autism to Decode Animal Behavior*, Orlando, Florida: Harcourt, Inc.

Grean, Stanley (1967) *Shaftesbury's Philosophy of Religion and Ethics*, New York: Ohio University Press.

Gruen, Erich S. (1974) *The Last Generation of the Roman Republic*, Berkeley and Los Angeles: University of California Press.

Haddock, Bruce (1974) 'The History of Ideas and the Study of Politics', *Political Theory*, Vol. 2, No. 4: 420–431.

Haddock, Bruce (2005) 'Contingency and Judgement in Oakeshott's Political Thought', *European Journal Of Political Theory*, Vol. 4, No. 1: 7–21.

Hamilton, Alexander (1787) 'The Federalist IX', in Bailyn (1993a): 339–344.

Hardin, Russell (1999) *Liberalism, Constitutionalism, and Democracy*, Oxford and New York: Oxford University Press.

Hayek, F. A. (1960) *The Constitution of Liberty*, Chicago: The University of Chicago Press.

Hayek, F. A. (1973) *Law, Legislation, and Liberty, Volume I: Rules and Order*, Chicago: The University of Chicago Press.

Hayek, F. A. (1978) *New Studies in Philosophy, Economics and the History of Ideas*, Chicago: The University of Chicago Press.

Hayek, F. A. (1979) *Law, Legislation, and Liberty: Volume III*, Chicago: The University of Chicago Press.

Healy, Gene (2008) *The Cult of the Presidency*, Washington: Cato Institute.

Hegel, G. W. F. (1896) *Philosophy of Right*, Preface, trans. S. W. Dyde, London: Prometheus Books, available at Marxists Internet Archive, www.marxists.org/reference/archive/hegel/works/pr/preface.htm (accessed June 3, 2010).

Hoppe, Hans-Hermann (1988) 'Utilitarians and Randians vs Reason', *Liberty* (November): 53–54.

Horton, John (2005) 'A Qualified Defence of Oakeshott's Politics of Scepticism', *European Journal Of Political Theory*, Vol. 4, No. 1: 23–36

Hooker, Richard (1989) *Of the Laws of Ecclesiastical Polity*, ed. A. S. McGrade, Cambridge, England: Cambridge University Press.

Hutchins, Robert M., G. A. Borgese, Mortimer J. Adler, Stringfellow Barr, Albert Guérard, Harold A. Innis, Erich Kahler, Wilber G. Katz, Charles H. McIlwain, Robert Redfield, Rexford G. Tugwell, and Committee to Frame a World Constitution (1948) *Preliminary Draft of a World Constitution*, Chicago: Univ. of Chicago Press, available at *Questia*, www.questia.com/PM.qst?a=o&d=505583 (accessed Mar. 17, 2009).

Jacobs, Jane (1992) *The Death and Life of Great American Cities*, New York: Vintage Books.

Jefferson, Thomas (1975) *The Portable Thomas Jefferson*, ed. Merrill D. Peterson, New York: Viking Press, Inc.

Jefferson, Thomas (1989) 'First Inaugural Address', from *Inaugural addresses of the presidents of the United States: from George Washington to George W. Bush*, Bicentennial edition, Senate document (United States. Congress. Senate); 101-10, Washington: U.S. G. P. O.

Johnston, Zachariah (1788) 'Speech to the Virginia Convention', in Bailyn (1993b): 751-756.

Jolley, Nicholas (2005) *Leibniz*, London and New York: Routledge.

Ketcham, Ralph, ed. (2003) *The Anti-Federalist Papers and the Constitutional Convention Debates*, New York: Signet Classic New American Library Penguin Group.

Kirk, Russell (1987) *The Conservative Mind: From Burke to Eliot*, 7th rev. edition, Chicago and Washington: Regnery Books.

Kukathas, Chandran (1993) Untitled Review, *Political Theory*, Vol. 21, No. 2: 339-343.

Lee, Arthur (1787) 'Cincinnatus V', in Bailyn (1993a): 114-121.

Leeson, Peter J. (2007) 'Better Off Stateless: Somalia Before and After Government Collapse', *Journal of Comparative Economics*, Vol. 35, No. 4: 689-710.

Le Glay, Marcel, Jean-Louis Voisin, and Yann Le Bohec (1996) *A History of Rome*, trans. Antonia Nevill, Oxford: Blackwell Publishers Ltd.

Levinson, Sanford (1988) *Constitutional Faith*, Princeton: Princeton University Press.

Levy, Leonard W. (1963) *Jefferson and Civil Liberties: The Dark Side*, Chicago: Ivan R. Dee, Inc.

Lintott, Andrew (1993) *Imperium Romanum: Politics and Administration*, London and New York: Routledge.

Lintott, Andrew (1999) *The Constitution of the Roman Republic*, Oxford: Oxford University Press.

Livius, Titus (1905) *The History of Rome*, Vol. 6, ed. Ernest Rhys, trans. Rev. Canon Roberts, London: J. M. Dent and Sons, available at www.mcadams.posc.mu.edu/txt/ah/Livy/Livy42.html (accessed May 29, 2008).

Livius, Titus (2002) *The Early History of Rome*, 3rd edition, trans. Aubrey de Sélincourt, London: Penguin Books.

Machiavelli, Niccolo (1882) *The Historical, Political, and Diplomatic Writings of Niccolo Machiavelli*, trans. Christian E. Detmold, Boston: J. R. Osgood and Company, available at www.oll.libertyfund.org/title/775/75949 (accessed Mar. 15, 2009).

MacIntyre, Alasdair (1973) 'The Idea of a Social Science', in Ryan (1973): 15–32.

MacIntyre, Alasdair (1973) 'Is a Science of Comparative Politics Possible?', in Ryan (1973): 171–188.

MacIntyre, Alasdair (1988) *Whose Justice? Which Rationality?* Notre Dame, Indiana: University of Notre Dame Press.

MacIntyre, Alasdair (2007) *After Virtue*, 3rd edition, Notre Dame, Indiana: University of Notre Dame Press.

Madison, G. B. (2006), 'Hermeneutics and Liberty: Remembrance of Don Lavoie', in *Humane Economics: Essays in Honor of Don Lavoie*, ed. Jack High, Cheltenham, UK and Northampton, Massachusetts: Edgar Elgar, 141–163.

Madison, James (1787) *The Federalist*, No. 10, in Dunn (2006), 362–369.

Madison, James, Alexander Hamilton, and John Jay (1987 [1788]) *The Federalist Papers*, ed. Isaac Kramnick, Middlesex, England: Penguin Books.

Madison, James (1794) 'On the Memorial of the Relief Committee of Baltimore, for the Relief of St. Domingo Refugees', Library of Congress: American Memory project, available at www.memory.loc.gov/cgi-bin/query/r?ammem/hlaw:@field%28DOCID+@lit%28ed00423%29%29 (accessed Jan. 23, 2010).

Marshall, John (1967) *John Marshall: Major Opinions and Other Writings*, ed. John P. Roche, Indianapolis and New York: Bobbs-Merrill Educational Publishing.

Martin, Luther (1788) 'The Genuine Information VIII', in Bailyn (1993a): 645–651.

McDonald, A. H. (1966) *Republican Rome*, New York and Washington: Frederick A. Praeger.

McDonald, Forrest (1985) *Novus Ordo Seclorum: The Intellectual Origins of the Constitution*, Lawrence, Kansas: University Press of Kansas.

McIntyre, Kenneth B. (2004) *The Limits of Political Theory: Oakeshott's Philosophy of Civil Association*, Exeter: Imprint Academic.

Mead, Walter B. (2005) 'The Importance of Michael Oakeshott for Polanyian Studies: With Reflections on Oakeshott's *The Voice of Liberal Learning*', *Tradition and Society*, Vol. XXXI, No. 2: 37-44, available at www.missouriwestern.edu/orgs/polanyi/TAD%20WEB%20ARCHIVE/TAD31-2/TAD31-2-fnl-pg37-44-pdf.pdf (accessed Dec. 12, 2008).

Meyers, Steven Lee (2009) 'Benchmarks in Wartime: As Reliable as Promises', *The New York Times*, Nov. 28, available at www.nytimes.com/2009/11/29/weekinreview/29myers.html?_r=2&hpw (accessed Dec. 8, 2009).

Minogue, Kenneth (2002) 'Hayek's Prophetic Scepticism', *New Criterion*, May 1, available at

www.questia.com/read/5000764926?title=Hayek%27s%20Prophetic%20Sce
pticism (accessed Dec. 11, 2009).

Nardin, Terry (2001) *The Philosophy of Oakeshott*, University Park, Pennsylvania:
The Pennsylvania State University Press.

Oakeshott, Michael (1933) *Experience and Its Modes*, Cambridge: Cambridge
University Press.

Oakeshott, Michael (1948), letter to Karl Popper, 28 January, Hoover Institute
Archives, available at www.michael-oakeshott-
association.com/pdfs/mo_letters_popper.pdf. (accessed Jan. 28, 2009).

Oakeshott, Michael (1962), File 1/3, introduction to lecture by Eric Voegelin at
LSE, Oakeshott Collection, British Library of of Political and Economic
Science, London School of Economics and Political Science.

Oakeshott, Michael (1975) *On Human Conduct*, Oxford: Clarendon Press.

Oakeshott, Michael (1976) 'On Misunderstanding Human Conduct: A Reply to
My Critics', *Political Theory*, Vol. 4, No. 3: 353–367.

Oakeshott, Michael (1991 [1962]) *Rationalism in Politics and Other Essays*,
Indianapolis: Liberty Fund.

Oakeshott, Michael (1993a) *Religion, Politics and the Moral Life*, ed. Timothy
Fuller, New Haven and London: Yale University Press.

Oakeshott, Michael (1993b) *Morality and Politics in Modern Europe: The Harvard
Lectures*, ed. Shirley Robin Letwin, New Haven and London: Yale
University Press.

Oakeshott, Michael (1996) *The Politics of Faith and the Politics of Scepticism*, ed.
Timothy Fuller, New Haven and London: Yale University Press.

Oakeshott, Michael (1999) *On History*, Oxford: Basil Blackwell Publisher
Limited.

Oakeshott, Michael (2004) *What Is History? And Other Essays*, ed. Luke
O'Sullivan, Exeter: Imprint Academic.

Oakeshott, Michael (2006) *Lectures in the History of Political Thought*, ed. Terry
Nardin and Luke O'Sullivan, Exeter: Imprint Academic.

Oakeshott, Michael (2008) *The Vocabulary of a Modern European State*, ed. Luke
O'Sullivan, Exeter: Imprint Academic.

O'Grady, Mary Anastasia (2009) 'Honduras Defends Its Democracy', *Wall Street
Journal*, June 29, available at
www.online.wsj.com/article/SB124623220955866301.html (accessed Feb.
19, 2010).

O'Neill, Onora (1996) *Towards Justice and Virtue: A Constructive Account of
Practical Reasoning*, Cambridge: Cambridge University Press.

Paine, Thomas (1995a) *Common Sense*, Amherst, New York: Prometheus Books.

Paine, Thomas (1995b) *Collected Writings*, ed. Eric Foner, New York: The Library of America.

Payne, James L. (2006) 'Does Nation Building Work?', *Independent Review*, Vol. X, No. 4: 597-608.

Pettit, Philip (1997) *Republicanism: A Theory of Freedom and Government*, Oxford: Oxford University Press.

Plutarch (1899) *Plutarch's Lives*, trans. with notes and a Life of Plutarch by Aubrey Stewart and the late George Long, Vol. II, London: George Bell And Sons, available at www.gutenberg.org/files/14114/14114-h/14114-h.htm.

Plutarch (2005) *Fall of the Roman Republic*, trans. Rex Warner, rev. Robin Seager, London: Penguin Books.

Pocock, J. G. A. (1975) *The Machiavellian Moment: Florentine Political Thought and the Atlantic Republican Tradition*, Princeton: Princeton University Press.

Polanyi, Michael (1962) *Personal Knowledge: Towards a Post-Critical Philosophy*, Chicago: The University of Chicago Press.

Popper, Karl (1948), letter to Michael Oakeshott, 31 January, Hoover Institute Archives, available at www.michael-oakeshott-association.com/pdfs/mo_letters_popper.pdf (accessed Jan. 28, 2009).

Powell, Benjamin, Ryan Ford, and Alex Nowrasteh (2008) 'Somalia after State Collapse: Chaos or Improvement?', *Journal of Economic Behavior and Organization*, Vol. 67, Issues 3-4: 657-670, available at www.sciencedirect.com/science/article/B6V8F-4SHMCBM-1/2/b46d8ff766c19a68c8f66e13d7a349c1 (accessed Mar. 3, 2009).

Rand, Ayn (1957) *Atlas Shrugged*, New York: The Penguin Group.

Raphael, D. D. (1964) 'Professor Oakeshott's Rationalism m Politics', *Political Studies*, Vol. 12: 202–215.

Rawls, John (1999) *A Theory of Justice*, revised edition, Cambridge, Massachusetts: The Belknap Press of Harvard University Press.

Rawls, John (2005) *Political Liberalism*, expanded edition, New York: Columbia University Press.

Raynor, Jeremy (1985) 'The Legend of Oakeshott's Conservatism: Sceptical Philosophy and Limited Politics', *Canadian Journal of Political Science*, Vol. 18, No. 2: 313–338.

Reagan, Ronald (1974) 'We Will Be As a City upon a Hill', speech to the Conservative Political Action Conference, Jan. 25, available at www.conservative.org/pressroom/reagan/reagan1974.asp (accessed Feb. 2, 2010).

Reagan, Ronald (1989) 'Farewell Address to the Nation', Oval Office, delivered on January 11.

Richard, Carl J. (2008) *Greeks and Romans Bearing Gifts: How the Ancients Inspired the Founding Fathers*, Lanham, Maryland: Rowman & Littlefield Publishers, Inc.

Roberts, Peri and Peter Sutch (2004) *An Introduction to Political Thought: A Conceptual Toolkit*, Edinburgh: Edinburgh University Press Ltd.

Rothbard, Murray N. (1998) *The Ethics of Liberty*, intro. Hans-Hermann Hoppe, New York and London: New York University Press.

Rothbard, Murray N. (2005) 'The Heresy of Prudence', available at *LewRockwell.com*, www.lewrockwell.com/rothbard/rothbard65.html (accessed June 4, 2010).

Rowland, Barbara M. (1998) 'Beyond Hayek's Pessimism: Reason, Tradition and Bounded Constructivist Rationalism', *British Journal of Political Science*, Vol. 18, No. 2: 221–241.

Ryan, Alan, ed. (1973) *The Philosophy of Social Explanation*, Oxford: Oxford University Press.

Sacks, Oliver (1990) *Awakenings*, New York: HarperCollins Publishers.

Sandoz, Ellis (1994) 'Foundations of American Liberty and Rule of Law' *Presidential Studies Quarterly*, Vol. 24, No. 3, Conduct of Foreign Policy: 605–617

Schlesinger, Arthur M., Jr. (1973) *The Imperial Presidency*, Boston: Houghton Mifflin Company.

Schwitzgebel, Eric (2006) 'Most-Cited Ethicists in the Stanford Encyclopedia', available at www.schwitzsplinters.blogspot.com/2006/11/most-cited-ethicists-in-stanford.html (accessed May 19, 2009).

Scullard, H. H. (2006 [1959]) *From the Gracchi to Nero: A History of Rome from 133 BC to AD 68*, London and New York: Routledge.

Scullard, H. H. (1973) *Roman Politics: 220–150 B.C.*, London: Oxford University Press.

Scullard, H. H. (1980) *A History of the Roman World: 753 to 146 BC*, 4th edition, Abingdon, Oxon: Routledge.

Sebeok, Thomas A. (2001) *Signs: An Introduction to Semiotics*, Toronto, Buffalo, London: University of Toronto Press Incorporated.

Second Continental Congress (1776), 'Declaration of Independence', available at www.archives.gov/exhibits/charters/declaration_transcript.html (accessed Jan. 29, 2010).

Schutz, Alfred (1967 [1932]) *The Phenomenology of the Social World*, trans. George Walsh and Frederick Lehnert, Evanston, Illinois: Northwestern University Press.

Shotter, David (1994) *The Fall of the Roman Republic*, New York: Routledge, available at *Questia*, www.questia.com/PM.qst?a=o&d=108816571 (accessed Jan. 8, 2009).

Smith, R. E. (1955) *The Failure of the Roman Republic*, Cambridge, England: Cambridge University Press, available at *Questia*, www.questia.com/PM.qst?a=o&d=9017977 (accessed Jan. 8, 2009).

Smith, Steven D. (1998) *The Constitution and the Pride of Reason*, New York: Oxford US.

Snow, Dan (2001) *In the Company of Stone*, photographs Peter Mauss, New York: Artisan.

Spitz, David (1976) 'A Rationalist Malgre Lui: The Perplexities of Being Michael Oakeshott', *Political Theory*, Vol. 4, No. 3: 335–352.

Spitzer, Robert J. (2000) 'Saving the Constitution from Lawyers', in *Politics and Constitutionalism: The Louis Fisher Connection*, ed. Robert J. Spitzer, Albany: State University of New York Press, 185–225.

Stewart, Roberta (1998) *Public Office in Early Rome: Ritual Procedure and Political Practice*, Ann Arbor: University of Michigan Press.

Stringham, Edward Peter (2003) 'The Extralegal Development of Securities Trading in Seventeenth Century Amsterdam', *Quarterly Review of Economics and Finance*, 43 (2 Summer): 321–344.

Suarez, Ray (2006) 'Attacks in Iraq at All-Time High, Pentagon Report Says', *PBS News*, Dec. 19, available at www.pbs.org/newshour/bb/middle_east/july-dec06/iraq_12-19.html (accessed Mar. 5, 2009).

Taylor, Charles (1989) *Sources of the Self: The Making of the Modern Identity*, Cambridge, Massachusetts: Harvard University Press.

Teachout, Terry (2002) *The Skeptic: A Life of H. L. Mencken*, New York: HarperCollins.

Thompson, C. Bradley (1998) 'Young John Adams and the New Philosophic Rationalism', *The William and Mary Quarterly*, Third Series, Vol. 55, No. 2: 259-280.

Thoresen, Alberto Valiente (2009) 'Why President Zelaya's Actions in Honduras Were Legal and Constitutional', *Rebel Reports*, available at www.rebelreports.com/post/133319827/why-president-zelayas-actions-in-honduras-were-legal (accessed July 21, 2010).

Tollison, Robert D. (2009) 'On Good Government', *Review of Austrian Economics*, Vol. 22, No. 2: 127–130.

Tseng, Roy (2003) *The Sceptical Idealist: Michael Oakeshott as a Critic of the Enlightenment*, Charlottesville, Virginia: Imprint Academic.

Vincent, Andrew (2004) *The Nature of Political Theory*, Oxford: Oxford University Press, available at *Oxford Scholarship Online*, www.dx.doi.org/10.1093/0199271259.001.0001 (accessed Jan. 23, 2009).

Viroli, Maurizio (1999) *Republicanism*, New York: Hill and Wang.

Voegelin, Eric (1987) *The New Science of Politics: An Introduction*, Chicago and London: The University of Chicago Press.

Voegelin, Eric (1997a) *The Collected Works of Eric Voegelin: Vol. 19, History of Political Ideas, Vol. I, Hellenism, Rome, and Early Christianity*, ed. Athanasios Moulakis, Columbia and London: University of Missouri Press.

Voegelin, Eric (1997b) *The Collected Works of Eric Voegelin: Vol. 25, History of Political Ideas, Vol. VII, The New Order and Last Orientation*, ed. Jürgen Gebhart and Thomas A. Hollweck, Columbia and London: University of Missouri Press.

Voegelin, Eric (2000) *The Collected Works of Eric Voegelin: Vol. 11, Published Essays: 1953-1965*, ed. Ellis Sandoz, Columbia and London: University of Missouri Press.

Watkins, J. W. N. (1952) 'Political Tradition and Political Theory', *The Philosophical Quarterly*, Vol. 2, No. 9: 323-337.

Weber, Max (1992) *The Protestant Ethic and the Spirit of Capitalism*, London: Routledge.

Webster, Noah (1787) 'An Examination into the Leading Principles of the Federal Constitution', in Bailyn (1993a): 129-163.

Wheare, K.C. (1966) *Modern Constitutions*, London: Oxford University Press.

Wheelan, Joseph (2005) *Jefferson's Vendetta: The Pursuit of Aaron Burr and the Judiciary*, New York: Carroll & Graf Publishers.

Wikipedia (2009) 'Lichtenstein', available at www.en.wikipedia.org/wiki/Lichtenstein (accessed July 1, 2009).

Williams, Bernard (1981) *Moral Luck*, Cambridge: Cambridge University Press.

Winch, Peter (1990) *The Idea of a Social Science and Its Relation to Philosophy*, London and New York: Routledge.

Wittgenstein, Ludwig (1994) *The Wittgenstein Reader*, ed. Anthony Kenny, Oxford: Blackwell Publishers Inc.

Wood, Gordon S. (1998 [1969]) *The Creation of the American Republic: 1776-1787*, Chapel Hill and London: University of North Carolina Press.

Wood, Gordon S. (1991) *The Radicalism of the American Revolution*, New York: Vintage Books.

Wood, Gordon S. (2009) *The Empire of Liberty: A History of the Early Republic, 1789-1815*, Oxford: Oxford University Press.

Wood, Gordon S. (2011) *The Idea of America: Reflections on the Birth of the United States*, New York: Penguin Press.

Worthington, Glenn (2000) 'Michael Oakeshott and the City of God', *Political Theory*, Vol. 28, No. 3: 377–398.

Worthington, Glenn (2005) *Religious and Poetic Experience in the Thought of Michael Oakeshott*, Exeter: Imprint Academic.

Yoo, John (2005) *The Powers of War and Peace: The Constitution and Foreign Affairs after 9/11*, Chicago: The University of Chicago Press.

Young, Alfred F. (2006) *Liberty Tree: Ordinary People and the American Revolution*, New York and London: New York University Press.

Index

on Augustus, 134–35

on English civil war, 148–49

on gnosticism, 33n.4

on Locke, 149

on Roman republic, 104, 110–12, 139, 140–41

theory of representation, 110–12, 122

'The Voice of Poetry in the Conversation of Mankind' (Oakeshott), 62

Watkins, J. W. N., 69n.10

Weber, Max, 7, 9, 71

Webster, Noah, 158–59

Wheare, K. C., 77–81, 188

Wheelan, Joseph, 170, 171–72

'Why I Am Not a Conservative' (Hayek), 64–69

Wilkinson, James, 170, 171

Williams, Bernard, 88

'Will of the powerful,' constraints on, 81

Winch, Peter, 9, 52–54, 132

Wittgenstein, Ludwig, 17

Wood, Gordon S., 154–55, 158

Worthington, Glenn, 36n.7

Written constitutions, 71, 76, 96, 98–99, 154

power of, 81

as *sine qua non*, 100

See also Constitutionalism, Oakeshott and; Constitution, U.S.

Yoo, John, 184, 185

Young, Alfred, 173

Zelaya, Manuel, 190